Praise for *Igniti*

"Delightfully written, Rowan Bombadil's *Igniting Intimacy* is a practical guide to the magic of enriching your relationships—with yourself, with others, and beyond. It's not a sex manual, relationship guide, or typical 'sacred sexuality' tome. Bombadil brilliantly avoids some of the pitfalls of this genre: platitudinousness, new-age credulousness, cultural appropriation. Instead, *Igniting Intimacy* is pragmatic, straightforward, and jam-packed with insights, exercises, and practices that will help you connect and live more fully, happily, and erotically."
—Patricia Johnson & Mark Michaels, coauthors of *Partners in Passion: A Guide to Great Sex, Emotional Intimacy, and Long-Term Love*

"Rowan's book is full of love and generosity. I feel as if they are sitting next to me, holding my hand, sharing with me from their vast storehouse of knowledge and experience. Thank you, Rowan!"
—Betty Martin, creator of The Wheel of Consent

"In *Igniting Intimacy*, Rowan Bombadil offers an honest but gentle template for spiritual relationship that is accessible even for those who are suspicious of the whole concept. If you're making your first tentative gestures in the direction of spiritual sex and love, this much-needed book is a kindly and nonjudgmental guide to lead you through it at your own pace. From self-compassion to ecstatic energy, Bombadil creates a safe container for singles and partners to explore new paths of body-and-heart openness."
—Raven Kaldera, author of *Hermaphrodeities: The Transgender Spirituality Workbook* and editor of *Sacred Power, Holy Surrender*

IGNITING
INTIMACY

About the Author

Rev. Rowan Bombadil (they/them) is a UK-based queer sex witch, psychosexual coach, and interfaith minister, dedicated to bridging the binaries between sex and spirit. Their work inspires individuals and groups of all genders, orientations, and bodies toward a more radical, creative, and intersectional vision of conscious intimacy. In their coaching, ceremonies, workshops, and events, Rowan seeks to facilitate personal and planetary transformation through pleasure. A nerd as well as a sex geek, Rowan's other passions include their ever-expanding library (nonfiction, high fantasy, poetry, and graphic novels), punk rock music, walking on the land, and practising radical intimacy with the people they love. They're also something of a fire fiend, trained in firewalk facilitation and ritual fireplay.

SEX MAGIC RITUALS
for Radical Living & Loving

IGNITING INTIMACY

REV. ROWAN BOMBADIL

Llewellyn Publications
Woodbury, Minnesota

FIRST EDITION
First Printing, 2019

Cover design by Kevin R. Brown
Editing by Holly Vanderhaar
Interior art by Antonio Páramo Gómez

Llewellyn Publications is a registered trademark of Llewellyn Worldwide Ltd.

Library of Congress Cataloging-in-Publication Data
Names: Bombadil, Rowan, author.
Title: Igniting intimacy : sex magic rituals for radical living & loving /
  Rev. Rowan Bombadil.
Description: First edition. | Woodbury, Minnesota : Llewellyn Publications,
  2019. | Includes bibliographical references.
Identifiers: LCCN 2019037417 (print) | LCCN 2019037418 (ebook) | ISBN
  9780738759227 (paperback) | ISBN 9780738759333 (ebook)
Subjects: LCSH: Magic. | Sex--Religious aspects. | Sex.
Classification: LCC BF1623.S4 B66 2019 (print) | LCC BF1623.S4 (ebook) |
  DDC 133.4/42--dc23
LC record available at https://lccn.loc.gov/2019037417
LC ebook record available at https://lccn.loc.gov/2019037418

Llewellyn Publications
A Division of Llewellyn Worldwide Ltd.
2143 Wooddale Drive
Woodbury, MN 55125-2989
www.llewellyn.com
Printed in the United States of America

For my father, who gifted me with a love of books

For Barbara, who gifted me with sex magic and lineage

And for Benjamin, who gifts me with love not in spite of, but because of

A Note of Gratitude

This book represents the fulfilment of a lifelong dream, and would not have been possible without the support of some extraordinary humans. As such, I'd like to take a moment to offer my heartfelt thanks:

To my editor, Angela Wix, for her guidance and good humour, as well as her apparently infinite reserves of patience!

To my line editor, Holly Vanderhaar, for her delicate and thoughtful handling of my work, and for being such a delight to work with.

To Antonio Páramo, for illustrating this book with sensitivity and style.

To the team at Llewellyn, particularly Jake-Ryan Kent, Lynne Menturweck, and Andy Belmas, for turning a manuscript into a book, and giving it wings to fly.

To everyone who has given me permission to cite their precious work and personal stories—Barbara Carrellas, Betty Martin, Roxana Padmini, Lola Houston, Andy Davice, Kate Napier, Rosie Enorah Heart and J.

To everyone who has held my hand or kept me company at different points through this process—particularly Olivia, Jo, Lys, and, of course, Barbara.

To Adam, who so generously directed me to the crossroads of prayer and surrender.

To MJ for the gift of writing retreats, and for giving me a glimpse of what it is to have, and to be, a first reader.

To Elise, Barbara and Kate, for being family on the other side of the pond.

To Max, Martin, and their rambunctious offspring for being family on this side, and for being awesome.

And to Miranda and Benjamin, who keep me alive, and make my life a loving place to be—thank you. I love you more than words could ever hope to tell.

Finally, a small paean of appreciation for some of the voices that return me to myself (and are not mentioned above): Brené Brown, Brian Fallon, Bruce Springsteen, Frank Turner, Joanna Macy, Julia Cameron, Mary Oliver, Patti Smith, and, of course, Sir Terry Pratchett.

Disclaimer

Neither the author nor the publisher is engaged in providing medical, therapeutic, or other professional services. This book does not attempt to give medical diagnosis, treatment, prescriptions, or suggestions for medication in relation to any disease, pain, injury, or physical or mental condition. The information included in this book should not cause pain or unusual symptoms. Consult a qualified professional to obtain a diagnosis for any physical or mental symptoms you may experience.

Contents

PLAYTIME—Table of Exercises

PART III: MAKING LOVE WITH ALL THAT IS

Foreword by Barbara Carrellas

I remember the day I discovered sex magic. Louise Hay, my mentor and friend, had suggested we all send love to a person or a place on the planet that needed it. Always an overachiever, I concluded that if love sent by thought was effective, love delivered via an orgasm might be even more powerful.

There were a lot of people and places that needed love and healing back when I started practising sex magic in the late 1980s. I decided to focus on sending individual doses of orgasmic healing energy to my friends with AIDS, and collective orgasmic energy to South Africa, to support the fight to end apartheid.

I learned countless lessons through my sex magic practice. First off, I learned the unsurprising fact that an erotic connection is a powerful motivator. Unlike other practices that require discipline to practice regularly, it was easy to show up for my sex magic rituals. Secondly, the results of my sex magic practice appeared in the real world in ways I didn't expect. Suddenly (magically, you might say), people and events showed up in my life that gave me concrete ways to support my sex magical intentions. Opportunities to support and care for people with AIDS doubled and the connections I already had deepened. A job suddenly appeared, ironically, to work for white South African producers on Broadway. This gave me opportunities for real activism, such as refusing to import goods made by black South Africans being paid slave wages.

But the biggest transformation was personal. I felt empowered in ways that felt new. I felt a part of movements that were bigger than me. I felt more connected to the collective power of humanity. I felt like a part of the solu-

xxii Foreword by Barbara Carrellas

tion. Sure, I got angry sometimes, but the anger was more energizing than the hopelessness I had so often felt. It was as if the sex magic I was sending out was coming back to me multiplied. It was like I was plugged into a vast network of inspiration and possibilities.

Perhaps you've experienced a moment that gave you a glimpse (or maybe even an entire download) of possibilities so vast that your entire belief system was upended. For many of us, this magical moment happens during orgasm—an orgasm so deep, intense, or prolonged that we can pull back the veil between the worlds and get a glimpse of the network of life at the intersection of sex and spirit. If you have picked up this book, you most likely have either an innate suspicion or a long-standing belief that sex and magic and empowerment are inextricably connected.

Perhaps you want to figure out what exactly created the explosion when sex and magic collided for you. Maybe you want to know how you got to that intersection. Or how to get back. Or how to stay there longer. Or how to bring others with you. Or how to meet others there. Perhaps you want to know what else is possible. Maybe you're looking for your first taste of the possibilities of sex magic. Maybe you just want to know if you're normal or crazy.

Magic is the art of transformation. It's the ability to imagine an alternative existence and then create and sustain that existence. Sex is one of the easiest ways to experience magic in action. Sex magic both requires and creates in us the ability to see, hear, feel, taste, smell, and just plain know that there is a fragile yet unbreakable connection that binds us together as humans, and binds us as humans to the rest of creation. When enough of us can imagine an alternative existence we inevitably, collectively, create that reality.

We need the magic of sex and spirit more than ever in these times. In a world increasingly defined by what we don't want, by separation and division, by seemingly irreconcilable differences, and a dire disconnection from the Earth, we need a road map back to oneness. *Igniting Intimacy: Sex Magic Rituals for Radical Living & Loving* is a vehicle that can put us back on the path.

The magic we need in these times must be fierce, fearless, and practical. The thoughts and prayers offered in trite social media posts following disasters will not cut it in these dangerous and divisive times. We need a sex magical practice that can simultaneously hold a radical acceptance of the ways things are with an equally radical trust in transformation. We need to learn to create powerful intentions for our sex magic and then back up those intentions with the permission to enjoy the results. We need the courage to explore intimacy not just with ourself and others, but also with Earth and divinity.

This is not sex magic for sissies. And you can't do it alone. When I wrote *Urban Tantra: Sacred Sex for the Twenty-First Century*, one of my magical intentions was to connect with sex magicians of all races, abilities, gender identities, sexual preferences, and spiritual proclivities who would like to celebrate, mourn, play, and create with me. One of the first people to step up was Rowan Bombadil. Rowan's fierce commitment to nurturing the connections between sex and spirit informs and inspires their entire life. This book is the magical manifestation of their passion.

This book is for you, whoever you are. The language is inclusive and the content inviting and inspiring. You'll learn new ways to relate with yourself, beloveds, friends, family, and the world. You'll get to discover and define your own personal meaning and style of intimacy, not only with people, but also with the planet and with divinity. And—whether you identify as straight, queer, or something else entirely—you'll reap the boundless benefits of queering love, sex, ritual, and of course, magic.

Best of all, opening this book invites you into community—a powerful community of people waiting to include you, accept you, empower you, celebrate you, and enfold you in a magical embrace. Welcome home. Blessed be.

—Barbara Carrellas, Author of *Urban Tantra:*
Sacred Sex for the Twenty-First Century

Introduction

Welcome, dear reader, to this playbook.

What is a playbook? I hear you ask. That's one of the questions I intend to address in this introduction. Since this is a playbook about sex magic, I'll also be exploring what sex has got to do with magic, and what magic has got to do with sex, along with a few other questions you might conceivably have at this stage of our acquaintance.

Before I elaborate: If you decide to read on, you'll discover that I'm a great believer in the power of intention. Intention, for me, is the seed from which magic, pleasure, and creativity grow. So it seems appropriate to begin by stating my intention in writing this book, and to thereby give you a chance up front to see if it aligns with your intentions in reading it.

My intention in writing this book is to inspire you toward radical relationship: with yourself, with other people, with the world we share, and with the life you live. And with an unconditionally loving Divine, if that's something you're drawn to.

I hope that this book will empower you with the tools to forge new paths to intimacy with any of the above you choose—and also entice you into surrender, so that those intimacies can take you both deeper and higher than you have been before.

Oh, and I also plan to teach you how to do magic—magic that's practical, accessible, applicable, and pleasurable. Magic to liberate your sexuality and creativity. Magic to transform not just the way you love, but also the way you live.

Are you with me? Awesome. Let us begin…

~

Let me take a moment to clarify what I mean by magic.

Magic has traditionally been defined as using one's will to manipulate natural forces toward a desired outcome. It has differed from prayer in that it relies as much—or more—on power within the individual as it does on external grace.

In my experience, however, the divide between these two isn't as wide as that would imply. I have found that magic is less about power over, and more about power with.

Here's how I discovered this. Some years ago, I was traversing a particularly difficult time. Business was nonexistent, my finances had hit rock bottom, and my relationship was turning into a nightmare that seemed to have been spawned in the inner circles of hell. But I'm a born coper, so I soldiered on regardless, pulling myself back up each time I felt knocked down, and trying to hatch some new scheme to solve the crisis.

A few months in, an old lover paid me a visit. After the inevitable questions had arisen about what the hell was going on with me he mused for a moment, and then asked me if I had tried praying. I said something suitably defensive to the tune of "it hasn't been bloody working." At this point he made an astute observation about me refusing to give up, and how he found prayer to be most effective from a place of surrender.

"Why don't you just admit you can't do this?" he asked.

It's probably worth mentioning at this point that I was raised by a single parent in an atmosphere of fierce independence. It was an environment where the achievements of single-minded hard work were rewarded, while needing others was looked down upon as a sign of weakness or vanity. Old habits die hard. As such, it is a mark of how desperate things were at the time that I was evidently willing to try anything, because I retorted with:

"OK. Fine. I can't do this."

It was, dear reader, as though a skylight had opened somewhere inside me. As the days and weeks passed, my situation got slowly but steadily better. I realised that I had fallen into a habit of treating the Divine as something of an occasional consultant; when things went wrong, I would demand of the God/dess that they be fixed, and fixed just so at that. After which, I would return to my mission of "getting by" all by myself, and put the Divine back in its box for another rainy day. Somewhere along the line, I had come to the conclusion that my divine parent must want from me what my earthly one had—independence and a good work ethic—and that these might make me worthy of a grain of love and support every now and then.

Since that day, I have based my spiritual and magical practice around the realisation that the Divine is less like an overstretched single parent, and much more akin to an annoying best friend. The kind that knows what you want before you do, and has already contrived a nifty shortcut to get you there. Since she has an opinion about everything, and I've found out the hard way that those opinions are worth listening to, I try to keep the lines of communication open, stay willing to ask for help, and be prepared to be surprised by her love.

This is why, when I talk about magic these days, I describe it as an act of co-creation.

$\sim$

That experience of co-creation also had a radical impact on my work. The year after that skylight opened, I launched Making Love with God—a body of work that encompasses my practice as a psychosexual coach, as well as a series of intensive workshops on The Art of Sex Magic. The latter teach participants the fundamentals of sex magic ritual, while giving them a taste of both their innate erotic and creative superpowers, and the experience of using those superpowers in collaboration with the Universe. It is those same aims I hope to achieve with this book; the structures I'll be sharing with you, and the structure of the book itself, are inspired by that body of work.

The text is divided into three parts, each of them based on an aspect of Making Love with God:

Making Love with Self deals with the art and practice of radical self-love and solo sex magic. It focuses on that relationship which is the foundation of well-being, and of all other relationships—your relationship with yourself. It invites you to discover the divinity that resides in you, and to treat yourself accordingly. It also introduces some of the basic practices that support the exercises threaded through the rest of the book.

Making Love with Each Other explores some of the ways magical techniques can deepen and transform intimacy. It offers consensual and creative ways to connect, communicate, and co-create pleasure. It looks at how you can use ritual practices to sustain and strengthen your relationships. And, of course, it offers a range of possibilities for practising sex magic together.

Making Love with All That Is widens the frame of intimacy, using sex magic to transform our relationships with the natural world, the god(s) of our understanding, and life itself. It introduces practices like ecosexuality and erotic ecstasy, and explores the possibilities sex magic opens up for falling in love with living.

You'll find more on what to expect from the shape of this playbook at the end of this introduction. For now, let's take a look at why magic—particularly sex magic—is such a powerful tool for effecting changes like those described above.

Magic invites us to get clear about what it is that we desire, and ritual provides us with a way to express that desire to the Universe. For me, it's also a way back into relationship with myself and with the cosmos, and back into my creative flow. I may receive a response to my wishes—or I may receive something entirely different that ultimately fulfils the same need, or reveals that something else was needed instead. Either way, I'm clearer in myself, re-connected to the fact that I'm loved, and better able to orientate myself toward my desire—while also being more receptive to the fulfilment of it from "out there." And usually, if I've indulged in a spot of magic, I've also had a wonderful time.

Rituals like the ones I teach through Making Love with God are made up of the following components:

1. Creating Safe/Sacred Space
2. Invocation
3. Setting Intention
4. Raising Energy
5. Release
6. Surrender
7. Giving Thanks

One of the most important of these is Raising Energy. We raise energy in order to set our desire alight with it. Freestyle shaman Jan Fries, one of my favourite voices on this subject, also talks about the use of exhaustion as a way to shut the logical mind up so that we can plant the seed of our desire in the depths of ourselves.[1] States of heightened energy and/or exhaustion—what we might also call altered or trance states—have traditionally been achieved in a number of ways: physical practices such as dance or drumming; emotional crises, allowing the self to be cracked open by emotion; or breath and awareness practices such as rhythmic breathing, meditation, and journeying.

In short, magic requires a boost from intense physical, emotional, and consciousness-raising activities. Which, of course, is where sex comes in. One of the wonderful things about conscious and consensual erotic activities is they have the potential to stimulate all of the aforementioned parts of us—body, emotions, breath, and awareness—making them the perfect fuel for ritual.

Quite apart from how neatly it slots into the traditional requirements for sources of magical energy, sex is also an effective ritual tool for the following two reasons:

First, it is the most human, and perhaps the most common, avenue to altered states, moments of bliss, and a taste of something more—something like oneness, whether with parts of ourselves, with our lover(s), or with the cosmos. In their book *Radical Ecstasy*, Dossie Easton and Janet Hardy talk about engaging in intense erotic practices for the purpose of getting out of our skin and back into a state of oneness which we recall from before:

"All of us spend the first few weeks of our lives … [getting] a firm grasp of where we end and the rest of the world begins. And then many of us spend a great deal of the rest of our lives in a frantic scramble to dissolve those walls again … We think that radical ecstasy, as we experience it, is a way to pull down the walls that keep us apart from each other and the rest of the universe."[2]

Getting a taste of that oneness during peak sexual experiences is something many people experience whether or not they have even bothered to

---

1. Fries, *Visual Magic*, 21.
2. Easton and Hardy, *Radical Ecstasy*, 19-20.

think about what "came before." Whatever your definition of divinity may be, I would argue that we yell "Oh God yes!" for a reason.

Second, sexuality lies at the heart of our greatest creative potential as human beings. We can beget new life with the help of our genitals. I propose that harnessing that power for making change in our own lives is not that big a step to take.

Oh, and it feels fabulous (if it isn't feeling fabulous, hopefully something farther along in this book will be able to help you change that). And the more pleasurable magic feels, the more we are likely to open up and surrender to the blessings the Universe has been patiently waiting to give us.

~

So sex has a lot to offer magic—and I'm delighted to share that magic gives back as good as it gets. Dream with me here, people—imagine how it would be to treat sex like a magical ritual, or a sacred act. What might change? Let's start answering that by looking at some of the components I mentioned above through an erotic lens.

Creating Space

Imagine if, instead of hoping that sex will just occur of its own accord in the midst of our busy daily lives; instead of expecting our partners to be fully telepathic masters of knowing when and how to be sexual with us; instead of waiting for desire to spring perfectly formed from our shared bed after an evening of discussing topics like bills and school runs, and then assuming there must be something wrong with our relationship when it doesn't…

Imagine if we all understood that sex isn't a lightning bolt, it's a practice—and like any practice we wish to perfect and fully embody, it takes time, space, and energy. Imagine if setting aside that time, space, and energy was a sacrosanct act for which all parties were responsible, and to which all parties gave their full attention. Imagine if part of our week was dedicated to setting aside time, and to creating a beautiful and sacred space, in which to meet with our partner(s) intentionally.

Intention

For me, intention is the most powerful slice of the magical pie. I have noticed that, for myself and my clients, sometimes just having a moment of clarity around what is desired will get things shifting of their own accord, before any magical act has even been done. I have also noticed how intention transforms atmosphere and action. Later on in this playbook we'll be exploring conscious communication methods, and I will note what a marked difference it can make to begin a conversation with "My intention in having this conversation with you is … (e.g., for us to feel closer, to create understanding, to feel more heard by you, etc.)," as opposed to just diving into the deep end of a tricky topic.

Setting an intention for an action transforms what follows. Imagine how it would be to agree on your intention before embarking on erotic acts together—rather than just diving in the deep end of your partner's genitals and hoping you both want the same thing. "Scary," I hear some of you say. OK, so what happens if I want to be spanked and pounded and taken till I'm seeing stars, but my partner was envisioning a nice soothing cuddle? Are we more likely to get what we want by coming together with such different desires and keeping quiet about it, or by sharing them and seeing if one or both can be met now, or scheduled for a little later?

Raising Energy

What this component of magic brings to sex is sensitizing us to energy, and to the flow between us. As burgeoning magicians, we increase our awareness, not only of our own flow, but also of other people's. By tuning in to our innate embodied wisdom we are better able to know not only where we are at, but we also become more aware of what is happening for our partner, as well as what is flowing in the space between us.

By following the energy that we find between us, rather than attempting to stick to some preordained path that sex is "supposed" to take, we can become more connected, discover new pleasures, and find new depths of intimacy. We discover that sex is not a straight path to a particular goal, but more akin to that feeling of jumping waves in the sea when you were a kid. We also build the energy between us, which ultimately means more pleasure, and a potentially more lasting and ecstatic …

Release

Bringing ritual practices to our erotic interactions liberates our climax. These practices liberate those of us for whom physical climax is a distant, difficult, or undesirable prospect from the pressure of having to perfect or perform it regardless, and offer us alternatives for peak experiences. They liberate those of us for whom orgasm is localised and limited to have more full body, full being experiences. And they liberate us from the confines of our bodies, and offer us an invitation to shoot out of our skins and into the stars.

Surrender

Surrender is not just a vital component of magic and sex magic rituals; it is also medicine. And it isn't just medicine for our bodies, for our pleasure, for our relationships—it is medicine for our time. Surrender is the antidote to the anxious malaise of pleasing, perfecting, and performing. It is the being to our culture's incessant doing. It sits on the other side of the scales from creativity to create a sustainable and satisfying existence. Practicing surrender in our erotic pursuits expands our capacity for receiving, for pleasure, for ecstasy. And it also serves as a signpost toward self-acceptance, open-hearted relating, and a life well-lived.

Presence

Above all, the greatest gift that magical practices have to offer sex is presence. In ritual practices, we cultivate a presence to the moment; to our physical, sensual, emotional, intellectual, and spiritual selves; to what is unfolding within us and around us. Imagine what someone who can get present enough to listen to the whispers of their own intuition, or become entirely absorbed in the textures of a fallen leaf, can do when they turn that level of attention to a lover's skin.

Yum.

$\sim$

The above hopefully begins to address the questions of why sex, why magic, and why sex magic. Further answers include the following:

- A more embodied and integrated (love) life, a greater sense of wholeness
- Visions, out-of-body journeys, pretty lights, and other assorted forms of sober ecstatic experience
- The expansion of pleasure and sensation, the deepening of intimacy and love
- Sex, eros, and love-making beyond the confines of gender, genitals, and skin
- Dreams come true

But why Making Love with God? What has the Divine got to do with sex magic?

Yes, it would be a hell of a lot easier for me to market this book without throwing the God word in there. For so many of us, the G-word and sex do not mix well, for all kinds of valid, and often painful, reasons. But here's the thing. If you really engage with this work—or with this play as the case may be—you are highly likely to have experiences that are, quite frankly, divine.

As I write this, I am thinking fondly of a few staunch atheists who, during different workshops, have come back from doing erotic breath work or vision work, and started talking about the kind voice they heard speaking to them while they were "out there."

So, here's a disclaimer: By engaging fully in sex magic practices, you run the risk of experiencing visions, shapeshifting, catharses, and, of course, that energy I keep mentioning that can feel like life force, or like a force of nature, or like a state of union with your lover and/or the cosmos. Above all, you run the risk of experiencing yourself, as I did in the story I shared at the start of this introduction, as *loved*.

When I use the word God/dess, it's that love that I'm referring to.

I see sex as the most human, the most pleasurable, and the most direct path to communing with the cosmos—or at least, with the energy that underpins, overflows from, and makes up the cosmos. In this book, I will be inviting you to explore, (re)connect with, and trust that energy as it is manifest in yourself, as it is manifest in your lover(s), as it is manifest in the world around you, and as it is manifest in the silence between all these things.

I won't be touching much on the G-word again between now and the third section of this book, so please do take a deep breath, and unclench those butt-cheeks if the last few paragraphs have been difficult for you.

That being said, when I do use words like the G-word, you're welcome to be self-responsible spiritual adults, and replace them with whatever word works for you—be it Universe, Spirit, Higher Self, Deep Mind, Love, or any deity, ancestor, or fictional character of your choice. My recommendation would be that it be a word that you associate with unconditional love. It is my hope that, in reading this book, you stumble into the direct experience of being loved—not in spite of who you are, or who you love, or what you desire, but because of those very things.

Some further questions answered

What do you mean by sex?

By sex I mean any activity that, for you, stimulates erotic energy, and that is practised with the consent of everyone involved. As you'll discover, I see the erotic as expanding far beyond the confines of what our culture still tends to think of as sex. Our current cultural model of sex—linear, performative, goal-driven—is similarly unsustainable and ultimately unsatisfying as the capitalism which created it, and it is setting us all up for boredom at best, and failure at worst. For the purposes of our time together, the only things you'll absolutely need to create your own sex magic practice are breath, and a willing imagination. Everything else is an add-on. That being said, I promise we will be exploring plenty of add-ons!

What do you mean by energy?

I mean that charge that we often experience most clearly during moments of intense erotic connection or activity, or peak moments of aliveness. This is the stuff we build to fuel our intentions in ritual, and I also think it's the stuff our world is made of. This can, however, be a question that is best answered experientially—so feel free to skip to page 128 for some experiments in feeling and playing with energy.

What is a playbook?

A playbook, at least in this instance, is a book that is a little less preach, a little more practice. It's less interested in telling you how it is than in inspiring you to find out for yourself. Less interested in talking at you than in entering into a conversation with you, and inspiring further conversations between you, yourself, others, and the Universe. Accordingly, you will find that the text is generously interspersed with exercises designed to encourage you to have your own experiences, and draw your own conclusions. As such, this book is most effectively approached the way you might approach learning a new skill or practice: with an open mind, with a willingness to suspend your disbelief and try new things, and with something with which to take copious notes!

Who is this playbook for?

This playbook is for anyone who wishes to make their erotic lives more magical, to build a magical or spiritual practice that incorporates pleasure, and/or to access and liberate the creative power of the erotic in themselves. That being said, it differs in some key ways from many other books on sex and magic.

First, it has been written with a more intersectional audience in mind than many books on these topics. At the time of writing, the worlds where consent, consciousness, sex, and spirit intersect are still predominantly white, middle class, nondisabled, and fairly binary in terms of gender and sexual orientation—although pioneers like Kim Loliya, Afrosexology, and members of the Urban Tantra graduate community are working to change that. While it is my intention to create work and spaces that seek to continue that change, inevitably the material in this book will be coloured by the lenses of my own intersections of oppression and privilege (genderqueer, raised as female, emigrant childhood, white, nondisabled, educated by Western standards), as well as by the language currently in use around diversity in my communities. Said language is changing daily, and will certainly be outdated when some of you read this. As such, I won't be able to fully meet all of you, and all of your diverse needs and desires, on the page. That being said, there will be no assumptions of gender (I'll be using the singular "they" pronoun throughout), sexual orientation, or relationship style from me to you. I have tried to be mindful of different bodies in the exercises, and to keep things like physical positioning, etc., fairly flexible. And I have endeavoured to keep any suggestions for resources optional, or included options that are low cost.

Second, you are likely to come across things in this book that don't at first appear relevant to either magic or sex. That is because the bias at the heart of this book is relationship—with ourselves, with our beloveds, with the Earth, and with life itself—and the premise that learning to love in radical new ways will transform our lives into more pleasurable and magical places to be. So while you're welcome to skip over all that stuff about sitting with feelings, listening to yourself and others, and getting into your body, in order to get to the sexy magic stuff, I can guarantee the experience of the latter will be infinitely richer if you put in the time with the former first.

Third, the underlying principles of this book are that sex—in the expanded sense in which I defined it above—is sacred, and the sacred is sensual. That pleasure is our birthright, and that dedicating time, space, resources and energy to expanding that pleasure, and learning the skills we need to do so, is a radical act. And that the Universe supports, celebrates, and participates in that pleasure.

Some further notes on structure

Playtime

When you see the word "Playtime," it indicates that an exercise is starting. I'm using the term "Playtime" to remind you to approach the exercise with curiosity and kindness to yourself/each other, and see it as an invitation to try something out rather than a challenge to "get it right." The exercises in the book do build on each other and refer to each other, so as much as possible, try and give the basics a bash before diving into the more complex rituals that appear later on in each section.

Practical Magic

Occasionally, you will encounter stories told in the first person and the present. These recount personal experiences that I've had with the aspects of the work we're exploring in that chapter, and as such they offer you a window onto what that work might look like in practice. I am including them to inspire your own practices, and also because sometimes the places that doing this work takes us are simply impossible to describe. By sharing my own experiences with you, I hope to give you a glimpse of the horizon of infinite possibilities sex magic can open up.

Messiness Alerts

You will also notice these popping up occasionally. They are there to remind you that this work is powerful psychosomatic stuff. It can elicit intense responses, unearth long repressed feelings, and bring you face to face with aspects of yourself, your relationships, and your life that cause you various degrees of discomfort. In short, if you engage in this work, things are likely to get messy. Messiness Alerts are there to give you a heads-up, and reassure you that surrendering to the mess is a vital part of the process. And they are there to remind you of two core principles of this book: Play and Practice. As I mentioned above, the invitation here is to play. And the more you play—the more you practise the techniques, or make the techniques your practice—the more likely it is that they will open doors for you into embodiment, pleasure, love, and transcendence.

If the messiness starts to feel overwhelming, or if you just feel like you would appreciate a skilled companion on this chapter of your erotic journey, don't be afraid to reach out for help—this work can be therapeutic, but it isn't therapy. Check out the Resources section at the back of this book for leads to some fantastic psychosexual practitioners.

Without further ado then, let's get radical...

Part I

Making Love with Self

We begin our adventures in sex magic with Making Love with Self.

This is in part because to start with the self, especially the aspects of the self that our culture teaches us to devalue and override, is a radical act. Specifically, it's relationship as a radical act. By cultivating loving relationship with all aspects of ourselves, we release the creative power previously trapped within aspects that have been lying dormant or repressed. We also empower ourselves with the tools to connect authentically—not only with ourselves, but also with others. Radical acceptance of ourselves, and then others, allows us to sidestep the competition capitalism relies on, and enter into authentic connection and collaboration to make the changes we wish to see in the world.

It's also important to start here because we cannot relate to others if we can't relate to ourselves. Let me be clear: I'm not repeating the old adage that we can't love, or be worthy of love, until we love ourselves. As you'll discover in the second part of this book, I believe that those around us have vital parts to play in our journeys toward self-acceptance, and vice versa; I don't think we can make those journeys alone. What I am saying is that we can't hope to sustain open, co-creative, and fulfilling relationships with other people if we're not willing to tend to our relationship with ourselves as well.

Finally, the self is the starting point because the extent to which we are willing to encounter and embrace ourselves corresponds precisely with the depths to which our experiences of intimacy can go, and the heights to which our pleasure can take us.

～

In this section, we're travelling within to meet our inner pantheon. I'll be inviting you to practise treating yourself as a sacred being—partly because I happen to believe that you are one, but also because the way that believers treat their favourite God-friends corresponds precisely with how I hope to encourage you to treat yourself.

I recall an occasion when I was hanging out with my favourite God-friend —and by hanging out, I mean sitting in front of my altar and offloading my latest woes. Eventually I asked my God-friend: "How can I love myself more?" The answer arrived in my thoughts, clear and emphatic: "Act like it."

If you like, you can think of this chapter as a manual in "acting like it."

The three things I'm going to be encouraging you to cultivate toward yourself as a sacred being are *faith*, *worth*, and *celebration*.

Chapter 1

Faith

Let's start with a little game. Fill in the following sentence ten times—quickly, without thinking about it too much, and certainly without censoring yourself:

If I trusted myself, I would …

Now read through your answers. How much of what you have written is already present in your life and actions should give you a rough idea of how much you trust yourself.

For some of you, the very possibility of self-trust may feel alien. Western culture is built on hierarchical infrastructures that are not served by all people trusting themselves equally. Instead, we're encouraged to put our trust in other people. At the time of writing, those are usually people who display more of the following qualities than we do: whiteness, "masculinity," wealth, heterosexuality, rationality, physical stamina, and coming from a higher so-cial class and/or level of education—all of which are currently synonymous and symbiotic with social and/or cultural and/or political power. We are taught to look to those more powerful than ourselves for answers, rather than looking within, or figuring things out co-creatively.

Even if we're among the segment of the population whose judgment is considered valuable at any one time, the proportion of our faculties that we are encouraged to place our trust in is relatively limited, since as a culture we prize our intellectual capacities above all others. Indeed, we're often en-couraged to apply rational thinking to the exclusion and detriment of all our other faculties—our instincts, our emotions, our physical senses. Few of us receive an education in locating and deciphering—never mind trusting—these other facets of ourselves. Science may be talking about the second brain in our gut, but we still locate wisdom firmly in the head.[3] Not many of us would think to look for it in the gut, let alone in our genitals.

And yet … most of us have experienced that moment when we get home from, say, a social event, flop down, and think "I knew I shouldn't have gone to that. I had a feeling the evening would go to shit." If you think about it, I bet you can think of a whole bunch of other times when you've had "feelings" that have turned out to be painfully—or perhaps delightfully—on point. If you think about it some more, you could probably point to the area of the body where that feeling, that tension or flutter or nausea, manifested itself.

I have found in my capacity as a psychosexual coach that the body never lies. For example, if someone is struggling to have sex—whether with themselves, or with someone else—I have observed time and again that invariably the body is trying to flag up an underlying reason for them not wanting to have sex in this particular instance. This is either because there are emotional issues that aren't being addressed in the relationship they're in, or because the sex they're having is not currently worth wanting. If you're in this position with a partner, this may be a scary thing to be reading—but I'm not suggesting that what the body is flagging up is insurmountable. Instead, I'm suggesting that your body holds the key to what is happening for you, and learning to listen to your body can help you unlock that knowledge.

There is a cornucopia of knowing and clarity available to us in our bodies—innate wisdom that has the capacity to enrich every aspect of our living and loving. All that is required is our undivided attention, and a little faith in ourselves, to plumb our own depths, and get to know ourselves.

Accordingly, one of the first items in our playbook is going to be learning how to "listen in" to our bodies. Before we go there however …

Let's talk about breath (baby).

---

3. Sonnenburg and Sonnenburg, *Gut Reactions*, 138.

Breath

Your breath will be your guide in the journey you're about to embark on, and it forms the backbone of pretty much every exercise in this book. Of course, at times you'll be layering it up with all manner of deliciousness—but that doesn't make it any less important. On the contrary, breath fuels deliciousness, just like it does every other sensation we receive.

Here are some of the keys to deliciousness that breath offers us:

- Breath offers our awareness a way into our body. Even when we have become detached from our embodied selves, when we are resisting big emotions or physical pain happening therein, or when we are locked out of parts of ourselves by distress or disease, breath can get us in and begin to unlock the vaults of energy, power, and eros that lie within.
- Breath expands—not just our lungs, but also any sensations we receive and feelings we have, and by extension our capacity for pleasure and joy.
- Breath helps us to process big feelings and intense sensations. It helps us to sit with the difficult stuff that life throws at us, to engage with and process emotional pain and trauma, to make peace with what is—however challenging that may be.
- Breath gets us high. It allows us to have ecstatic, transcendental, transformational experiences. It also allows us to manipulate energy, to give and receive it, and to change our erotic shape—thus infinitely expanding the horizons of our sexuality, and even our gender.
- Breath helps us to be in the moment—to step out of the frustrations with yesterday and the fears about tomorrow, and, in the words of happiness expert Srikumar Rao, "accept the Universe exactly as it is." [4]

In light of the above, and of the fact that one or other of the practices that follow will feature in many of the exercises in the rest of this book, I invite you to give each of the below a try as you read through them. Think of them as experiments, rather than something to get right, and take note of how your body feels after each.

---

4. Rao, "Plug into Your Hard-Wired Happiness."

Energising and Releasing Breath

The breath I use the most is an Energising and Releasing Breath.

Why: Breathing in through the mouth provides us with more oxygen, and—by extension—more energy. Breathing out in this way helps us to release physical and emotional tension, and be that little bit more present in the here and now.

How: Begin to take full, deep, easeful breaths in through your mouth. As you breathe in, imagine the breath is an old friend you're embracing after a long time apart. As you breathe out, allow yourself the luxury of a sigh. As you breathe in, imagine that you draw yourself more fully into your body, making yourself more welcome in the present moment. As you breathe out, notice and release any tension around the eyes, the jaw, the neck. As you breathe in, invite more of your body to expand with the breath, including your abdomen and belly. As you breathe out, drop your shoulders down your back. As you breathe in, yawn, and then allow your palate to stay open and receptive—so that the back of your throat feels open in the same way it does when you feel big emotions like joy, or when you know you're about to cry. Breathe out, and allow a little noise of relaxation and satisfaction to escape you. Yum.

Processing Breath

I also frequently call upon the Processing Breath.

Why: The processing breath is designed to help us release emotional upheaval that is getting stuck in our system. The term "processing" is frequently used to describe the process of engaging with, feeling, releasing, and integrating intense experiences or emotions. This breath helps us get things moving again, so that we can then take a step back, take stock, and behave in a more conscious and choiceful fashion.

How: It is best done is an upright position, either standing, kneeling, or seated (e.g., cross-legged). Begin by breathing right down into the part of you where the emotional tumult is—often somewhere around your belly or your chest. Take a few deep breaths there, and simply acknowledge what you're feeling. Then, when you're ready, imagine that you can gather all of those big feelings up with your breath. As you breathe out, imagine the feelings (you may see them as colours or shadows, or feel them as a churning mass) rising up from your belly, and flowing out of your mouth. You can open your mouth wide and expel air forcefully, pulling a fierce face to reflect how you're feeling—or you can pull your lips into an O, as though blowing out a candle, and expel the breath forcefully in a long-drawn out exhale. It can help to shake your body or stamp your feet while you're doing this, particularly the area where the feelings seem to be stuck.

You can add a good cleansing cry to this breath (and it's a great breath to call upon if you feel that need for catharsis welling up, and you really want to go into it)—or scream into a pillow for a bit if you'd rather the neighbours didn't know how pissed off you are!

Toward the end of your processing, you might like to imagine your exhale is happening through your heart, and have a sense of letting go of this feeling that has been getting stuck in you lovingly, and appreciatively. After all, it's likely it was there to give you some useful information.

Breath of Fire

Why: This breath is useful for raising our energy or inner "fire," which we'll be doing a lot of later on in this book. It is awakening, enlivening, and many of us have done something like it during fast exercise or steamy sex.

How: Focus on your outbreath, and make it a little faster and sharper than it would normally be. As you breathe out, consciously contract/pull in your stomach muscles (this breath often features in martial arts or yogic traditions where the focus is on building up the energy in the *hara* or core). Then allow the in breath to flow in of its own accord, and repeat. Once you have the hang of it, speed the process up a little more, and keep going for a minute or so, before bringing the breath back to normal, and noticing how your body feels in the aftermath.

Heart/Sex Circuit Breath

Why: This breath is a great connector. Like any breath, it reconnects us with ourselves, but it also has the ability to connect different parts of us with each other—e.g., our hearts with our erotic selves. You'll see it featuring later in the book in many of the exercises involving connecting with other people, and it can be used to connect with other entities as well—more on that later.

It's a great one for building energy during pleasure, and has an abundance of potential uses in sex magic.

How: The aim of the breath is to create a circuit between the heart centre and the erotic centre of the body—with the conceit that the former is located in the chest, and the latter in the genitals. You can either breathe in through the genitals, imagining the breath flowing up your spine into your chest, and then breathing out through the chest, imagining the breath flowing out of your heart and back down your torso to your genitals… or you can go the other way, breathing in through the heart, imagining the breath flowing down your spine to your genitals, breathing out through the genitals, and imagining the breath flowing back up to connect with your heart. I suggest trying each direction for two to three minutes, ideally standing or sitting upright. Allow your body to move a little with the breath if that feels right, and just notice how your body feels after trying each direction.

Breathing the Heart/Sex Circuit Solo

Bottom Breath

Why: This is a great breath for slowing right down, and coming into the body, and into the place and time the body is currently inhabiting, more fully, and more fully focused.

How: When introducing this breath to a group, Barbara Carrellas will often begin by saying, "Put your head in your ass." Which is to say, breathe deep, and take your awareness down to your anus. As you breathe in, imagine you can push your anus out to kiss the chair beneath you. Then release on a long, slow, outbreath. And repeat!

Rooted Breath

Why: I use this breath particularly when I'm feeling overwhelmed, stressed, or in any way out of body. It's a really great one to use if you or someone you're with is feeling hyper, ungrounded, or a little too "heady"—I tend to get my best friend doing it when I can tell she needs a really good cry. I also use it in a professional context when I'm working with clients or groups, and I call upon it if I'm in a confronting situation, or having a difficult conversation.

How: Take a deep, full breath, breathing through the overwhelm and into the warm, welcoming darkness of your belly. Keep breathing into there. As you breathe out, bring your attention to your feet, and imagine roots dropping from the soles of your feet into the Earth below. As you breathe in, become aware of the solidity of that ground, of how steadily and constantly it supports and carries you. As you breathe out, drop those roots a little deeper; see/feel them sinking/snaking down through mud and tree roots and silt and water and rock. As you breathe in, notice the generous abundance of warmth and love flowing up those roots to you from the Earth. As you breathe out, let those roots drop still deeper, and release any weight from your heart and mind that you do not wish to carry at this time. As you breathe in, feel yourself supported. As you breathe out, allow the ground to take your full weight, so that you may be more completely here, without fear, knowing that you are carried, supported, held.

~

Breath is this secret ninja magic wand that we all possess, are all already experts in using, and can all access at any given moment. One of the best things we can do for ourselves and each other is remember to breathe.

Listening In

OK, back to learning to trust ourselves. As I said, breath is our guide in this process. As you become more practised in using these techniques, you'll be able to strip them down to just breathing your attention toward any part of your emotional or physical body you wish to gain deeper understanding around. In these first explorations, we're going to use the threefold map of head, heart, and body to direct our flow of attention.

⋙ PLAYTIME ⋘
Head, Heart, Belly

Get yourself sitting comfortably, arm yourself with a way to take notes, and start to breathe deeply—perhaps using the Energising or the Bottom Breath. In this first experiment, you're welcome to focus simply on getting a sense of what is moving in you right now. Many of us live our lives in very out-of-body ways, or have been taught to distrust our carnal or emotional selves. Crossing the divides set up by these habits and beliefs can feel strange, even scary, and often takes time, patience, and self-kindness. That being said, you could also bring a question that you've been struggling to get clarity on to the Listening In process, and see what answers emerge from your head, heart, and belly.

Deep breaths. Take a moment to focus on your outbreath, making it long and luxurious, and allowing it to carry away with it anything that might be coming between you and your body—anxiety or mental chatter, for example. As you breathe in, imagine that you can breathe yourself deeper into your body, and let your attention follow your breath.

Once you're feeling a little more "in" your body and the present moment, start to focus your attention. The easiest way to do this is focus your breath, imagining that you can "breathe into" different areas of your body, much as you would normally breathe into your lungs. Begin with the head, where most of us are used to thinking of our mind residing. Breathe, gently invite your attention into that part of your body, and start to "listen." "Listening" in this case means offering as much of your attention as you can to your mind, and being open to any messages that might arise from it.

When it comes to inner work of this sort, the kind of messages you receive will likely depend on which of your five senses you tend most rely on for information. Some of you might receive images, while others may hear or see particular words; still others may simply get a "feeling" or impression. Even if what you receive seems faint, give it your attention rather than sliding down that all-too-slippery slope of "getting it right." Remember, this is a playbook, and we're just playing; allow yourself to be curious, and follow what faint threads you find. Taking notes as you go may help you to clarify what is arising in each area.

Keep breathing. Keep listening. Notice the qualities of the mind, the ways in which it offers you information, how that information feels to you, and how accurate you feel it to be.

Once that feels complete, take your breathing deeper, and invite your attention to drop down into your "heart." I locate my "heart centre" in the middle of my chest because of a background in working with the maps of the chakras. You may feel it resides in your literal heart, or somewhere quite different. Set the intention to listen to your heart, and see where you're drawn to go.

Repeat the process. Let the breath make a little space within for you to inhabit. Give yourself the full gift of your attention. And listen. Notice what's here, how this area feels—closed or open, stuck or flowing, full or quiet—what the particular qualities of the heart are, and the flavour of information it gives you.

Once that feels complete, and you have some notes, deepen your breathing once more, and draw your consciousness into your belly. Breathe. Make space. Listen. The belly is the centre of your instinct, your "gut feelings," your deep knowing. And if that sounds a bit too hippy dippy, check out recent scientific studies on what is being referred to as our "second brain," made up of the one hundred million neurons embedded in the walls of our guts.[5] That stomach of yours is a thinking creature. And the information that you glean from it may feel a lot like the "having a feeling" that we were talking about

5. Sonnenburg and Sonnenburg, *Gut Reactions*, 138.

earlier. So listen, take note, and see what it has to tell you. When that feels complete, take some deep breaths, come back to where you are, and see what you have written.

∽

In my experience, the belly is the place where we find our big Yeses, and our big Nos. Many of us have grown up, live, or work in environments where our Yeses and Nos don't count for much, or have been actively discouraged. In order to go against these "gut feelings," we've had to detach ourselves from this part of our body, and, to an extent, shut it down. However, in shutting down our gut, we also risk shutting down the energy that lives below it—our sexual energy and our life force. These are also connected to our capacity to be angry, empowered, and creative. Thus, for example, putting ourselves in a professional situation that goes against our instincts may lead to a loss of clarity, inspiration, and motivation—while putting ourselves in a relationship that doesn't "feel right" at that basic level can lead to a loss of libido and feeling "out of body."

The body never lies. In learning to Listen In, we give ourselves a shot at working with, rather than against, it and at reintegrating ourselves back into our personal power and drive, and bringing those energies to bear on our lives and love lives once again.

More ways to listen in

Here are two further ways to unlock and listen to the truths of the body. The first can be applied to any aspect of the self, and the latter centres more specifically on the erotic self, with a focus on the genitals.

≽ PLAYTIME ≼
Automatic Writing

Why: You're having this recurring emotion that's been driving you and everyone around you crazy. Or, you have this feeling that you can't quite put your finger on, but it's been around for a while now, and you sense it's important. Or you're feeling distant from a particular part of yourself, and you'd like to reconnect. In short, it's time to have a chat with a specific aspect of yourself, and see what it has to say. This technique can be useful if a quick "Listen In" just isn't quite giving you the answers you need.

How: Grab your favourite way of taking notes, and get comfortable. And much like you did in the exercise above, take full deep breaths, and begin to bring your attention to the part of your body where you can feel this feeling lurking.

What is this thing you're needing to have a chat with called? Is it Fear? Your Inner Kid? The Black Dog? Once you can feel where it is, write "Hello, [e.g.] Fear" at the top of your page. Underneath, allow it to respond. Let the dialogue unfold from there.

I made that sound simple, didn't I? I should clarify that often, especially when talking to my Fear, the first response I get back is along the lines of "grunt," "growl," or even "fuck off." Doing this can take a certain amount of perseverance—alongside, of course, a willingness to use your imagination to have a chat with a feeling or other aspect of you as though it were a sentient being! What this technique offers is a direct way of communicating with, and subsequently integrating, a part of ourselves we've been trying to separate off from.

I recommend completing the process only when you have come to something that looks like an agreement with this particular "gremlin." For example, you might be asking your fear to pipe down while you make this next big career move. In order to do so, your fear may need you to take a long soothing bath every day, ask for more cuddles from your loved ones, or jump up and down to heavy metal music while it has a bit of a tantrum! Find a way to come to an agreement, make an ally of your demon, and move forward.

⇒ PLAYTIME ⇐
Talking Genitals

Why: This is a useful exercise if you think your genitals might have something they need to tell you—either because of past trauma, or because of current challenges. It might also help you to get a sense of what you desire sexually if that's a topic you struggle with. You can do a simple version of it along the lines of the Head/Heart/Belly exercise, but "Listening In" to and making notes from your genitals instead. Or …

How: Arm yourself with a pile of cushions, and get comfortable on one. Take some time to breathe deeply, and find your way into your body on the breath. If things are sounding a little loud in there, you could do a quick "Listen In" to Head, Heart, and Belly, before bringing your attention to your genitals.

After you've spent a little time breathing your attention into your sex, place one of the cushions in front of you, and imagine that you are sitting opposite a mirror image of yourself. You are, so to speak, inviting yourself to sit down for a chat—and you will be speaking on behalf of your genitals. Once you have a mental image of yourself seated in front of you, bring your attention back to your genitals, and invite them to speak to the "you" that is on the cushion before you. Allow them to voice how they are feeling, any grievances they have, anything they need or desire from you in future, and speak out loud on their behalf. If any big emotions come up, keep breathing, and allow them to be expressed.

You may also want to ask your genitals if there is anyone else they need to speak or vent to—e.g., a partner, a parent, or someone from your past. If this is something you're drawn to, make sure you consider the Messiness Alert coming up at the end of this section, and check in with yourself that this feels like a safe way to proceed. If it does, get a different cushion, place it in front of you, and imagine that person coming and sitting in front of you. This image of the person is a reflection of their higher self—it cannot harm you, and it is simply here to listen to you. Again, speak aloud, express your feelings, vent as much as you need to—and yes, you can punch the pillow a bit if that helps!

When that feels complete, thank anyone you have invited to sit with you, yourself, and your genitals. Check in with the latter to see if there are any agreements you can come to before you finish. Perhaps take some time to make a note of anything that has particularly stood out.

$\sim$

Having access to your own guidance isn't just crucial for your relationship with yourself and others; it also allows for the development of qualities such as discernment and reflection, and fosters your ability to make choices, build your own code of ethics, and to nurture your innate wisdom. If your life has been founded on the voices of others, but the prospect of Listening In strikes a chord, the first thing I can recommend is practise. On a day-to-day basis, this could look like

- Taking five to ten minutes at the start of the day, or during a lunch-break/traffic-jam/walk/bath, to breathe deeply, and notice what arises when you focus on your head, heart, and belly
- Setting a timer on your phone to go off one or three times a day, and ping the question "How am I feeling?" onto your screen for you to breathe into for a couple of minutes
- Noticing when you're having an emotional response to something during your day, and taking a moment to breathe into it, and see what's underneath it—almost as though you could peel back the layers of each feeling to reveal another

♥ Messiness Alert!

Remember that, as you make Listening In a daily practice, you may come up against feelings and behaviours that have had a lifetime to build up. Be gentle with yourself and exercise patience and curiosity, rather than pushing for any particular goal or outcome. Keep breathing, keep practising—and get into the habit of treating your feelings as valid and welcome. Give yourself permission to seek professional help if any of these practices bring something up that you don't feel equipped to hold by yourself.

~

So here you are, hopefully breathing a little deeper, paying a little more attention to your precious self, and starting to get a sense of what the weather is like in your inner landscape. Inevitably, the next question to arisc is: What to do with this new information you're gleaning?

Chapter 2

Love

You've been practising listening to yourself, and you're starting to hear yourself loud and clear. You've gotten your own attention, and now you're providing yourself with all manner of new information about how you're feeling. This is where self-love comes in to guide how you process that information—specifically, in the form of self-worth.

Self-worth

Self-worth invites the conviction that anything you're feeling is first and foremost valid, and also a source of useful information and potential creativity—because you are a fundamentally worthy being, with wisdom in your heart and ancient stardust in your bones. A child of the Universe, no worse or better than any other being, and no less worthy of being heard and seen and listened to.

Whilst it is possible we are all born with this conviction, very few of us are raised with it. Just as it doesn't suit our hierarchical culture for us to trust ourselves, it doesn't suit our capitalist culture for us to love ourselves. Instead, we internalise convictions very different to the above, often based on hand-me-down shoulds and shouldn'ts, sins and shames. It doesn't take long for the voices we hear externally telling us what we can't, what we mustn't, where we're failing, where we're too much, and where we're not enough to become our own, internal voices—voices we turn against the parts of ourselves deemed unworthy. As a result, many of us don't have a recollection of what it feels like to love ourselves. Not having prior experience to draw upon makes it harder to imagine why self-love might be a practice worth cultivating—and is also precisely the reason why practice is required.

The meditation that follows was created during a heart circle I was running, on an evening when the majority of the participants were wrestling with big emotions. It takes the Listening In you've been practising one step further. This time you don't just listen, you actively offer compassion and love to an aspect of yourself you would rather avoid.

⋙ PLAYTIME ⋘
The Uncomfortable Thing Meditation

Listen In, and find that which is most uncomfortable for you right now—most worrying, heavy, fearful, hurting, resistant.

Find that which is most uncomfortable, focus on that uncomfortable thing, and breathe with it.

Give it your full focus, offer it your absolute attention, allow it to fill your whole awareness.

And breathe.

If you find yourself slipping sideways into other thoughts, or attempting to skip over, under, or around the uncomfortable thing to avoid how it feels, gently, tenderly, invite your attention back to it, and breathe.

Offer this uncomfortable thing the kind of attention
—curious, compassionate—
that you would offer a child
a child that you loved
a child that was hurt
or was asking you a difficult question.

Offer the uncomfortable thing the kind of attention that you would offer a beloved child
and breathe.

Offer this uncomfortable thing the kind of attention
—wondering, tender—
that you would offer a lover
a lover you adored

a lover needing comfort

a lover you were caressing with your eyes, and with the tips of your fingers.

Offer the uncomfortable thing the kind of attention you would give your beloved

and breathe.

Offer this uncomfortable thing the kind of attention you would offer a god made manifest before you

a divine being whom you trusted

a divine being who loves you

a divine being who is whispering ever so softly the answers you have been seeking for so long.

Offer the uncomfortable thing the kind of attention you would offer a god. Listen.

Breathe.

Offer the uncomfortable thing the kind of attention

you always longed for as a child

wished for from your lovers

prayed for from your gods

because this uncomfortable thing is part of you,

is you in this moment,

and as such is as deserving

of compassion, attention, and love

as you are

intrinsically, naturally, constantly,

no matter where, when, or why.

Offer this uncomfortable thing the kind of compassion, attention, and love,

that are your birthright as a child of this world

and breathe

breathe

breathe.

∽

As you've probably gathered, your willingness to breathe with what is happening in each moment is key when it comes to self-love and self-kindness as well. Consciously receiving the gift of breath is a fundamental act of self-care. Taking a few conscious breaths can bring us back to our centre, settle us in our body, and connect us to our truth. And it is a statement: we deserve life, we choose life, we receive life, and we're going to occupy the space that it takes for us to breath in, and out, and stay alive.

Notice also that breath gives us a tool with which to face feelings we might otherwise be too afraid to feel—for example because we have been taught to judge ourselves harshly for having them, or because we fear losing control in the face of big emotions. Whether because of messages we receive about our physical, sexual, or emotional selves, or experiences that impact those selves in ways that cause us pain and/or shame, throughout our lives we erect walls in our inner landscape. We dissect ourselves, drawing lines between, e.g., the heart we were taught to think of as pure and the erotic self we were taught to think of as dirty, or between our day-to-day thoughts and that experience we never had the space or support to process.

Breath supports us to cross those walls when the time is right, and brave those encounters. Breath helps us to move through the impulse to turn away from our precious selves, and find our way into the centre of the part of ourselves that we have been so afraid of—to get really settled down in there, to fully embody the feeling in question. By offering the feeling our full attention, and by allowing it move freely in our body, we're finally giving it a chance to fulfil its purpose. We're finally giving it room to breathe.

No intense feeling arises without a purpose. It's there for a reason—whether to help us process a loss, to point us in the direction of our desires, to encourage us to speak out against the injustice we have suffered, or just to inform us that we need to have a damn good cry and get a good night's sleep. Emotion is often described as "energy-in-motion"—and when we "act as if" these big feelings are valid and worthy of our attention, they are at last able to move, to be in motion, and to release the energy we've been expending in trying to keep them at bay.

Practical Magic: *As I am writing this section, you come into the room we affectionately call our "geekery," where our conjoined libraries share shelf space with art, board games, and a host of dragons, and crowd around the* *desk where I'm working. You've had a rough few days with depression, stress, and insomnia, and I have a hunch you might be ready to surrender to what you're feeling. I sit with you on the couch, and suggest as much, and you ask me to help. "Where are you breathing into right now?" I ask.*

You indicate your collarbone. Curled up around you, I place my hand just below said collarbone, and instruct you to breathe into the place where my hand is; I tell you that is all you have to do. The tears come very quickly. When I sense it's time to encourage you to take the breath, and the corresponding centre of attention, deeper, I move my hand lower. Heart, solar plexus, finally down to the belly.

All the time, I breathe slowly and steadily along with you, because we have a natural instinct to match our breath to someone else's if we can hear it. And I encourage you to keep going, reminding you that you are allowed to feel what you feel.

Eventually, your breathing changes, and you sigh deeply. I cuddle you, and then put you to bed, and tuck you in, trusting you will finally be able to get the rest that you have been missing.

~

Most recipes for self-love come down to noticing, trusting, and honouring our own thoughts, feelings, and intuitions. In this chapter, greater emphasis will be placed on the latter two, since Western culture already prizes intellect so highly. I want to be clear that I am not implying that, in order to effectively value yourself, you must put yourself at the whim of your every emotion. If anything it's my experience that, by facing our feelings head on, and forging friendships with our emotions and intuitions, we become better equipped to both express what is happening to us in any given moment, and to then make choices based on all the information we have at our disposal—without being sabotaged by feelings we're either repressing, or allowing to run us ragged.

I also want to note that the intellect that is so valued by our culture is still to a great extent that of a certain class of people. As such, if your intellectual capability and labour has historically been devalued, undermined, or dismissed, feel free to apply the principles of this section to your own personal ingeniousness as well.

⋙ PLAYTIME ⋘
A Grief Ritual

Sometimes we come up against a wall of emotion so intense that it leaves us feeling as though our world has been turned upside down, and we no longer know how to move through it. At times such as these, I take the kind of compassionate attention described in the meditation above to a different level, and create a grief ritual.

A grief ritual is a piece of time and space gifted by you to your big feeling. If your big feeling doesn't feel like grief, you might do an anger ritual, or a despair ritual. The important thing is that you are weaving a container in which to give yourself permission to have that big feeling. Permission to feel fully, to allow your emotion to sweep through you, until such time as it noticeably shifts or softens of its own accord.

Your ritual should include the following components:

- A designated time slot. Deep indulgence in our emotions for the purpose of hearing and healing them takes time. This won't always be the kind of ritual you can do spontaneously at the time that the need arises. What you can do is grab your diary, allocate a "feeling" slot, and keep it sacrosanct.

- Safe space—for you, as well as for your environment and anyone that shares it with you. Make sure that your ritual is going to be safe from intrusion, and that it won't intrude on anyone else.

- A way to allow your feeling to move. Demanding of yourself that you cry or rage as soon as you're all set and ready to go may not prove effective, particularly if time has passed between the source of how you're feeling and your ritual,. However, journaling, moving your body/raising your voice to some appropriate music, thumping or screaming into a pillow, or simply breathing into the place in your body where the feeling is, can all support you in getting deep enough into that emotion to really inhabit it, and let it do or say what it needs to.

- A way to process that feeling. Yes, just crying counts. I'm reminded here of the concept of crygasms—inhabiting the process of crying with such commitment and conviction that it moves past being about a "difficult" emotion, and becomes an almost ecstatic experience in its own right.

The point is—go for it! You can also write down your feeling—possibly following that by tearing or burning up the paper you've been writing on as a way to release the words and the feelings contained therein; you can dance or shake your feeling; you can invite the image of someone you feel hurt by to come and sit on a cushion opposite you, and let them have it till you're all talked/yelled out; or you can simply breathe, breathe, breathe with the body that is yours and that is feeling, until you notice a shift.

- An anchor. Something to hang onto once you've committed yourself to riding the waves of emotion. For me, this is usually my altar—which is, incidentally, a big chunk of tree trunk, and a pretty damn solid thing to hang onto. Yours might be a pillow, a childhood toy, a figurine, a crystal, a lucky charm. Whatever it is, give yourself something to keep you anchored to the ground, your body, and this world while you're feeling, and to support you in coming back when you're done.

- A letting go. Something to signify releasing what you're feeling, or its cause. Just to be clear here, the primary purpose of this ritual is not to "get rid" of that nasty feeling that's been bugging you and that you want gone. The primary purpose of this ritual is to treat the feeling like an honoured guest, and take the time to hear what it has to say, and what it needs. However, it's likely that some flavour of release will unfold, and, given enough space to move, emotions generally shift into something new. You may wish to close your ritual with something that signifies and honours that release—burning or scrunching up the paper you've been writing on; slowly, mindfully, tenderly cleaning your body; or burying the (biodegradable) remains of whatever you've used in your ritual in the earth.

Of course, not everything we discover when we start listening to ourselves is something we're going to want to release, and even those things that we do elect to try and process are likely to bring with them clarity and direction that we want to take action on.

As you establish relationship with yourself, and you start to act as if your feelings, your thoughts, your personhood, your self, have intrinsic value, it is likely you are going to start itching to make change. You might start asking questions of yourself and your life—why do I do this to myself? Why do I let this person do that to me? Am I really OK with doing this for eight hours a day? Where does love/joy/pleasure fit into my life, and how can I have more of it? Why did I never give that thing I love doing/thought I would love doing a real shot?

The changes you're going to want to make are probably going to relate to one of the following things:

Self-care—how you treat yourself

Boundaries—how you allow or ask others to treat you

Creativity—how you treat the time and energy you have available to you, and, ultimately, how you ask life to treat you back.

It's very tempting during times of personal change to want to throw the pieces of your life up in the air and let them fall into fresh conglomerations, or to feel defeated because that doesn't feel like an option for you. It's particularly hard when we have very limited resources—whether of the monetary or energetic variety—and it seems like abundant resources are what is required for us to be able to get the help we need and change our lives for the better. It's not just the anticipation of facing big feelings, or fear in the face of the unknown, that can make the path to change look like the more daunting or difficult option.

At times like these it's important to remember that Small is Beautiful.

I see this play out with my clients. I have a habit of assigning "homeplay"; I usually see my regular clients once a fortnight, and suggest between one and three small things for them to try in between sessions. Because this gives them a small number of specific things to focus on, change takes root, slowly but surely, in their day-to-day lives. It may be subtle at first, but it is these small shifts that add up to significant and lasting change. I sometimes suspect that changes that have been built up with this five-minute practice here, or tweaking that way of communicating there, have a much better chance of being permanent than the kind of change that throwing one's life up in the air might effect.

Great change, then, is implemented not just by life's big bangs, but with small, daily actions; actions that may seem like sweet nothings, and yet have the power to become regular habits that transform a lifetime, and the person living it. And the best way to demonstrate self-worth is through small and regular acts of self-love.

Which brings me once again to practice, and how perfect its effects can be.

Self-care

Despite what advertising would have us believe, self-care isn't a series of activities mostly involving spending money. Self-care is a collection of fundamental beliefs that radically shape our way of life—a philosophy for living, if you will. Those beliefs pertain to our own worth, and whilst they are likely to be unique for each of us, this is what they boil down to:

I am as worthy of love, life, and belonging as everyone else. I deserve to be here. My needs are valid; my ideas count; my feelings are worthy of being seen, heard, and tended to; and my creative contribution is necessary.

As a practice, self-care consists of acting on this philosophy. Many of us have been raised to look outside ourselves for love, affirmation, success, and other things that confirm our worth and help us find meaning and pleasure in our lives, rather than pay attention to what is happening within. As such, moving from the habit of comparing ourselves to others in order to establish our worth, to actively believing in our own intrinsic worth, is something of a journey. This is where practice, and acting "as if," come in again.

To practise self-care is to maintain awareness of ourselves as we move through the world, to keep the lines of communication we looked at earlier open, and to act on what arises from those conversations.

Again, I'm not suggesting acting out our every emotion or whim. What I am suggesting is that our thoughts and feelings are valuable and deserve our attention. When we give our inner world the time of day, then we can feel more fully, and act responsively and responsibly on what we feel. Feelings move from being our enemies to becoming our allies. They thus move from being likely to flare up or overwhelm after being repressed for too long, to becoming integrated parts of ourselves that we can clearly and cleanly express and make choices around.

I'm also not suggesting acting on compulsion. At the time of writing, it is my belief that we do not live in a people-friendly culture. Our world is instead focused on profits, and in order for profits to rise sacrifices must—it would seem—be made. These include our time, our energy, our money, our creative capacities and emotional reserves, and, increasingly, our sanity. Or, as Sarah Knight so eloquently puts it in her TEDx Talk "The Magic of Not Giving a Fuck," our Fucks (time, money, energy).[6]

The faster our world moves, and the more it takes us away from the things that make our lives meaningful—relationships, creativity, pleasure, play—the harder it is to inhabit. The more we become distanced from the cycles of the natural world, the more we buy into a flawed paradigm of constant progress and need to numb ourselves in order to be part of that paradigm, to be an effective cog in the machine. We all have ways of numbing our inconvenient feelings, and whether they're addictions or just bad habits, they all carry a degree of compulsion. Unfortunately, it's not possible to selectively numb our feelings; by applying salves and stoppers to our grief or anger, we also take the kick out of our pleasure, and dull down our joy. In inviting you to listen in and act on what you find there, I'm not necessarily inviting you to act on the voice that is shouting the loudest for the TV remote—though that voice is also valid, and sometimes exactly the one we need to listen to! Rather, I'm inviting you to listen deeper, until you find the voice that is speaking to you most tenderly. Follow that.

Finally, I want to acknowledge that many if not all forms of self-care are a privilege. It is much harder to attend to our inner voices when, for example, our basic needs are at risk of not being met, or the people in our environment are shouting too loudly for us to be able to hear ourselves. Taking time to Listen In when it seems like there are not enough hours in the day to do everything that is being demanded of us can feel like a luxury—though I promise you it will not prove a frivolous one. Self-care is not exercising our privilege in order to avoid what is happening in our world, although it must sometimes look like switching off for a while. Rather, self-care is doing what needs to be done so that we may be the best vessel for the change that each of us wishes to create and see in the world. As civil rights activist Audre Lorde

---

6. Knight, "The Magic of Not Giving a F***."

writes: "Caring for myself is not self-indulgence, it is self-preservation, and that is an act of political warfare."[7]

In order to discover what self-care is for you, you will need to start paying generous attention to the parts of you it's likely you have been taught at one point or another to overlook—the tender bruised parts, the furious parts, the sweet juicy parts, the animal parts, the feelings in the gut parts. The heart and belly and sex parts. These can tell you much more about what nourishes you, what you need, and how to gift that to yourself daily, than any billboard ever will.

The Listening In practices that we explored earlier in this book can support you in opening those lines of communication with yourself, and discerning what your feelings, needs, and instincts have to say in any given moment. That in itself can be a radical shift in perspective. But even as we come to know ourselves, and figure out what really sustains us, there is still a divide between those realisations, and acting on them—especially when there are factors in our environment that discourage us from doing so. The bridge between understanding what we need, and acting on it, is trust in and love for ourselves. I'm pleased to report, however, that you don't need to have that whole self-trust/self-love thing down, done, and dusted before you can practice self-care—because practising self-care, or, if you prefer, acting as if you trust and love yourself, reinforces the possibility that you can, and that you do.

So as you get into the habit of pausing and asking "How do I feel/What do I need?," a follow up question might be "And what would I do about that right now if I loved myself?" If that question doesn't quite sink in for you yet, alternatives might be "What would I do about that right now if I completely trusted myself?," or "What would I do about that right now if I knew I was worthy of love and belonging?" The answer is likely your next step.

It's also worth having some self-care practices up your sleeve for those moments when you become aware that you are desperately in need of a time out, a boost in resources, or just a little joy burst.

---

7. Lorde, *A Burst of Light*, 131.

≷ PLAYTIME ≶
My Self-Care Tool Kit

List ten activities or experiences that make you feel nourished/comforted/rested.

Next to each one, note:

Do you need anything in order to do it?

Does it cost money or is it free?

How much time will it take?

Can you do it by yourself?

Does it nourish your mind, body, heart, sex, or spirit?

Then list ten activities or experiences that leave you feeling inspired, renewed, alive, and do the same again.

Now, drawing inspiration from the above, get creative, and make yourself a physical self-care kit. This can be as simple as a list of five or ten direct actions you can take to soothe, nourish, or uplift yourself in any given moment; slip the list into your wallet or coat pocket, or pin it somewhere you can see it when you need to.

Or, you can create a real-life kit, filling a shoe box with objects, reminders, and treats that will inspire you to self-care. Mine might include a candle, a notebook and pen, a book whose words reassure me, a homemade tea or tincture, a Pocket Dragon figurine, chocolate, a loving card from a friend, and something to put in a bath.

If you travel a lot, or just don't have a whole lot of space, it's a great idea to make a portable self-care kit to take with you on the road or squirrel into a nook somewhere.

While I was training toward my ordination as an interfaith minister, I embarked on a project exploring how spiritual counselling could be of service to sex workers. For my case study, I worked with a colleague who is often on the road, giving workshops and sessions in different cities. She was finding it hard to stay grounded, and to remember her worth, when she wasn't at home and doing her regular practices. As her final assignment, I invited her to create a portable altar, something that would contain the things she needed to support her in doing her practices and practising self-care on the road. A few months later, we were both teaching at the same event. On the last day, she said she had something she was excited to show me. It was her portable altar—a tiny antique box picked up in a thrift store, containing a tea light, a square of chocolate, a lucky penny, and a sex workers' rights badge. The affirmations we'd been working on together were written out on thin slips of paper stuck to the inside of the lid. Voilà! One portable self-care kit, a pocket-sized reminder of self-love. What would yours look like?

Self-love

You will soon find that some of the most radical acts of self-love involve other people. Specifically, as you begin to listen to yourself, act on what you hear, and reassign your time, resources, and love—or, to use Sarah Knight's excellent shorthand, your "fucks" [8]—accordingly, it's highly likely that the following things will happen to a greater or lesser extent:

- You will keep more of your fucks for yourself.
- You'll take some fucks back from areas of your life where other people expect you to just keep on giving them.
- As you start giving a fuck about you, you'll start giving one about how others treat you.
- And, inevitably, you're going to realise that there are some people who just need to be asked, in the nicest possible way, to fuck off. Or told, if that whole nice thing doesn't work out.

The responses you receive to the above, and the changes you realise you need to make, may well seem scary at first—especially if:

You're used to being a giver, a coper, a "nice guy," a "perfect parent," a "rock": and you're used to being appreciated and validated for being one. But the thing is, you only have so many resources available—and in order to reassign some to you, you're going to have to give a few less to others. If you're used to basing your self-worth on the external affirmation of others relying on you, looking to you, and thanking you, you're going to have to practise believing in your intrinsic worth double-time to keep up. But I promise you, you are worth the love you have to give—not to mention the love some others have probably been waiting to take a turn at giving you. And you will be much better placed to give with ease, happiness, and grace when you get into good habits around replenishing your own resources.

---

8. Knight, "The Magic of Not Giving a F***."

You lose people as a result of your self-loving actions: Yes, this happens.
It can suck. And it can be scary. I've watched clients, deep in the process
of self-discovery, immersed in the hard work of self-acceptance, having
to grapple with the terrifying prospect of the growing distance between
themselves and their people, with no new circle of confidants emerging
quickly enough to fill the breach. As if gathering up the courage and conviction to act like you have value wasn't hard enough, we often have to
start that journey by ourselves. Others will join you, I promise. Also, just
because people from your past aren't on precisely the same path right now,
it doesn't necessarily mean they won't be willing to accompany you if you
share what you're traversing, and ask. And there's nothing like asking for
our vulnerable, heartfelt needs from those we love to get us acting like
we're worthy of love.

You realise that a fundamental aspect of your life routinely devalues you:
This can be tough if it's an aspect such as a job that you rely on to pay the
bills. It's especially tough if it's a significant person—a family member who
you don't have the dubious luxury of cutting ties with, or a close friend or
partner whose presence in your life you had counted on being a permanent fixture. It's hard, when we're used to being treated a certain way, to
imagine that things could be different—so we're likely to keep trying to
make things work, rather than cut ties and lean into the unknown. If the
relationship in question can sustain some big conversations and some be-
havioural adjustments, or some new boundary setting, in order to reflect
your intrinsic worth a little more, great. If not, you may have to allow for
the possibility that you deserve better.

～

As you begin to attend to the whispers and callings of your inner world,
you will begin to identify the following in relation to other people: Needs,
Boundaries, Desires, and Values.

Needs

The concept of need has an unfortunate rep in our culture. The idea of being
"needy" in relationships is anathema, and, on a wider scale, the basic needs
of the many are often treated as unnecessary—usually in favour of profit for

the few. And yet we all have needs, without which we simply cannot move through our daily lives. Likewise, we all have needs in relationship, without which we cannot be expected to relate in an open, loving way. Some of these are fairly universal, while others may be a little more personal, based on our history and circumstances.

Our needs are the conditions that allow us to relate in an open-hearted manner. And not unlike our most primal needs for food and rest, when our relational needs are not being met, there is a sense of recurring hunger, exhaustion, or longing, which keeps on surfacing—however much we work on ourselves or talk it out. When a pattern like that emerges, it's likely signposting an unmet need. If that is the case, no amount of self-work will make that need go away, just like you can't talk yourself out of feeling hungry. In those moments, what we need is the radical self-love to bring our need to the relationship and ask: Can this be met? Your need is valid, and it isn't going anywhere—so if the answer is no, you'll have to work out whether that need can be nourished without causing damage to the situation, or whether you need to leave the situation in order to nourish you.

Where in your life, or your relationships, do you feel consistently hungry?

Boundaries

Our boundaries are the lines—physical, emotional, or mental—that we need others to respect, in order for us to be in connection with them. If you're not sure where your edges are, or you are so used to having them overstepped that they are somewhat frayed, take some time to think about when you feel safe, and when you don't, and the conditions that are present in each instance. That feeling you get in your belly when you don't feel safe is there to tell you that a boundary is being crossed.

Where in your life do you feel unsafe to connect or communicate? What circumstances, behaviours, or people do you need to set a boundary with in order for that to change?

Many of us have not been encouraged to heed that feeling, or have had our boundaries expressly crossed, or entirely stripped away from us, at some point in our history. Or we've become used to inhabiting the role of givers or carers, healers or listeners, and not made time to explore and express where our own edges are.

I recall working with a client on the subject of expressing boundaries, needs, and desires. She described the process as one of shifting her boundaries out from under her skin, where she had learned to keep them as a child, in order to please and appease the adults around her. Through our work together, she was able to expand her boundaries out from her body—which in turn finally relaxed, once it no longer had to be constantly on guard. Her boundaries became lines she was aware of, which she could choose to invite people over, or keep them on the other side of, according to her needs in the moment.

Here are some other things to remember about your valid, lovable, kickass boundaries:

- Some boundaries stem from the universal human need to feel safe, to have agency and choice, and to have personal space and privacy. Some boundaries stem from—or are intensified because of—trauma or other painful past experiences. The latter are not less valid than the former; given time, safe space, and the opportunity to process and to reclaim the parts of you that were previously violated, they can change—but they must do so at your pace, rather than at the insistence or pace of anyone else.

- Your boundaries will flex and shift based on environment, energy levels, mood, relationships, timing—and that is absolutely appropriate. It's totally valid to have different edges when you're tired and hungry, or when you're in an unfamiliar place, or right after having an argument, according to your needs in each moment.

- You get to change your mind. You are not required to have the same boundaries you did last year, last week, or even a moment ago, if your body is telling you that something can or should change. That being said, I recommend the practice from parts of the BDSM/kink world, whereby the boundaries that are agreed to at the start of a "scene" are the ones that are adhered to throughout said scene—even if one or both of the players decide they want, for example, to take more risks or get more intimate halfway through. Changing your mind about boundaries when in an altered state—even if it's just produced by endorphins—is rarely a good idea. Keep it for the next "scene."

• You are allowed to have different boundaries with different people. You are not obliged to share with one friend what you have with another. You are not obliged to hug everyone in the room if the room you walk into happens to contain one person you wish to hug. If you find yourself in a threesome, you are not obliged to lick a part of one person's anatomy, just because you were up for licking the other person's. Your job is not to be a walking democracy where everyone is entitled to an equal share; your job is to make the choices that will allow you to be your most open-hearted self in each connection—and sometimes, that requires the other person to stay on their side of the sofa/room/country.

Knowing that our boundaries are known and will be respected is one of the factors that can make it much safer for us to express our desires.

Desires

If our relational needs are the basic requirements for us to be in connection, our desires are the things that make us want to be there. Desire is that which overrides our fears, our past experiences, our "knowing better," and inspires us to move into connection with others again and again. This includes our desire for belonging, our desire for companionship, our desire for pleasure, and our desire to become even more of the person we have the potential to be.

Once we're in connection, having the freedom, encouragement, and opportunity to express our desires can lead to more of what drew us to connection in the first place: more intimacy, more co-creation, more pleasure, more shared adventures. However, even with these parameters in place, expressing our desires does not come easy for many of us. Like our boundaries, desires are not necessarily something we're given a language for. Indeed, I myself have lost track of the number of times when parents, partners, teachers, and colleagues have explicitly or implicitly discouraged me from expressing my desires, or branded them as somehow "too much" or "wrong"—messages echoed in the institutions and culture around me. One of the reasons consent is such a hot topic at the time of writing is that so many of us are not taught to express our desires cleanly and kindly, but rather to get them by manipulation, subterfuge, taking, or allowing, all in the name of the spontaneity and performance we have come to associate with romance.

A fundamental need I have in relationship, with myself and others, is for my desires to be welcome. I see that same need playing out in my clients and workshop participants when I witness the profound impact that being in spaces where the expression of desire is welcome has upon them. Whether or not we always choose to act upon our desires is another matter, but we all need to experience our desires being heard, and seen as valid. This allows us to get more comfortable in our skin, and gives us space to either follow the flow of our desire—or, if that desire carries an inherent risk, to unpack it, and see what it's about, and whether it's worth following anyway.

To follow the flow of desire is to take a moment to pause, breathe in, listen to your body, and ask "What would feel good to me, right here, right now?" and to follow the answer you receive. It's worth pausing again in a little while, and asking "What would feel even better to me, right here, right now?"—and then keep following. This is a beautiful practice to get into—whether in your resting, your self-care, your erotic encounters, or your daily decision-making. Obviously the practice needs to be within your own consent, and take into account the consent and well-being of your personal ecosystem—your partnerships, family, environment, financial security, etc.

Unpacking desire is sometimes accompanied by recognising that following the desire in question comes with risks—either to yourself, to your lifestyle, or to your relationships. When this is the case, you may wish to take the time to explore what your desire is about, what the root of it is, what the likely outcome might be, and how well it sits with your needs and values.

And then ask yourself the big questions:

How does the prospect of following this desire feel to my head/heart/belly?

What would I need to make doing so safe? If I can't, can I follow this desire in a different way that would be safer?

Values

I mention values above. Values are a little more subtle than absolute necessity, or the Nos and Yeses of our boundaries and desires. They are also less fluctuating than the latter—though they can change throughout our lifetime. And they are often less conscious—though bringing them into consciousness can contribute to a life well-lived. Interestingly, they play a much more significant role in the sustainability of our relationships with other people than, for example, our individual tastes and even desires—things we often base initial attraction on. When it comes to choosing to share our lives with other people, unless we share some common values, it is likely that the initial enthusiasm of shared tastes or hobbies, or physical attraction, will erode in the face of differences at such a fundamental level.

Barbara Carrellas talks about the arguments we have that are caused by differences in values being fundamentally different from other arguments —often profoundly shocking, recurring, and difficult or impossible to fully resolve.[9] This is because our values are not only core beliefs that are fundamental to our identity and life choices; they are also intricately woven through our behaviour, through the way we move through the world on a daily basis, and through the way we choose to live. And, inevitably, through the way we relate to other people.

Getting to know our values can support us in making choices in our living and loving that are fully aligned with who we are. Below are some questions that will hopefully help you to get a sense of yours. These are best worked on with a journal to hand.

Think of the worst arguments you've had, the ones that left you feeling uncertain, uncomfortable, or untrusting of the friend, partner, or family member you were having them with; the ones that left you with the feeling that this connection might not be sustainable—or that, in hindsight, were the beginning of the end. What were you fighting for—or, put another way, what were you personally fighting in favour of?

Think of a time when you felt particularly proud of yourself or something you were doing, or that you look back on with particular pride. What were you doing, and what were you doing it for?

Think of an activity that felt deeply meaningful to you, something you felt fully present with and engaged in, or fully yourself doing. Something you'd do again, even if you had to do it for free. What were you doing, how did it make you feel, and what was your purpose or intention in doing it?

What can you absolutely not live without?

What do you most wish for those you love?

~~~~~~

9. Carrellas, *Ecstasy Is Necessary,* 30.

Once you've written the answers to the above, revisit each one. Some of them may already be revealing the values underlying them. Some of them will have yielded answers that are things, experiences, circumstances—in which case, ask yourself "What does that thing or experience give me?" Keep asking that until you come to something that seems like a value. Once you've done this with each answer, go back through, and circle any values that stand out to you or recur.

Now you have your initial list of values. There may be some that feel like different versions of the same thing; for example, justice, equality, and compassion all come up for me at the moment when I do this exercise. If this occurs, group them together, and pick the one that feels truest to you, or most jumps out, to assemble a final list; for me, this is currently compassion, because I figure if we were all more compassionate to one another, then justice and equality would follow close behind.

If you want to take this even further, you can have a go at putting your values in order of priority, and then checking in to see how aligned your daily life feels to these at present on a scale of one to ten.

~

We'll be diving into the acute delights of communication more deeply in the next section. For now, I just want to remind you why starting sentences with words like "I need," "No thank you," "I'd love to," and "I believe" is worth doing.

Each one of those sentences has the power to be a radical act of self-care, an affirmation of self-love, and a validation of our own worth—and a step in the direction of a life we love to live.

By honouring our own needs, boundaries, desires, and values, we give others permission to honour theirs, and we have the opportunity to find creative ways to incorporate both into our relating, rather than just "your way" or "my way"—which makes for a richer and more fulfilling relationship for everyone. Our connections are enriched when we bring ourselves bravely and brazenly to the table, and are often poorer for the moments when we stay silent.

And if you're still resisting all of the above, because taking care of others is just to intrinsically bound up with your identity, self-worth, and the way you move through the world, remember this: if it really is your job, and yours alone, to save the world/your beloveds/your family/your clients, who the fuck is going to do that when you've disregarded your needs, allowed your boundaries to be trampled, failed to find ways to nurture yourself, and let others define what is important to you, till you're in a broken down heap of tears and tiredness, and you're so far out of resources you can't imagine ever recouping them again? If others must be so very reliant on you, you'd better make damn sure you've put in the self-care necessary to be able to keep giving from a place of grounded kindness, rather than from a sense of obligation no one could ever possibly hope to repay.

Just saying.

≳ PLAYTIME ≲
The Power of "May I"

One of my favourite tools when it comes to communicating tender subjects such as our edges, our needs, our longing, is the phrase "May I."

I love these two words for the following reasons:

- They invite the listener to get present with the speaker
- They give the listener a chance to consent, whether to conversation or physical contact
- They make the listener an ally in what is about to be communicated/done—rather than a surprised or unwilling recipient, who all too easily becomes an opponent

Furthermore, these wonderful words can be used to communicate all the things we have just been exploring. For example:

May I ask you for something? (a need, a boundary, or a desire)

May I share something with you? (a need or a value)

May I speak with you about something that's been troubling me/that's important to me now/sometime soon? (a need, a boundary, or a value)

May I do something to you? (a desire)

Replace "something" with whatever is up for you in each moment, and don't be afraid to tell your listener how you would like to be heard (more on that on page 106).

~

The other area that building relationship with ourselves inevitably impacts is our creativity, and how we direct our creative energy.

To be clear, this is not just directed to the self-identified artists among you. We are all innately creative beings. All of us. And we all express that creativity in different ways. For some of us it absolutely looks like what our culture tells us it looks like: from bold, sprawling graffiti, to tiny, emerald-bright watercolours; from the tactile joys of hands slick with clay, to the slap and scrape of cement and plaster; from sequins and pearls, to words to notes to symphonies. And that's beautiful. But that's not where creativity ends.

The Renaissance did us a lot of favours, but one unkindness it left for future generations was taking art out of the hands of the craftsperson—who could be anyone, from a guild master, to an apprentice, to an elder at her spinning wheel—and put it in the hands of a chosen minority, with supposedly god-given gifts, that we have come to call Artists. It's always a dangerous thing when something precious, nurturing, and transformative lands in the hands of the few, rather than the many. In this case, the danger is to our psyches, our inner world, and to our very life-force, which is so profoundly, fiercely creative. In believing that this creativity stuff is for other people—with more resources, education, opportunities, inspiration, and that oh-so-dangerous word, "talent," than us—we shut down a part of ourselves which is intrinsically intertwined with our own aliveness.

To be creative is to follow our flow into making something that we are called to bring into the world. Deep listening allows us to tap in to our flow, and to hear what is being called forth from us. And yes, that could absolutely be an exquisite aria—but a lullaby can also be exquisite, as can a nut roast, or a mural for a child's bedroom wall, or a cosplay outfit, or a daisy chain.

Sure, many forms of creativity take a certain amount of practise—but the need to practise is not equivalent with "Oh no, I couldn't possibly, my sister is the artistic one." As someone who was headed happily down the exhibiting artist route before sex and god took the wheel out of my hands, I promise you, it was practise, years of practise, that got me there. There was no "it just comes naturally" about it.

Which doesn't, of course, mean that it's not a god-given gift. I just don't buy the idea that God/dess discriminates with that one! Rather, I think that our creative flow is as innate as our life force, or as erotic energy is for many of us—in fact, I suspect that they are at the very least intrinsically inter-twined, and possibly even the same thing. In "The Uses of the Erotic," Audre Lorde writes: "When I speak of the erotic, then, I speak of it as an assertion of the life force of women; of that creative energy empowered." [10]

So how can you access that creative flow? We'll be looking later on at ways to explicitly combine creativity with pleasure; for now, here are some mundane ways to tap into the magic of creativity.

Get into your body: Combine the intention and practice of listening to yourself with a physical activity—ideally one that allows you the luxury of turning your attention inward. Examples that can be done for free might include walking, running, dancing, slow exercises/stretches, or moving a part of your body that feels moveable today in whatever way that part of you wants to move. Get into a habit of combining physical movement with attention, intention, and that enquiry you've been practising—what's up for me right now? How am I feeling? What do I want to follow? What do I want to release? And breathe. Keep returning to the breath. This is practising embodiment. Specifically, it's practising connecting your aware-ness into your physical self—and your physical self is usually where your flow is to be found.

Give yourself permission to play: Most of us have a thing we've always wanted to try, but never made time for. It might be that big dream that you've had since you were four, but which you put away with childish things a long time ago. It could also just be a fleeting curiosity—"saxo-phones are sexy instruments, aren't they? I wonder what it would be like to be able to play one;" "My neighbour looked happy for weeks after he completed that cycling tour of the greenways in Catalonia; must feel great to be able to do that!"; or even just "Ghost sure made pottery look like fun!" I encourage you to pursue one thing you're curious about, in a way that feels manageable to you, without any expectation or goal—oh look, another way in which creativity is like sex! Don't try to make Great Art; I'm not saying that won't be what emerges, but that's not what I'm encour-aging you to do. What I'm encouraging you to do is have a go, experiment, play.

---

10. Lorde, *Sister Outsider*, 55.

Pick a daily practice: To commit to a daily practice is to intentionally open the line of communication between yourself and your flow once per day. Given time, it's likely to result in that line of communication being available to you whenever you need to call upon it. The practice that has served me faithfully most mornings for most of the last decade is the Morning Pages practice suggested by Julia Cameron in *The Artist's Way*.[11] The practice is essentially writing three pages every morning upon waking, allowing whatever is in you to come out and, as Julia so perfectly describes it, "rest on the page."

Other daily practices to help you access your creative flow could include—

A daily sketchbook. This can be brought out on a commute or a walk, in a lunch hour or a lecture, when you look out the window or before you go to sleep. It can be a direct depiction of what you're looking at, or capture the memory of something you saw during the day. You can take five minutes or thirty.

Scrapbooking. Pick up one or two items during your day, and add them in a way that pleases you to the items you picked up the day before. This can be 2-D in a scrapbook, or 3-D in an installation, or online/on your device using an appropriate app. Or collage: collect images each day (from magazines, free newspapers, postcards, social media, your browsing history), and collage them together in whatever way you feel.

Short poems, verses, haikus, single sentences, each one taking no more than five to ten minutes, scribbled or recorded at the end of the day.

Taking a daily photo, of the same thing, or of a different thing each day that catches your attention.

Growing potted plants that need daily care.

A daily dance. A dance that's just for you.

$\sim$

Storyteller and researcher Brené Brown writes: "Wholehearted living is about engaging in our lives from a place of worthiness ... Yes, I am imperfect and vulnerable and sometimes afraid, but that doesn't change the truth that I am

11. Cameron, *The Artist's Way*, 9.

also brave and worthy of love and belonging."[12] I hope that the exercises in this chapter have inspired you to treat more aspects of yourself as worthy, and offered you at least a glimpse of the life-changing possibilities of radical self-love. In the next chapter, we dive into ritual as a container for self-love—specifically in the form of self-pleasure ...

---

12. Brown, *Daring Greatly*, 10.

Chapter 3

Celebration

So we've explored what it means to listen to ourselves, and how to exercise faith in what we hear ourselves saying. We've experimented with the art of self-love, and practised care and compassion for the more neglected aspects of ourselves. You've stuck with me, whilst hopefully building, or beginning to build, a significant and change-making relationship with yourself.

And I'm delighted to announce that, as we arrive at the subject of celebration, we begin at last to touch on the theme of the erotic that caused so many if you to pick this book up in the first place. Because what better way to celebrate ourselves that to dedicate ourselves to the study of our own pleasure?

Reclaiming the body

Before we can begin to revel in the rites of self-pleasure, however, many of us need to embark on a journey of reclamation. We must travel from where we find ourselves, to where we find our bodies. We must tenderly retrieve our bodies from the places where they are being displayed, have been abandoned, or were stolen away to. We must take them by the hands, and walk together into a new relationship called integration. And when we have built a haven for our bodies to rest, and established the parameters that ensure their safety … then we can settle slowly and intentionally down into our own skin, and truly begin an enquiry into pleasure.

A lot of us receive the message very early on, in one form or another, that our bodies are "for" other people. Depending on parameters such as the gender we were brought up with, our cultural and religious environs, the footsteps we are expected to follow in, early sexual experiences, and, of course, any experiences of emotional or physical abuse, we internalise beliefs around how our body ought to be in order to compete, conform, or command attention. Whether we're striving to look attractive or express modesty; to stand out or blend in; to disguise our social class, or express our religious values; to "pass" as a particular gender, age, race, or class…Our bodies, and how we arrange and decorate them, are constantly in dialogue with other people. For many of us, much of that dialogue is spent trying to please, appease, or pass.

This is all the more true when it comes to our pleasure. Few of us, at least in the West, receive any real sensual education. I love watching my amazing friends who are parents as well as sex educators teaching their children about consent, presence, and embodiment, and I look forward to the time when these paragraphs are made obsolete by future, wiser, generations. However, up until now, the journey toward pleasure has been an individual journey, often traversed in private, in the spaces betwixt and between. Often this journey is taken with snippets of incomplete informational input from the media, educators, parents, peers, porn—and it can be a vulnerable, imperfect, and messy process. When we are navigating uncharted waters with incomplete maps and low-level mood lighting, it often takes us a long time to notice how deep those waters run.

Sex and sexual activities are not only innately vulnerable, but also fundamentally psychosomatic experiences. They touch not just our physical bodies, but also our energetic and emotional ones. And so it is that, while we're navigating those deep waters, the experiences we have all too easily influence the course we chart—or indeed, whether we wish to sail at all.

As you continue to journey into your body, and particularly as you begin to build a more intimate relationship with your own sexuality, it's likely that, unless you have been startlingly fortunate, you're going to come across wreckage. We often store the vestiges of intense or traumatic emotional experiences in and around the genitals, or other erogenous zones. As you hone your capacity for self-compassion and listening to those part of yourself, stuff may come up, looking to be healed.

One of the things you may encounter is all the ways in which your desires, sexual drive, and erotic energy have been disallowed, dominated (nonconsensually), or devoured by others, and disowned by you. The places where your erotic self has been labelled as too little, or too much, and the places where you have sought to reshape or restrict (or do away with altogether) that molten core at the centre of who you are.

In the process of reshaping, repressing, or removing our physical and/or sensual selves for the sake of other people, we lose sight of—or look away from—our own needs, boundaries, preferences, desires. Our embodied erotic selves. The exercises that follow are designed to help you catch sight of yourself again, and bring your precious, wild, molten self back into focus.

⋗ PLAYTIME ⋘
Who Am I For?

List ten (nonsexual) things you do with your body. They can range from the mundane—getting dressed in the morning, shaving—to the miraculous—aerial aerobics, rock climbing.

Then, next to each thing, without overthinking it, list who you do those for. It's OK for those answers to be simple—"because my lover likes the way it smells"—convoluted—"initially, because my sister pressured me into joining her, but now mostly because it feels good"—or unexpected—"because of that boy in third grade who mocked my upper arms." The point is not to censor yourself, and to simply notice what arises.

When you've made your list, you might want to scan through it, and, in those instances where another person is involved, ask yourself: "Would I still want to do that if not for them?"

Now do the same for ten things you do in sexual encounters.

Read through what you've written. Are there any patterns emerging? Anyone who has a little more impact on, or control over, your physical and sensual self than you realised? And if so—are you happy with them having that measure of control?

Complete the following sentence ten times without overthinking it or censoring yourself:

If my body was a divine gift just for me, I would …

Do the same with:

If I were to have sex purely for my own pleasure, I would …
Go and do at least one of the things you have listed now!

~

For some of you, doing the exercise above, or just reading through the introduction to this chapter, may have brought up memories of times when you
felt your body, your pleasure, and your erotic agency were manipulated, mis-
treated, or simply taken without your consent. Some of you will be reading
this with an awareness either of precisely the moment when you shut down
your erotic self, or a strong sense that that moment happened, even if you
can't pinpoint when it was.

Hopefully you know that kind of experience is a great reason to get professional help, ideally from a therapist who incorporates the body into their
work, and has experience working directly with sexual issues (see the Resource section at the end of this book for recommendations). And hopefully
you'll believe me when I tell you that you deserve to get the help that you
need, and that your pleasure and your sexuality, and the core creative energy
that is bound up with them, are absolutely worth it.

The exercise that follows is one I have used for years, both personally, and
with clients who have experienced emotional or sexual trauma. It's a form of
what is referred to as Soul Retrieval by modern shamanic practitioners.

♥ *Messiness Alert!*

As I mentioned above, depending on your past experience and current
well-being, some of the exercises in this book might be best done in the company of a trusted therapeutic professional or support person. This next piece
is one of those. If you are drawn to try it, but are concerned about where it
might take you, consider doing it with support, or having support available
in the event that it does bring up more than you can hold.

⇾ PLAYTIME ⇽
Retrieving the Sexual Self

Carve out some time and space where you will not be disturbed.

Use whatever methods you wish to create "safer space." This could be as
simple as lighting a candle and asking that the most benevolent force you can

think of watch over you for the duration of this exercise—or as complicated as building a pillow fort, settling down in the centre of your fort with a cup of steaming cocoa, and imagining the entrance guarded by a legion of angels with flaming swords. You could even ask a friend to check in on you once you're done. Whatever feels effective and relevant for you right now.

Get comfortable, and take some deep breaths. Take the time to release any mental chatter with the outbreath, and follow the breath into the body with the inhale.

When you're feeling safe, grounded, and as centred as you're able to, gently begin to notice where in the body you're most strongly aware of the feelings the Who Am I For? exercise brought up. Give that part of you your attention, perhaps placing a hand there. Imagine that you're able to breathe deeply into it. You may find you feel an impulse to withdraw your attention, to slide around or away from that part of yourself. Instead, if you can, breathe yourself deeper into the feeling—as though your awareness could settle down into it as into a hot bath, and just breathe with how that feels.

This may be as much as you can manage for now—which is absolutely fine. If that's the case, see if you can breathe with the feeling until you have a sense of something shifting a little. Then bring yourself gently back. If there are big feelings, and accompanying tears or sound, allow those to flow until they feel complete. Then do something that nourishes you: make a cup of tea, have a bath, do some gentle exercise—and give yourself time to integrate what you just experienced.

If, once you have located the part of you that's holding the stuff of your past, you think you can keep going a little longer, gently ask yourself whether there is a place, and maybe a time, associated with this feeling you're breathing into. A place where a little piece of you was lost or left behind. See what arises. You may find you just get an impression of a place, or you may find a particular memory surfacing.

Use your mind's eye to look around, to see or sense where this place is, what it looks like, what is happening in it. And then look around for the you who is still here. That version of yourself will probably look as you did at the time of the experience. Notice where you are, what you look like, what you seem to be feeling.

And then, when you're ready, envision your current, adult self stepping into that space. If you feel nervous about doing so, take any support with you that you need—a guardian, a protective animal, an ancestor or good friend—and have them enter the room with you. If someone else is in the room, you may need to stand up for the past you, to speak out on your behalf. When it feels right, take yourself by the hand (or pick yourself up if you're very small), and consciously imagine leaving that space, and closing a door on it, and anyone inside it—a door with a lock to which only you have the key.

Before you come back to real time, take your past self to somewhere safe in your mind's eye. Comfort, reassure, hug yourself, have a conversation, do whatever you need to do to feel complete. And then, slowly and with purpose, imagine breathing or hugging that past you into your body, until they are part of you once more.

Take your time coming back. You may need to grieve, or process, or even just sleep. Give yourself whatever aftercare you need—drink plenty of water, get something to eat, wrap up warm, talk to a friend … In short, make sure you're fully back in your body, and you know what day of the week it is, before you do anything else.

～

Depending on how that experience went for you, here are some ways in which you may wish to further the process of integrating that particular part of you that you have reclaimed:

- *Re-connective conversation:* Find a photo of yourself at the time the experience you recalled occurred—or an object or memento that represents that time—and have a conversation with that aspect of yourself. Grieve together, remember together, and work out how you might want to move forward and forgive together. You may find the Automatic Writing process on page 26 useful for this.

- *Cutting the ties:* See page 199 for a practice that can help you cut the psychological, emotional, and energetic bonds tying you to anyone from your past who caused you harm, and/or who your erotic self is struggling to move on from.

- *Create a shrine:* Make an altar or shrine in your home for the part of yourself you are reclaiming. You can be as creative as you wish, and make your shrine either a pure acknowledgement of yourself when you traversed the experience you revisited in the exercise—perhaps some photographs surrounded with things that represent love and healing to you, for example—or you can make it a more active representation of the qualities you're intend to reclaim in reconnecting with that part of yourself—playfulness, pleasure, personal power, and so on. Give your shrine a few minutes of attention and love each day, either resting your eyes upon it for a while, lighting a candle, blowing it kisses, or pausing to listen in and see whether that part of you has anything to share with you in that moment.

Sacred self-pleasure

If in the Who Am I For? exercise earlier you started to glean the shapes and curves of your own desire, I invite you to bring those with you as we dive into the subject of self-pleasuring.

For many of us, our first forays into self-pleasuring follow the "quick and quiet" rule. Masturbation becomes something to be gotten over with before we are discovered, or before the shame sets in; a bite of forbidden fruit in exchange for a small burst of pleasure and relaxation. Combine this with the theory that our first erotic experiences set the scene for our erotic lives, and it's not hard to see how so many of us have ended up with an experience of pleasure that is localised to our genitals, transient, and reliant on holding our breath and/or constricting our muscles. Often, we feel ourselves to be at the whim of pleasure, rather than in collaboration with it; orgasms either arrive too quickly or appear out of reach; and that *something more* we once sensed might be possible in sex never quite makes itself known to us. Quick and quiet moves from being a necessity to becoming a habit that we don't know how to change.

The exercises that follow are designed to support you in changing old habits, experiencing pleasure in new ways, and coming into collaboration with your embodied erotic self.

Let's take a moment to explore your relationship with masturbation. And just to be clear—what follows makes no presumptions about what that looks like for you. We're delving into this not because there is a "right" or "wrong" way to have pleasure, but rather to support you in giving yourself pleasure that is more choiceful, more embodied, and more sensational, should you so wish. So approach the questions below with curiosity and playfulness, and without censorship:

- *What one word or sentence would you use to describe self-pleasuring?*
- *What one word or sentence would you use to describe how you self-pleasure?*
- *Who is it for when you self-pleasure?*
- *Who is it for when you resist self-pleasuring?*
- *What was your first experience of self-pleasure?*
- *What have your best experiences of self-pleasure been like?*
- *What about the worst ones?*
- *What, if anything, do you enjoy about self-pleasuring?*
- *What, if anything, frustrates you about it?*
- *What, if anything, disgusts you about it?*
- *How would you like self-pleasuring to feel in the future?*
- *How would you like to feel about self-pleasuring in the future?*
- *Is there anyone else you would like to share your self-pleasuring with?*

Notice if any themes emerge—and see if a vision is beginning to take shape for you of what self-pleasuring might be—if the experiences you're already having can be improved on, of course. While that vision is taking shape, it seems as good a time as any to let your genitals get a word in as well...

⋙ PLAYTIME ⋘
Talking Genitals II

Note: if for reasons of gender or other dysphoria, looking directly at your genitals is not something that fits within the self-care bracket for you, feel free to use the Listening In techniques from Talking Genitals I on page 27 instead, or to just skip right over this exercise.

Equip yourself with a way of making notes, and a small mirror (one with its own stand if possible), and carve out some private space and time for yourself. You'll need to have direct access to your genitals for this exercise, so get cosy in something suitably loose and open—and then sit in a way that feels comfortable, with your back supported, and your tools to hand.

Take a few moments to get present with yourself—taking deep, luxurious breaths—and check in with you. When you're ready, position your mirror in front of your genitals, and begin by just looking at your reflection. Notice any judgments or discomfort as they arise, and see if you can breathe them out, one by one, until you're just witnessing yourself with gentle curiosity.

If you find this initial stage difficult, remember your genitals are not all that you are; they do not define you, or your sexuality or gender. They're simply a facet of your physical self, just "what you have to work with" right now.

Observe and breathe for at least five minutes.

When you feel that you're as present as you're able to be with yourself, begin a conversation with the reflection before you. Greet your genitals, and allow the response to arise uncensored. If it feels easier, use the Automatic Writing technique from page 26 to allow the dialogue to unfold.

Take the time to ask your genitals how they are feeling, what they are currently desiring, and about the kind of holding or touch they might be longing for (if any). Ask them how they feel about your self-pleasuring habits, and whether they would like anything to be different, or more or less of anything in particular. Remember to keep an open mind, listen carefully, and allow yourself to be surprised by the answers you receive.

When the conversation feels complete, thank your genitals, make notes, and bring this gently to a close in whatever way feels appropriate.

~

Having engaged in compassionate conversation with yourself, and your genitals, that vision of the self-pleasuring experience you desire is hopefully beginning to take shape. Here's one final thing to try before we get down to making that vision manifest.

⇶ PLAYTIME ⇷
Turn-On Tables

Grab some paper and a pen, and create columns, one for each of the five senses (or for each of the senses you have access to).

Under each heading, list at least ten things that stimulate that sense, and also happen to stimulate you sexually.

For example, under Touch, I might list sunshine on my skin and running my fingers through cropped hair; under Smell, sweat and vetiver; under Hearing, Nina Simone's "Sugar in My Bowl" and having my name called in the throes of passion, etc.

Make sure you list things that don't rely on another person (chocolate), as well as things that do (watching a lover unbutton their jeans). As ever, the first rule of the game is to have fun!

Masturbation matters: an aside

Before we dive into making your self-pleasuring visions manifest, I want to say a little bit about why I'm taking the time to delve into the delicious depths of masturbation with you. It's not just because doing so might provide you with a safe space in which to run your first experiments in sex magic—though I certainly hope that will be the case. It is also because of the vital place self-pleasuring occupies in holistic (by which I mean that which touches on our whole selves, or renders us whole) sexuality.

Masturbation is widely looked down upon as the poor second cousin of "sex"—and by sex we usually mean PIV intercourse. Still loaded with religious and social stigma, and for many of us the place where we first learn sexual shame, masturbation rarely features in saucy scenes on the screen, gets described in juicy detail in mainstream literature, or finds itself drawn upon to flesh out the lyrics of passionate love-songs. On those occasions where it does feature, it is rarely depicted in a positive light—indeed, depictions often uphold the "quick and quiet" rules we were touching on earlier. Masturbation may have played an invaluable part in the sexual liberation movements of the 1970s through the work of trailblazers like Betty Dodson—but it is still far from being liberated from the place of second-class citizen in the erotic echelons.

One of the tasks that faces us as conscious sexual beings and erotic magicians is a shift in mindset around the hierarchies to which we confine sex and sexual activities. We must allow for the possibility that no one sexual activity between one or more consenting adults is more valid or valuable than another. Masturbation is a great place to begin that shift—and here are some reasons for cultivating a renewed appreciation for self-pleasuring:

- It's a safer and self-consensual place to start—not just when you first set out on your sexual journey, but also on those occasions when you need to start that journey over again. Significant events in our lives such as loss, illness, or trauma can cut us off from our sexual selves—and so can the busyness of daily life, or the built-up resentments in long-term relationships. When you need to begin again, to rekindle, to remember, to rediscover, self-pleasuring gives you a safe enough harbour from which to set sail.

- It allows us a way of taking responsibility for our desires and taking charge of our pleasure—in general, and in those instances when sharing those kind of pleasures with others is not an option, which may be the case for a shorter or longer period of time, in or out of relationship. When this is the case for us, we can get creative, have dates with ourselves, affirm and enjoy our erotic identity, and never risk losing it because we stopped using it.

- It gives us a space in which to explore, experiment with, and develop our sexuality. Whether this is tentatively trying a new sensation to find out if it's for us (e.g., nipple clamps); developing a skill (e.g., delaying ejaculation); or simply finding out what we like in detail, for our own pleasure, and also so we can communicate it to our lovers (e.g., "circular strokes about two millimetres below the clitoris please!"), masturbation ensures that we always have the opportunity to continue to evolve as sexual beings.

- It allows for moments in which our sexuality is for our own pleasure only, rather than a gift, performance, or obligation to another. I cannot stress enough how important those moments are.

- It is also a beautiful thing to share with a partner, opening up new possibilities in shared pleasure and play.

- It's the safest safer sex—and sometimes that level of safety is what you need in order to have an erotic encounter with someone.
- And, last but most certainly not least, as you are about to discover, it is an excellent tool for magic!

Sacred self-pleasure, continued

It's time to go ahead and set a date with yourself, and dedicate some of your sweet energy and time to feeling good—because you can. I'll be talking more about the importance of dates for maintaining erotic flow in intimate relationships later on in this book. For now, suffice to say, consciously carving out space and time for love and pleasure is just as important when it comes to building your connection to your erotic self. By allocating time in your schedule to your own pleasure, and by guarding that time with the same care that you would a slot allocated to spending time with a dear friend or lover, or pursuing a new skill or a favourite hobby, you send yourself a clear message about how much you value your erotic self. So grab your diary and make a date with you—and keep it! Don't go postponing as soon as the first request comes in from Auntie Mabel to help repaint her kitchen. You're busy. You're worth it.

Having carved out time, when that time rolls around, it's always a good idea to create a conducive space. Draw on your Turn-On Tables for inspiration, and set up a space for yourself that is clean, private, and includes some of the elements you listed in the exercise. As much as you can with the resources available to you, create an environment that makes you feel comfortable in your own body, and encourages you in getting sensual in your own skin.

Depending on how easeful or possible self-pleasuring feels for you, you may wish to start your explorations into your own pleasure with the first two of the exercises that follow. They offer a way to dip your toe into embodiment, and the possibilities of pleasure and sensation, without being overtly sexual.

The third exercise invites more explicitly sensual and sexual touch, though still with the intention to get embodied and feel the (self)love.

You can choose one, two, or all of them, flowing from one to the other organically, if it feels safe and scrummy for you to do so.

⪢ PLAYTIME ⪡
Beginning

Whichever of the following options you choose at this time, begin by getting comfortable (in whatever state of dress/undress you wish) and taking some deep breaths. Breathe until you feel a little less in your head, and a little more in your body. Notice any feelings or fears that arise, and breathe with each of them, before gently sending them off to play elsewhere.

When you're feeling more present and relaxed, put your attention into your heart, and just breathe with whatever is present there.

If, as you breathe, you find some tenderness, some compassion, some warmth, some love—send that to yourself. Imagine it flowing round your body as you breathe out. Let your body start to fill up with love.

If you have a sense of a higher power of some sort, of a source of love that feels unconditional, imagine that your heart is cradled in that greater heart. Breathe in some of that unconditional love. Imagine it flowing round your body as you breathe out.

When you have as clear a sense of your own lovedness as possible, and your breathing has relaxed and deepened, then you are ready to begin.

⪢ PLAYTIME ⪡
Loving Hands

This exercise is based on Betty Martin's Waking Up the Hands structure.[13]

Rest one hand on your lap if you're sitting up (in which case, make sure your back is supported), or on your belly or on the pillow next to you if you're lying down. This resting hand will be your receptive hand. Your other hand will be your active hand.

Take some full, deep breaths.

Begin to touch your resting hand with your active hand. Really explore your resting hand fully with your fingertips, discovering all its textures and contours and edges, finding out where it is hard, where soft, where callused, where silken.

Check in and make sure you're still breathing deeply. Slow down the speed at which you're touching your hand.

---

13. Martin, *The Pleasure in Your Hands*.

After a little while, consciously choose to touch your resting hand in a way that your active hand enjoys.

Check in and make sure you're still breathing deeply. Slow down the speed at which you're touching your hand.

Notice if you're experiencing any pleasure in your active hand. See if you can build on that. See how much you can enjoy exploring your own skin.

After three to five minutes, consciously change your focus. Ask yourself how your receptive hand wishes to be touched, and "listen" through the fingertips of your active hand for the answer.

Check in and make sure you're still breathing deeply. Slow down the speed at which you're touching your hand.

Consciously choose to touch your resting hand in a way that feels good to it.

Check in and make sure you're still breathing deeply. Slow down the speed at which you're touching your hand.

Notice if you're experiencing any pleasure in your resting hand. See if you can build on that. See how much pleasure you can experience just through your hands, just because.

Do not be deceived by the simplicity of this exercise. It can be profound. Keep breathing, keep listening to your skin, and spend at least ten minutes on the whole experience. Set a timer if necessary.

Notice if there was a difference in the quality of your touch when you were focused on your active hand feeling good, or your receptive one. Notice if you enjoyed one more than the other.

⋙ PLAYTIME ⋘
Loving Skin

Now that your hands are a little more "awake," it's time to take this to a different part of the body.

Breathe, listen in, and identify an area that feels like it might actively like to be touched.

As before, begin by touching with your active hand, in a manner that feels good to that hand.

Remember to repeatedly check in with your breathing, and slow down your touch.

After three minutes, "listen" through your fingertips to see how this part of your body, this stretch of skin, would like to be touched—and do that.

See how many good feelings you can give yourself just via this one stretch of skin, this one part of your body. Just because.

If you decide to flow from this exercise into the next, you may wish to allow this touch to slowly expand to take in other parts of your body.

⋙ PLAYTIME ⋘
Making Love with Self

So, here you are. You've created your space, carved out your time. You're comfortable and breathing deeply. You're as connected as you can be with the sense that you're loved.

The primary invitation here is to be as present as possible with yourself in each moment—rather than slipping into old habits, or assumptions about how your body or pleasure does or should work. The invitation is also to explore and experiment, rather than reach for a specific goal. The moment you reach for something over there, you risk no longer being here in your skin.

In order to facilitate this, I offer you three recommendations:

- Remind yourself to breathe deeply and fully. Doing so will help you relax and receive, and it will also allow sensation to build and flow around your body, and release tensions in body or mind.

- Every few minutes, pause, and ask yourself: "What would feel good to me now?" Allow the answers to surprise you and entice you in new directions. Follow them.

- Use everything in your power to spread the pleasure, and allow energy to move around your body. As well as deep breathing, you may wish to add a breathing technique such as the Heart/Sex Circuit breath. Other ways to expand pleasure and move energy include sound, movement (particularly of the pelvis), sensations, and squeezing and releasing the pubococcygeus muscle. What we are aiming for here is precisely the opposite of the "quick and quiet" rule—so feel free to use whatever you need to liberate your erotic self!

As our intention here is one of awakening and inhabiting our physical selves and senses, I don't necessarily recommend using a sex toy at this point.

See if you can find your way deeper into the simpler sensations offered you by your own hands. However, if reasons of desensitisation, dysphoria, physical illness, or disability mean that your hands just don't deliver sensations you enjoy to you, the same rule applies: use whatever you need to feel good.

I recommend beginning in your heart as above, and coming back to your heart at the end, even if all you're doing is placing a hand there in the aftermath.

And I recommend listening to your body, not just during, but also after. Whether or not you find your way toward a physical or energetic orgasm, take the time to pay attention to what moves in you when you are in the tender "after" place, rather than rushing on to the next activity.

♥ Messiness Alert!

Chances are that, as you start to get present with yourself during pleasure, stuff will come up. Be gentle with yourself, make to time to reflect on and feel what arises for you—and resist the temptation to give up on yourself. That something more you hope for from your erotic life is out there—or rather, in you. A little perseverance, balanced with a whole lot of self-care, can go a long way.

Sex magic, solo

As we learn to breathe more deeply, to see what is moving in us more clearly, to touch more tenderly, we are also learning to perceive, move, and release energy—the kind of energy that is the primary ingredient necessary for magical ritual. In the preceding exercises, we started bringing some ritual elements to our erotic practice. Now it's time to find out what happens when we bring erotic elements to the practice of magic.

You may recall from the introduction that ritual magic as I work with it has seven components. They are:

1. Creating Safe/Sacred Space
2. Invocation
3. Setting Intention
4. Raising Energy
5. Release

6. Surrender

7. Giving Thanks

Creating Safe/Sacred Space

Creating Space is something we started touching on in previous exercises. It is the act of setting aside time and carving out private space for yourself, your magical working, and anyone or anything you intend to commune with during that working. It also means doing what needs to be done for the space you are using to become a liminal space—a space where you can connect not just to the physical, but also to the psychological, the emotional, and the spiritual aspects of yourself, and to the cosmos around you.

What it takes to define liminal space will vary from person to person. Like any magical process, it can be as complex as you wish—but like any magical process, it can also be stripped down to breath and imagination if necessary.

If you can, taking some time to tidy and arrange the space you'll be working in can be a great way to start. You may get a sense as you do so that you're clearing your internal space as you clear your external space. You can also cleanse your space energetically as well as physically. Ways to do this could include:

- Imagining your space filled with light, or a favourite colour, perhaps enclosed in a bubble of that light or colour.
- Walking round your space clockwise, and drawing a circle of light or colour with your left hand, encircling the space.
- Making sound. A simple hum works as well as a chant or a song. Chimes or singing bowls are popular, but anything that makes a clear, ringing sound when tapped will work just as well. Or just put on your favourite thrash metal and stomp and shake your way around the space until you and it feel a little more energised!
- Burning herbs. I confess I discovered Californian sage before I discovered cultural appropriation. By the time that conversation had started to happen—and gave me pause to think about taking a magical herb out of its traditional ritual context, and using it despite the fact that it comes from a culture that my own culture has historically oppressed—

I already had an established relationship with that plant as a cleanser and companion. If you can, build relationships with plants that are native to the land you live on, both because you will be able to have more ongoing connections with them—seeding, nurturing, and harvesting them, or foraging for them—and to avoid blunders like mine. However, if, like me, you find your plant friends in other cultures, take the time to think about how the purchase of those plants can enrich the cultures they come from: buy organic, use local suppliers, make sure your purchase benefits the community you're taking from, and so forth.

- Lighting a candle. Fire offers such an effective focus for ritual, partly because it is transformation incarnate, and transformation is so often what we are doing ritual for. You can make the simple act of lighting a candle a deeply meaningful act with your attention and intention; with silence or with words of intention or prayer; or by imagining that, as you do so, the light of the flame ripples out, like a pebble thrown in a pond, and creates a bright space for you to work in.

You may wish to think about decoration—or the absence thereof. What evokes safe and sacred space to you? Is it minimalism: a white cloth, a single candle flame? Is it an abundance of colours, textures, and artefacts? Is it photographs of your ancestors? Is it all about the background music? Is it the simple act of locking the door? What can you create that speaks to you of a space that is different from the everyday—a space that is *kadosh*, a Hebrew term often translated in the West as "sacred," but in fact meaning "set apart." Find a balance between something that is luxurious enough to be special, and easy enough to be something you could regularly repeat should you so choose.

Invocation

An Invocation doesn't have to be to a specific divine being—it's really just a way to remember that we are not alone, that we are part of something greater, and to allow for the possibility that something greater wants our good. You may wish to invoke a particular face of a deity, but you could just as easily invoke a quality, like Love; the presence of a person or creature who has passed on who made you feel safe when they were alive; a natural element you feel an affinity with such as the sun, the energy of springtime, or water; or simply, a shorthand for that possibility that we're all connected, such as All That Is or Universe. Call in something you'd welcome support from in your magical working—and that you feel could be suitably sex-positive to provide it wholeheartedly!

Setting Intention

Setting Intention is the component of ritual I'd choose if I were pushed to pick just one, because so often, it seems like intention is all it takes to make the magic happen! I've heard clients set a loose intention in one coaching session, and then come back the next one with an extraordinary story of how life lined things up to give them precisely the experience to meet that intention. I've made a note to do a ritual for a particular intention for myself, and watched the magic unfold long before I got round to it. I have come to see Intention as one of the primary ways to make any process conscious, and I'll be encouraging you to use setting intentions in all manner of ways during the course of this book to support intimacy, pleasure, and transformation. For now, I'll address it purely in terms of magical workings.

When it comes to magical workings, our intention is our statement of what we are doing the magic for—whether that is inner transformation, a change in our environment, a shift in global consciousness, a celebration of ourselves or a season or an aspect of our lives, or something we'd like to call into our lives. The first thing to be aware of when it comes to intentions is that they work best for magical purposes when they are in some way encapsulated. By this I mean they are short, sweet, and succinct. If you're playing with this magic stuff for the first time, I recommend choosing an intention that can be articulated in a single sentence for your first ritual. For example: "I intend to break through the blockages between me and my pleasure," or "I intend to welcome more joy into my life."

Of course, sometimes the thing you're doing magic for is not simple in the slightest—for example, when calling in a new partner or a new home, or something else that has lots of specific characteristics you're hoping for. Beginning your magical working with, "I intend to manifest a lover with brightly coloured hair, emotional intelligence, similar music tastes, good baking skills, tattoos optional, etc." does not make for easy ritual, nor does attempting to hold all these characteristics in your head at the same time throughout. In these cases, I think of what Jan Fries says about the intention being a seed that gets planted in the deep mind through the process of ritual.[14] The question then becomes how you can make your more complex intention into a seed, into some equivalent of a single sentence. What can you encapsulate it in? You need to find something to infuse with the qualities of your intention that can represent it in your ritual. You can find more details on seed—or sigil—magic on page 164.

At other times, we don't know the details of what we want, but we do know how we believe it will make us feel. We may be able to encapsulate this feeling in a sentence or image. Feeling is a powerful driver for ritual because it taps into our embodied and emotional selves and the energy contained therein. As such, doing ritual with a feeling as the specific purpose can be very effective.

All that being said, the first time you do this I heartily recommend a simple, single sentence intention that you're going to need to put minimal effort into remembering. Feel free to write it down, and place it prominently in your sacred space, if you so wish.

Raising Energy

Raising Energy is how we give life to our intention, how we quite literally infuse that seed with our life force to help it grow. And what is more fundamentally intertwined with our life force than our sexual pleasure, that which can beget new life, and which engages our physical, emotional, and psychospiritual selves in the erotic act? Which is why sex magic is so potent—as well as so much fun!

For your upcoming ritual, I invite you to raise energy by engaging in an erotic activity with yourself. Here are just some of the things that could mean:

- Using the Heart/Sex Breath Circuit we explored earlier to raise energy, and building it by moving it around your body and charging up both yourself and your intention

---

14. Fries, *Visual Magic*, 9.

- Using a breath practice like the Genital- and Gender-Free Orgasm listed on page 240, to build breath and energy
- Indulging in some erotic/ecstatic dancing to an ever-building beat
- Calling upon your favourite kinky methods to give yourself some intense sensation
- And, yes, self-pleasuring (whatever that means to you) with the use of your hands or toys

Or, of course, a combination of a couple of the above; for example, I like the combination of the Heart/Sex Breath Circuit with self-pleasuring.

The choice is yours; as long as you choose something you can engage your physical, emotional, and erotic self in, something that will build to a climax of either orgasm, exhaustion, or something like the clench and hold breath practice from page 242, then you're all set.

Release

Release is that moment of climax. Climax might mean orgasm, but it could also mean some other kind of physical, emotional, or breathful peak and release. The moment just before it is the moment to bring your intention or seed to mind one more time. When you release your climax, you also release your intention to the cosmos, to your deep mind, to the god of your understanding—or all of the above. The moment right after it is the moment from which your intention is no longer in your hands, and indeed is no longer your concern or your job. Your work is done. Your intention becomes the work, the food, the pleasure of whatever you handed it over to. Your only job now is to …

Surrender

Surrender is a crucial component that is missing from Western culture at the time of writing. Since we have collectively bought into the idea that each of us is going it alone, we cannot afford to lean back into the moment between completing one thing and moving on to another—because who else would tend to our to-do list if we did?

Magic is founded on the premise that we are a whole lot more interconnected than that. To Surrender—in other words, to allow for a moment that you are taken care of, and to bask in the afterglow of ritual—is a vital component of the magical process. It's the moment when you trust that it is not your job to fix everything, and you allow the rest of the world to step up to the plate while you rest, receive, and enjoy, secure in the knowledge that you have been heard.

Giving Thanks

Giving Thanks is a great way to close any ritual. If you're working solo magic, you can thank yourself, and whatever you invoked, for what you have just co-created. If you're working with a partner, as we'll be exploring in the next chapter, you can thank each other for the courage and presence it takes to make magic together. It's a good moment to ground yourself, to come back to the breath, and back into your body if your ritual sent you flying out into the cosmos or just made you a little lightheaded. Perhaps most of all, this is a moment to acknowledge that you have been heard, to give thanks for that fact—and to close your ritual, and move on, secure in the knowledge that all is taken care of.

⇉ PLAYTIME ⇇
Grounding

It's pretty much always a good idea to take a moment, or indeed as much time as you feel you need, to get grounded after any ritual process. What does grounded mean? It's a fancy way of describing a process that can feel like coming back to Earth, or coming back into your own skin; it basically means feeling like your normal self again, as opposed to being in an altered state, which is after all what ritual is designed to help us enter into.

I strongly discourage you from using any of these practices to try and achieve a permanent altered state; they are not designed to help you to permanently escape from this world, from your feelings, or from the responsibilities of your life and relationships. Instead, I offer them to you as a way to make your life more embodied, and thus more ecstatic; to take your relationships with yourself and others deeper; and to support you in taking a more creative approach to living, whilst also discovering that you are not in this alone. Agreed? Excellent. Here are some grounding techniques. Practice one or two of them right now, even if you're just skimming through this section.

Physically: As you return from the Surrender part of your ritual, you may wish to wiggle your fingers and toes, wriggle your spine and hips, and stretch in some way that feels comfortable to you. You might want to pat yourself down, drumming your hands gently but firmly over your body from the crown of your head, down to your feet. Stamping your feet can also be effective. Make a physical gesture to close your ritual—a bow to yourself and all that is, blowing out the candle, or just mindfully tidying things away. Have a drink of water, and eat something small, dense, and delicious.

Mentally: Focus on where your body meets the floor, or whatever you are sitting or lying on. Put your attention into that place. Notice that you're supported unconditionally by the Earth below. If you wish, you can imagine little roots running down from the part of your body that meets the floor, and nestling into the Earth below.

Breathfully: Breathe out slowly and consciously. Use the Bottom Breath or the Grounding Breath. Place your hands on the ground, and intend that as you breathe out, any excess energy or light-headedness flows down your arms, through your palms, and into the Earth—leaving you feeling more solid, present, and alive.

Putting it all together

Ready to give this ritual thing a go? Got a thing you're longing to call into yourself or your life? Wonderful! Here are some top tips and loving reminders to get you going:

Start by setting aside time and space—a little more than you would usually feel comfortable taking for yourself, but not so much that it you'll never repeat the exercise because it isn't sustainable. Give yourself that time and space as a gift.

A few other things that are good to decide beforehand: your intention and how you'll encapsulate it. What you're going to do to raise energy. What release might look like.

That being said, it's also OK to follow the flow of the ritual to a greater or lesser extent, and see what you feel drawn to do in each moment—especially if that whole Listening In thing is going well for you.

When you've created your safe and sacred space, begin with the breath, and don't do anything else until your breath is deep and regular, and you feel a little more present—even if it is just a little more.

Don't skip bits that our culture has taught us are unimportant, especially if you haven't done this much before. Ask for help in your Invocation. Lean back into the Surrender section, and let it last just a little longer than feels comfortable. Give thanks in whatever way you're drawn to do so, but do it. Come to each part of your ritual mindfully, with appreciation, and trust that it serves your purpose.

You only need to bring your intention to mind twice, first at the beginning of your ritual when you express it—out loud, in your mind's eye, in the form of a representative image or artefact, or by writing it down—and secondly just before Release, when you bring it to mind, imagine it lighting up with the energy that you've raised, and then release it to the universe/your deep mind as you climax. Imagine it flying out of your body, and disappearing from view. Your work is done. It's not your job anymore. Lie back, let go, surrender. Enjoy the sensations still moving around your body.

Finally, remember: There is nothing to get right, and this doesn't have to be the only ritual you ever do. Make some simple decisions if this is your first foray into this kind of practice, and if you find yourself dithering over what to do, take a breath, feel into the options, and pick one in the knowledge that you can try the others at a later date, or even change your mind in the middle of things if you need to. Give yourself permission to play, to try, to experiment. Explore how you can enjoy the small moments that make up the ritual, rather than putting pressure on yourself toward achieving a certain result. In some ways, sex magic is no different from sex; the fewer expectations you have of it, the more you'll be able to be present to the experience itself.

Above all, give yourself permission to enjoy yourself!

Solo sex magic practices

Julia Cameron's *The Artist's Way* has been transforming my life ever since I first started working through it in my early twenties. In this seminal book on (re)kindling creativity, Julia recommends two regular practices: one of them a scheduled daily practice, and one of them a more spontaneous weekly one. The funny thing is, I've yet to meet anyone who finds both of them easy to do; most people prefer one or the other. I notice something similar happening when it comes to sharing erotic practices with my long-term beloved: I thrive on my daily practices, and tend to push for regular and structured practices between us. My beloved, on the other hand, finds that kind of structure excruciating, and much prefers to schedule in our dates or magic

sessions on an ad hoc basis. This, needless to say, has required a lot of negotiation to navigate!

Solo Sex Magic Ritual

While I recommend giving both of the practices below a go, one of the
reasons I'm offering you both of them is because one of them is likely to fit
more comfortably with you and your schedule than the other. The first is an
invitation to create a daily pleasure practice, and do it for a predetermined
number of days. The second challenges you to set a luxury date with yourself
to explore and indulge more extensively. Try and have a play with both at
least once!

⋙ PLAYTIME ⋘
The Daily Dalliance

I particularly recommend giving this extended practice a try if:

- You're in the process of reconnecting with, or rekindling, your sexuality
- You're in a relationship where sex has become a struggle, or a point of
  resentment, between you and your partner

- You're doing magic for a fundamental shift in yourself or your life, of the kind that is an ongoing process; healing your relationship to pleasure or money, for example, rather than manifesting a new car
- You want to integrate pleasure into your daily life

Decide on a number of days for which you will run this experiment. I recommend a minimum of seven, and you could go up to a month or a year if you wish. Make it specific, and make sure it only just pushes what feels manageable for you.

Decide on an amount of time that is both available to you on a daily basis, and that allows enough time for you to build some energy, and, if you wish, release and surrender. I recommend between fifteen and forty minutes.

Decide on your intention for this daily sex magical practice—and yes, just affording yourself the luxury of a daily wank is perfectly valid, especially if you approach said wank with a degree of mindfulness and some nice deep breaths. Other possible intentions might include:

- Rediscovering your sexuality, and integrating pleasure into your daily life
- Reclaiming and empowering yourself as a sexual being
- Raising energy for a big shift, project, or global issue

I'm going to offer you some examples of what a daily self-pleasure practice might look like for each of the above:

Reconnecting with your erotic self

If you're in the early stages of building or rekindling your relationship to your own sexuality, choosing both a clear time-frame, and a specific activity that feels accessible and possible for you, will be particularly supportive in building an effective daily practice.

We all set goalposts when it comes to our sexuality—because a lot of the messages we receive about sex tell us it's a goal-oriented activity. For those of us feeling like our sexuality is alien or broken, or simply uncharted territory, these messages often set us up for failure.

However, if all you have to do is show up for fifteen minutes a day and breathe a Heart/Sex Circuit, or caress your nipples, that may help shift your focus from those goals that can feel so unattainable, to the job at hand.

So, pick a manageable timeframe, and an activity that feels like it stretches, but doesn't entirely skip over, the edges of what feels possible to you right now. You can always decide to change it to something more ambitious next week.

Once per day, do what needs to be done to give yourself privacy. Pick a small gesture that can serve to delineate sacred space for you (lighting a candle and stating your intention out loud, for example). Take some deep breaths of your choice, and give yourself a moment of stillness. Then set a timer and begin your chosen activity.

When the timer goes off, it may find you in a state of raised energy, release, surrender, or just sticking with it. Wherever you are, find a gentle way to let go of the practice for today, knowing you'll come back to it tomorrow. Thank yourself for showing up.

You're doing great.

Reclaiming your erotic self

If you are adopting a daily practice in order to empower or expand your erotic self, it's still advisable to pick a timeframe for your practice that feels manageable—but allowing yourself to overflow that timeframe on occasion might be just the right way to be generous with yourself. More important is picking the practice: Will you spend your time simply giving yourself permission to indulge in your preferred form of self-pleasuring? Or is there something you've been wanting to experiment with for a while? As long as it is a practice that you have the knowledge and resources to do safely, this could be a perfect opportunity to try it out—and if it isn't, can you phone a friend or take a class to get you up to speed?

Whatever exciting array of possibilities you have laid on for yourself, make sure that you find some small gesture to demonstrate, at the start of your practice, that this is now separate space. Take the time you need to establish the deep, full breaths of your choice, and affirm your intention to gift your erotic self with this time before you set your timer and begin.

When your practice is over, offer thanks to yourself for this gift, and affirm you will be back tomorrow. Take some time to transition from this place of pleasure back into real life (e.g., by having a stretch or making yourself a hot drink).

Making change with your erotic self

In this instance you have chosen to do a daily practice to create change. This could be a change for yourself—for example, I have chosen in the past to do a daily practice for the purpose of inviting more abundance into my life—or for a global issue, such as sending healing to our planet, or smashing the patriarchy. Once you've chosen your practice and your daily timeframe, the key question when it comes to this daily magic-making is the nature of your intention—what the change you're wanting to create or contribute to is—and how you will visualise and energise that intention.

Some options:

As in the first ritual we looked at, pick something that encapsulates your intention—an image of what you want, or the feeling it will give you, or a short sentence—and visualise/feel/state it when you start your practice, and when you end said practice, and let it fly off into the universe.

Or, pick a simple representation of your desire that you wish to feed with the energy you are raising: an object, a picture, a candle. Take some time to breathe with this representation before you begin, opening your heart to it, offering it appreciation and love. Then do your practice. When that is complete, offer the energy to your symbol. You can do this by breathing it out and into said symbol on the first exhale after you climax—or by coming back to the symbol once the ritual is complete, and offering it energy by touching it, or just gazing lovingly at it.

Or—and this is the most complex option, not to be recommended before you feel comfortable with one or both of the above—you can share your energy via your breath with the representation of your desire throughout the ritual. If your representation is external, you'll need to position yourself so that you can see it during your practice. If your representation is internal, it will need to be simple enough that you can hold it in your mind's eye.

How it works: Once you've created your space and affirmed your intention, begin your practice. Keep going, until you've built up a little energy/pleasure. Then, focus on your object. As you breathe out, imagine that the pleasure, or the energy, or the life-force that you're building flows into the object of your desire, lighting it up. Then breathe into the pleasure again. Once you've built enough energy and/or pleasure to take your focus off that during the in-breath, you can imagine a circuit of light/energy/pleasure/sparkles moving to your object when you breathe out, and back to you from said object as you breathe in.

Make sure that, when whatever you have chosen as the end of your ritual happens, you fully release the energy into the object with one final breath, and by imagining it lighting up even brighter, before you complete.

⋙ PLAYTIME ⋘
The Indulgent Date

This luxurious semi-regular practice could be the perfect choice if

- You're ready to prioritise your pleasure, and practice treating your erotic self as you wish to be treated
- You're longing to try out a new sexual something, and want to give yourself plenty of time to explore and enjoy
- You're in need of some serious and sensual you-time
- You want to carve out time for a sex magic ritual that's all about you
- You wish to reconnect to your sexual self in a slow, luxurious, and deeply honouring manner

When it comes to carving out the liminal space for this luxurious practice, time is of the essence—and by that, I mean it's essential that you gift yourself with as generous a time slot as you can. I recommend a minimum of two hours, but you could just as easily spend an entire morning, afternoon, or evening on this particular slice of self-loving. Giving yourself time in this manner—time when the coms are off, the door is locked, the kids are on a sleepover—means that you can pay each aspect of your date with yourself the kind of loving attention you so deserve.

For example, your date might include a sex magic rite, or it might look like one long, drawn-out, self-loving ritual. Creating Your Sacred Space might involve an extended process of tidying and transforming your bedroom, or taking a long shower or bath. Setting your Intention could be preceded by a period of reflection on what it is you're longing for in your life right now, or where you'd like to be this time next year, in order to formulate that Intention. Your Invocation could involve bopping or singing unrestrainedly along to that love song that perfectly describes the relationship you want to bring into your life. Raising Energy might include a long walk in the wilds, or taking yourself to dinner, or making art, or trying out a variety of new positions or tools for self-pleasuring. Surrendering could include a hot bath, or simply falling asleep. Grounding could involve cooking yourself your favourite food and watching that film you've been waiting to watch.

Get a date in the diary, and then create a cocktail of elements designed to entice you into your body and get your erotic energy flowing. Do so with the kind of care and attention you imagine putting into a first date with someone you are keen to impress, and longing to get more intimate with.

~

Congratulations.

You made it through the first stage of your sex magical odyssey. You've initiated radical relationship with yourself. You're breathing, listening, and loving a little—or a lot—differently, and hopefully you've found some pleasure and made some magic along the way.

For some of you, this will be enough. Others may wish to pause here and take time to revisit the last section in its entirety or in specifics. And others, I know, are curious—or downright impatient—to bring these newfound skills into relationship with other people.

So let's dive on in …

Part II

Making Love with Each Other

One of the great losses I see in our becoming a more urban and more atom-ised society is that it is now all too easy for us to forget that we are cyclical beings. In disconnecting from the natural world, with her rhythms and sea-sons, her ebb and her flow, we are no longer looking into a kindly mirror that reminds us that we too need to follow our own cycles—whether they are cycles of rest and growth, of grief and forgiveness, or of work and play.

One of the rhythms that we follow has been beautifully mapped out by Gestalt therapy in the form of the Cycle of Intimacy. This circular flow reminds us that, in order to be fully in relationship with another, in order to attain a state of Union with them, we need to be in a state of Isolation first. The word isolation can sound a little threatening, but what it means in this context is to be just with ourselves, and ideally to be actively engaged in relationship with ourselves, before we can really open up to another. The fact that the process of intimacy is depicted as a cycle also reminds us that, during the course of relationship, we need to keep returning to ourselves in order to be able to open to our beloved anew. Otherwise we are in danger of becoming stuck in the state of Confluence, a comfortable familiarity which is also a necessary component of relationship, but which can become stagnant or co-dependent if we set up camp and stay there.

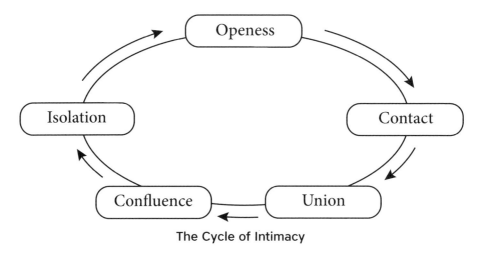

The Cycle of Intimacy

In the last chapter, we dove headlong and luxuriously into self-loving Isolation. The Cycle of Intimacy illustrates why it is necessary to have spent at least some time there, not just for our own well-being, but for the well-being of our relationships as well. Now we can explore how we apply tools like breath and deep listening, as well as the principles of sex magic, to open to another, to connect with them, and to enter a state of Union—as well as how to bring more awareness and creativity to the confluence stage of long-term partnership. All of this comes under the heading of what I would call Conscious Intimacy.

I define Conscious Intimacy as bringing *awareness, intention,* and *a sense of the sacred* to our relationships with others. Whilst those ingredients are fairly standard in discourses about conscious relating, experience also prompts me to add a carefully considered *ethical code*, and the *willingness to grow,* to the list.

To bring *awareness* to relationship is to apply the depth of attention and perception we develop through practices like Listening In, not only to ourselves within the relationship, but also to our partner(s), and to the space between us and them. It is to engage in connection with our full selves; to acknowledge that loving and making love to another often touches not just our feelings or our genitals, but the full spectrum of our physical, emotional, intellectual, and spiritual selves; to pay attention to how our interaction with the beloved makes us think and feel. And it is to pay attention to the space between us, and the flow, impulses, and intuitions that arise therein. Combined with caring and open communication on both sides, this can make for a depth of sharing we may not have experienced before.

Intention, as I've already mentioned, is the great transformer. It can transform a difficult conversation into a life-changing event, a simple touch into an ecstatic experience, and together time into quality time. It can also clarify and create the direction a relationship takes, without needing to detract from spontaneity or authenticity (intention, after all, is different from expectation). And it invites us to be more present with one another. When we're doing something together intentionally, we're more invested, more engaged, more here.

When I talk about bringing *a sense of the sacred* to our relating, I'm talking about two things. The first is simply treating our relationship with a sense of reverence and attention. I mentioned the term *kadosh* earlier on, which is used in Jewish tradition to describe a couple after they are married. It is translated as both "sacred" and "separate," and speaks to treating the connection between the beloveds as sacrosanct. Treating our partners—and other close people—and our relationships with them as though they were precious, and allocating time to focus on them and nothing else, plays a hugely important part in sustaining connection. That is one half of what I mean by allowing a sense of sacredness, of reverence, into intimacy.

The other half has to do with how I experience the concept of grace. Grace for me refers to the fact that, even in my darkest, most hurt, most furious, or just most failed or low moments, I am loved. I am loved, and there is help available to me, and things can move in my favour in wholly unexpected and seemingly miraculous ways.

Being in relationship is one of the hardest things we can do as human beings. Some relationships are certainly easier, kinder, more flowing than others, but all of them hit rocky patches at one point or another. In moments such as these, trusting that I am not alone in the chaos—that there is something bigger and wiser rooting for me and for us—can bring me great comfort, and even allow me to relax or reach out just enough at just the right moment for things to shift. To allow for the possibility of grace when in relationship is to allow for the possibility that there are forces moving in favour of our love that are bigger than our petty disputes and massive mistakes, that can help us find our way back together when we have come adrift—or help us come adrift in order to move on to more fulfilling lives and loves.

In my definition of Conscious Intimacy, I also include the need for some sort of personal *code of ethics* when it comes to relationships, as well as the *will to grow.*

A code of relational ethics can—and should—evolve over time, but I strongly recommend you start from somewhere. Having some clarity around how you intend to treat others and yourself in relationship, what you are and are not willing to bring to the table, what your deal-breakers and alarm bells are, etc., will not only make you a better partner, but will also help you and your potential partners make clearer choices about your connection. Your ethics are rather like your values—and indeed, the former will like as not reflect the latter. If your relational ethics differ fundamentally from those of a potential partner, it's going to cause friction pretty quickly.

There's little point in engaging in the practices of Conscious Intimacy if you're not willing to let those practices change you—or rather, if you're not willing to make the changes those practices reveal a need for. This isn't just a path to pleasure, it's also a path of *growth*. At its best, it shows us how to grow through pleasure, which can be truly revolutionary for a species that seems so very set on evolving in response to strife, pain, and suffering. While many of the practices illustrated herein can certainly extend or heighten a moment of pleasure, if you are willing to let them in a little deeper, they can transform a lifetime.

One of the main reasons many baulk at the prospect of Conscious Intimacy, besides the investment of time and energy which sustained intimacy requires (just like all the other important aspects of our lives), is that Conscious Intimacy asks that we allow ourselves to be seen, to make ourselves visible to our partners—from the folds in our skin, to the fears in our hearts. This can be a daunting prospect to those of us who experience any form of shame—which is to say, most of us.

However, what I have learned about Conscious Intimacy is that approaching our relationships in this manner—not just our intimate or sexual relationships, but also those friendships and family connections that can hold this level of transparency—gives us a fighting chance at continuing to grow and to love together, at traversing the unimaginable curve balls and causes for celebration that life throws at us, and at co-creating relationships that remain meaningful through the different stages of our lives. Since it is becoming increasingly clear that connection, belonging, and love are at the heart of what makes life worth living for most of us, developing tools that help us to sustain these things seems like one way to increase the quality of our existence.

Furthermore, Conscious Intimacy is *creative intimacy*. Listening and sharing, giving and receiving, seeing and being seen in these deeper and more delicious ways lead us not only to feel more connected, but also to be more choiceful. Inevitably, we find the ways in which hand-me-down relationship structures no longer work for us, as we discover the extraordinary, magical, revolutionary parts of us they are unable to contain. Openhearted, rooted in our love, the powers of our imaginations intimately combined, we can create new ways of relating that are tailored to our togetherness, and are as unique as it is.

Finally, the more we practise Conscious Intimacy, the more Love is available. Many of the ways in which we are taught to be intimate in our culture stifle Love. We're encouraged to be jealous, possessive, and monopolising. This can lead to disconnection from our partners, as well as friends and family; to repression; and to replacing affection with obligation. We're also encouraged to repress and/or act out our emotions, rather than work with them. By allowing our more uncomfortable emotions to rule us in this way, rather than making them allies in our relating, we never truly move through how we're feeling and back into love. Practising Conscious Intimacy, we can clear the emotional space between us, build trust, and find our way back to loving each other, time and again. We are also more in tune with the love we have for others outside our romantic relationships, and better equipped to appreciate and express it. This makes for deeper friendships, happier families, and more love in our micro and macro communities.

You with me? Let's go!

Chapter 4

Opening Up

So here you are, in a state of isolation. This state may be of the extended kind—arising from a period characterised by an absence of emotional and/or physical intimacy. Or it may be a briefer sort—the kind that arises from an argument, from withholding some part of yourself such as thoughts or feelings, or from time apart. If you're in a state of isolation because that feels like the only comfortable or attractive option, you're still welcome to read the below to see if anything inspires or intrigues—but I'm not expecting you to share my biases around intimacy with other people, and I hope this book will still be of service to you if you do not.

For the purpose of what follows, however, I am assuming a desire to move from isolation into connection. One of the things I most appreciate about the Gestalt vision of intimacy is that it acknowledges that, in order to do this, we must first open up to one another. It dedicates a fifth of the journey of intimacy to the process of opening, because opening to another is just that crucial, and just that terrifying.

Opening up is hard to do

Here are just some of the reasons why opening up to each other can be so difficult:

- We experienced people being closed as children. To a greater or lesser degree, we saw parents and/or guardians being closed and defensive with each other, or found them to be closed and stingy with their affections toward us. This is how we learned to relate, with guarded hearts and suspicious minds; this is how we learned to love, and these are the kinds of people we learned to love. And yet, there is more love available for us.

- We made the "mistake" of opening up once before, and it didn't work out so well for us. Someone was careless with our hearts or our bodies or both—or we were. Someone was cruel, or just not capable or clever or kind. We've been there, done that, and we don't want to get that t-shirt again, thank you very much. Or somehow, every time we try to open up, that's the t-shirt we end up wearing. And yet, there is more love available for us.

- Someone forced us to open up before we were ready. We were pushed to open up a physical, emotional, intellectual, or spiritual part of ourselves that we were not ready to visit or reveal, and we're afraid that could happen again. And yet, there is more love available for us.

- We've seen what happens to other people when they have risked opening up, perhaps even when they have risked opening up to us. Whatever we saw happen to them, it wasn't pretty, or dignified, or nourishing, and we don't want to risk that happening to us. And yet, love is available to us.

- We just don't know how, and we're convinced opening up is going to be yet another thing we get wrong. And yet, love is available to us.

- The people in our environment or lives at present are not people we feel safe, welcome, or desirous of opening up to. (If this is you, this is totally valid, and it's awesome that you've spotted it. You are encouraged to be discerning in your opening. It's OK to wait for the right people—and maybe be your own right people in the meantime as per the first section of this book.) And yet, love is available to us.

- And finally, and this could be the big one, and the underlying reason for several of the above: We're afraid to be seen. We're afraid to be known. We're afraid to be found out, in all our struggles and scars and silliness and fury and secrets and smallness and desire, especially by someone we're longing to be emotionally and/or physically intimate with. Which is to say, someone we find attractive, and/or love, whose good opinion we wish to keep. And yet, love is available to us.

⋙ PLAYTIME ⋘
Twenty Seconds of Insane Courage

Grab your journal. Visualise that moment of opening, whatever it looks like to you. It could be as simple as introducing yourself, as saying hello and risking eye contact; it could be sharing a part of yourself that the other person doesn't know about yet; it could be being the first to reach out after an argument or mistake or estrangement. In your mind's eye, take yourself to that place where you're poised to make contact, to be seen.

Once you're there, fill in the following sentences quickly and spontaneously. Don't overthink it. Let the words flow.

I'm afraid that
The risk I'd be taking is
This isn't worth doing because
My belly feels
My heart feels
What if

Read through what you've written. Does any of it sound familiar? Can you think of moments in the past when you've made decisions, let go of opportunities, or sustained losses because of your adherence to those fears and what ifs?

So, now tell me why you need to do this anyway. Same structure—don't think, just write:

I still want to do this, because
Connection is worth the risk because
What connection with other people gives me is
What connection with this particular person gives/might give me is
If I had Benjamin Mee's twenty seconds of insane courage,[15] I would

---

15. Crowe (dir.), *We Bought a Zoo*.

How to open up anyway

So how do we do it? How do we open or re-open to connection? How do we let another person in after what the last one did? How do we find those twenty seconds of insane courage?

First, we need a balance of readiness and willingness.

We need to be ready, because as we've discovered, isolation is precious and necessary, and whether it lasts half an hour or a year, the time when you're not ready to try trusting again is valid, and can be inhabited in a creative and self-loving manner. It might be a time to lick wounds and to heal; to retreat and to reflect; to emerge and to express; to rest, or to enter into a deeper understanding with yourself. It's OK to wait until we're ready.

And we need to find willingness, so that our emotional arteries don't become too hard, so that old wounds heal clean and don't scab over, so that we don't get too armour plated with wariness. So that we don't wait to be a kind of ready, which is more a kind of perfect, that we don't need to be in order to be loved. So that when love, or the beloved we argued with half an hour ago, comes knocking on our door, if it feels appropriate, we can take a deep breath, put down the book of the past that we've been thumbing, and open our heart to them anew.

When it comes to the act of opening up to another, if it helps you take those first steps, you can make a little ritual of it.

Start by using the power of intention. Either before meeting another, or as you sit down together, state your intention for the meeting: "It's my intention to allow myself to be seen today. It's my intention to be more open with you in this conversation than I've managed to be before. I'm willing to open my heart this evening."

Ask yourself whether you can create a safe and sacred space for this opening to happen. This could be about choosing where to meet someone, or asking for particular boundaries or needs to be honoured. My long-term beloved and I have a candle that we light when we're about to embark on conversations that are likely to require us to be particularly brave and vulnerable with one another, and a particular teapot we use to pour the tea for those talks. These small acts invite us to be present, to be here, and to be open with one another.

Do you need to invoke some support in opening up? This could be unseen support, but it could also be a friend who knows you're going to take that risk and is there to support you in doing so, or to hold you accountable to being honest, or to ask you how it went afterward.

What could help you build up the energy to be open? Is it the act of getting ready—an act that can be a hurried thing we do on autopilot, or a small rite of passage, depending on the attention and intention that we give it? Or is it having a conversation, or taking a long walk together, or asking the questions that reassure you that you're safe to open up? Or is it listening to a particular song that can serve as an anthem for you, or asking yourself what your relational hero would do, or imagining your brave, open, and connected self is standing in front of you, counting to three, and then jumping forward into that person and becoming them? Create a little energy raising spell for yourself, and go for it!

Opening up will, of course, look unique to each of us. It might be as brief as a ritual peak or release, but it may also be a messy, drawn-out process, and you may need to stick at it, and extend those twenty seconds into twenty minutes, or an hour or two, or even a lifetime. And it might not be met quite how you hoped, or needed, though I certainly hope it will.

But just in case it doesn't, and even if it does, don't forget the surrender and giving thanks portions of your little ritual. Make sure that there is time to rest, to take care of you or be taken care of.

Above all, take the time to tell yourself you're awesome. Even if you only managed a little openness, or things didn't quite go as you'd hoped, you still did it. You still stepped up, grabbed hold of your courage, and went for it. And you rock.

Finally, remember: small is beautiful. Opening up, being honest, telling someone how you feel, it all starts with just a single deep breath (or maybe three), and all it requires is one word at a time. Just one. Whichever one you have. Start there.

Chapter 5

Connecting

Having thanked our isolation for all that it has taught us, listened to the small or big unfurling in our hearts, and found the will to risk following it, we're now ready to connect more deeply with one another.

In the introduction to this book, I wrote about the gifts that magic—or ritualising our intimacy—has to bring to sex. I mentioned that the greatest of these gifts is Presence. I want to speak to why I see that as such a gift to our intimate relationships, and then share some of the invitations into intimacy that I've encountered in the realms of conscious sexuality for you to try with your beloveds.

Getting present

When we take steps to be present with another person, it can seem as though we're narrowing our attention onto the moment, the here-and-now. In fact, I find that, when I do this, it soon feels as though my awareness is expanding. By inviting all of my attention into the present moment, I bring all of my awareness into the now, where it expands to occupy the space between me and the other. There, I have three different avenues of information available to me. All three of these have something vital to offer our connection.

I am aware of myself. Often the first things I'm aware of, once I take the full breaths and the intentional steps to be here and to be in my body that is here, are all those things that are pulling me away from here—or all those things that are here that I've been resisting experiencing. Whether I am being distracted by unfinished to-do lists, or confronted with fear or frustration, by bringing my awareness here I will become aware of these things. And while this can be overwhelming at times—for example, if I'm confronted with a feeling or a truth that I've been assiduously avoiding—one thing it does do is give me choice. In becoming aware of what's stopping me from being present, I can choose what to do with it. I can talk about it with my partner, get heard or clear the air, or receive comfort or get it off my chest. I can find a way to welcome how I'm feeling into the space with me, to self-care and self-accept and integrate. Or I can take the action that will allow me to set things aside for now—write the to-do list, set the alarm, or make an agreement with myself to just let it go for the next two hours. I can address what is coming between me and being here, in order to get here, and be with the other person.

My awareness of myself allows me to move through the accumulated detritus in my psyche and arrive at my truth. At the truth of how I'm feeling, at the truth of my desires and needs, and at deeper truths of who I am. From this place of awareness, I can share myself more choicefully, and ultimately more fully. I am aware of my body, my sensations, my edges, my consent. I can tell what feels good, and what does not. Sharing these, and having them heard and respected, allows me to be even more here, even more present in my skin. Even more available to connect.

The second avenue of information I have is my awareness of my partner. The more I am able to be present with them, the deeper I can listen. I can listen to their words and support them to feel heard and validated; I can also respond to the desires and needs they express more effectively. I can listen to their body language, their expression, their energy body, which will also tell me things I need to know about how they are feeling in the moment. I can listen to my intuition and how it guides me to be with them. And I can listen to their skin, my fingers becoming antennae, sensitive detectors of how best to touch, to hold, to caress.

I am also aware of the space between us. This space is not just an empty space full of oxygen and other assorted atoms. In her TEDx Talk "The Power of Connection," Hedy Schleifer quotes the philosopher Martin Buber in describing the space between us as the space where our relationship is alive.[16] By listening to the space between us, especially when we listen with the "ears of our hearts," we can hear our relationship guiding us deeper into connection with the other. When we get hesitant, uncertain, even stuck, we can listen to the space between us, and therein find our flow again—the flow we share, the flow of our connection. That flow shows us how to connect next. The space between us is where a love that is greater than the sum of our hearts is at work. Listening to this love, we find it in us to love one another better.

The tools that follow are designed to help you invite your awareness into the space between you and your beloved(s), and connect with one another in that space. I recommend trying them as a series first, and then picking and choosing what works for you, or fits the needs of the moment.

As usual, we begin with the breath …

⋙ PLAYTIME ⋘
Threefold Attention

Stand or sit opposite your partner. Take a moment to synchronise your breath with theirs. A great way to do this is by starting by taking a deep breath each and letting out a big sigh, in order to empty your lungs, and begin to let go of those things that are stopping you from being fully here with one another. Then take three deep breaths together, in order to begin to find your way into a rhythm.

Once that rhythm has begun to emerge, close your eyes. Make sure you are both breathing in a way that is audible to the other, so that you can gently maintain that rhythm. If you can't hear your partner breathing, you may wish to have your eyes softly open, or have a hand on their body, so that you can discern the rise and fall of their breath. Keeping that common rhythm in your awareness, bring your attention inward.

Take a moment to listen to you. Try not to get stuck with any one thing that arises, instead giving each layer of yourself you become aware of a few breaths, reassuring that part of you that it's welcome, and then looking

---

16. Schleifer, "The Power of Connection."

deeper. Invite your awareness into your body with the breath, and just do a quick check in to see what is moving in you as you sit opposite your partner.

Come back when you're ready (if you want to ensure you come back at the same time, set a timer for two minutes or so), and gently extend your attention to your partner. Let your gaze be soft and open, ideally making eye contact with them, whilst also gently taking the whole of them in: their body language, their facial expression, and feeling or intuition you receive from them. Let them fill your attention for a moment. You can come back to you later, but just for now, let them be where the totality of your interest lies.

After another minute or so, let your attention move to the space between you. You can still maintain eye contact, but soften your gaze, and let your intuition, the knowing in your belly, guide you. Just notice how the space between you feels, and how that makes you feel. See if you can pick up any impulses or inspiration as you listen to that space. Notice how you feel guided to be and to act when you put your attention there.

Finally, take a deep breath, and bring your attention back to your connection with your beloved, knowing that your awareness is now engaged with all three participants in your connection—you, your partner, and your relationship.

⋟ PLAYTIME ⋞
Looking Deeper

Sit or stand opposite your partner. Gently synchronise your breathing, making your breath a conscious and intentional action, and speeding it up/slowing it down gently to find the place between your two rhythms where your breathing is aligned.

Make eye contact. When I'm guiding participants to do this in workshops, I often say something along the lines of "get courageous and curious enough to make eye contact with this person."

Notice what you see—whether it's the person you're besotted with, or the person who royally pissed you off by leaving their clothes strewn over the floor again last night; whether it's the bald patch, or the colour of their eyes that you can never quite find a name for. Notice what you see.

Now look a little deeper. Really lend your awareness to this person. Notice less of what you perceive, more of what you see. Look beyond your first rushes of feeling or judgment, beyond the facts of features. Look and see what is peering out at you from behind the eyes. Look deeper.

Soften your gaze. Allow for the possibility of being seen as deeply as you are seeing. Let your partner in with your eyes.

Breathe together. Keep looking deeper. See, and be seen.

Often, this is enough.

⋙ PLAYTIME ⋘
What's Here Now?

I came across this sweet way into connection and communication in a workshop for couples run by my wonderful colleague, nondual Kabbalistic teacher Roxana Padmini. It's a particularly useful one for those of us who live busy lives, with little time to process how we're feeling before we come into connection with our people.

Stand or sit opposite your beloved, breathing together and making eye contact. You can be in physical contact for this—e.g., holding hands, resting your palms on theirs, touching knees—or you can allow the same space between you as before.

Take it in turns to ask the question, "What's here now?" The partner who has asked the question simply listens, while the speaker takes a moment to listen in, and then responds with a simple word or phrase to describe how they're feeling. Take a moment to breathe together in acknowledgement of what has been shared, and then switch roles. The person who was just asking the question is now asked it, and takes the time they need to offer a simple, single word or sentence response. Keep switching roles and asking the question until you feel complete.

The invitation with What's Here Now is to keep breathing, keep listening to one another, and keep speaking the layers of what you are feeling in a simple way, in order to release them and find out what is underneath. Sometimes this or one of the other exercises will bring to the surface something that needs to be explored in more detail before it can be released. When this happens, you may wish to turn to one of the exercises in the Clearing the Space Between Us section on page 109.

⋙ PLAYTIME ⋘
Heart/Heart Circuit Breathing

Sit or stand with your partner, breathing and making eye-contact with one another. Let your breathing be full, and audible/visible enough for your partner to breathe in time with you.

Start to drop your awareness into your heart, whatever that means to you in the moment. As you breathe in, imagine that your heart opens a little, and as you breathe out, imagine it relaxes a little. Whatever you're feeling, make it welcome, let it be, and keep breathing with your partner.

When you feel like your attention is in your heart, allow for the possibility that, as you breathe out, you send some love, or energy, from your heart to your partner's—and as you breathe in, you receive some from them. What this looks or feels like is up to you. It might look like sparkles or light, or waves of electricity or heat; it might feel like warmth, or buzzing, or opening up; it might sound like a pulse or a violin; it might taste like sherbet. Just allow a small gift to move from your heart to theirs, and allow for the possibility that you might be receiving one back. If you're someone who finds it hard to express your feelings, you may want to focus a little extra on that flow of love from you to them when you exhale. If you're someone who finds it easy to give, and less so to receive, make sure you really let their love in when you inhale.

You may want to synchronise your breathing for this exercise, so that you breathe in as your partner breathes out, and they breathe in as you breathe out. That way you're both focusing on the same flow, which is likely to make it a more tangible, powerful experience. I find there comes a moment with this where I feel like my beloved and I are sharing the same life force.

Go for as long as you want to. (Try not to hyperventilate!)

Being seen

The experience of being seen is one of the greatest gifts we can give another human being. It's hard to imagine how profound, how powerful, the simple act of looking can be. If we can witness another without judgment, perhaps even with love, we have the chance to play a part in that person feeling welcome in this world. If that person also happens to be our partner, we give a gift not just to them, but to ourselves; not just to us, but to our relationship.

We've already touched on how vital for our well-being a sense of belonging is. Most of us will, at one time or another, come to know the ache of feeling separate, rejected, unwelcome. For those of us who live with a degree of difference to what our culture presents as the norm, the awareness of our supposed difference or "otherness" can be an acute presence in our lives. Many of us build our identities on that difference in an attempt to reclaim our dignity, to celebrate ourselves. Some of us spend our lives fighting for acceptance and recognition in the spaces between "us" and "them." If we're not careful, we become so attached to being "other" that we don't give ourselves the chance or the time to also find and rest in belonging.

Nothing tells us we belong quite like being seen—particularly being seen in our vulnerability, our fear and pain, in those states in which we most fear judgment and rejection. As part of my ministry within the queer community, I've held rites of passage for gender transition, in which the recipient adopts a new name or identity, or celebrates taking hormones or having surgery. Watching the recipients of these rituals step more fully into themselves—the selves they experience themselves to be—and watching what happens when they do so while witnessed by a circle of people who love them, has shown me the power of being seen as we feel ourselves to be in a way that nothing else has. The following words were gifted to me by the recipient of the first of these rituals I created:

> *As I stood in the middle of that circle, I felt more love than I have ever felt before. I felt held, seen, and respected in ways that I did not know could be possible, and also so grateful for the many wonderful beings that I have in my life. I experienced a sense of belonging and appreciation that will stay with me for many years to come. That will offer me strength in darker times and help me remember that, however lonely I may feel, I am never really alone.*

As a queer-identified person myself, the moments in the early days of my relationship with my long-term beloved when he made it clear in word, deed, and desire that he loved and wanted me not in spite of my queerness, but because of it, remain some of the most profound moments of my life.

We are not islands. We have a part to play in each other's journey of self-acceptance, and witnessing one another at our most tender, at our most furious, at our most joyous, at our most cracked open, is one way we can do that.

When we take the time to see each other without judgment or condemnation, we give each other permission to be.

When we feel disconnected from our beloveds, when we are withholding our thoughts, feelings, or trust from one another, the first thing that goes is our eye contact. Consciously and intentionally making eye contact with someone we love is one way to start cutting through the crap that accumulates between us in our day-to-day lives. It gives us a way out of our own world and a window into theirs, which is a recipe for compassion. Hiding from one another isn't an option anymore, so we're more likely to finally get down to sharing our feelings. And taking the time to really look at each other, to see each other afresh, helps us see past the grievances of the moment, and remember the person we love who is struggling through this uncharted territory of togetherness with us.

So take a deep breath, people, and look up.

Being heard

Not unlike witnessing one another without judgment, deeply listening to another person can have life-changing results. This is particularly the case when we find a way to do so without making what they are saying about us, slipping into judgment or hurt, or "listening to respond"—which is to say, eagerly awaiting the moment when they pause to catch their breath so we can jump in. Like the breath, our ability to hear each other is an underrated superpower most of us carry around with us every day. Like the breath, it can transform a situation.

We're about to dive into some ways to deepen our communication with one another. Before we do that, here are some of my favourite ways to listen:

Ears in the Heart

I first encountered this concept in the work of the late Bill Kirkpatrick, Anglican priest, AIDS activist, and pastoral care pioneer. Bill's writings invite the listener to place their ears in their hearts, thereby bypassing the head with its concerns and judgments, and putting the work of listening in the place where resides our capacity for love and compassion.[17]

To do so, let the breath be your guide. Breathe, feel your chest area expand, and let your attention drop into the space created by your breath. As you breathe, you can imagine that you feel your heart opening a little more to the person in front of you, or envisage an ear there, reaching to catch their words. If you notice yourself being distracted by judgments or hurt again, come back to the breath, and invite yourself back into the listening space in your heart.

The Listening Tree

Ever sat beneath a tree to think stuff through? Notice how having that solid, silent, yet tangible presence at your back allows your thoughts more space to expand and flow? This way of listening is about becoming that presence for another. It's especially useful when the person in question has something vulnerable, scary, or trauma-related to share.

See roots sinking down into the Earth—from your feet if you're standing, spine if you're sitting. Feel yourself held, supported, grounded. Know that you're welcome on this Earth, and see if you can also hold the knowing of that about the person who is speaking as well. Often, when we are in shame or fear or hurt, we forget that is the case. Having someone hold that knowing for us plays a powerful part in us remembering.

Without losing your connection to those roots, get as present as you can with what the person you are listening to is saying. Remember to breathe deeply, and particularly focus on your out breath. This will have the combined effect of gently encouraging the other person to breathe more, which will help them to release some of the tension around what they're saying— and it will make it easier for you to let their words slide down into your roots below, and out into the Earth. Let the Earth take the weight of what is being said, and just focus on listening in a silent but solid way. You can do this while maintaining eye contact, or while sitting side by side if that feels too confrontational, or while being in physical contact such as holding the other person while they speak.

17. Kirkpatrick, *The Creativity of Listening*, 113.

The Empty Cauldron

This is a way of listening that has a more creative intention, in which we make ourselves the vessel for the other person to have space and time to think things through. As such, it is quite a creative way of listening. It's also a good one for those of us who tend to jump in and respond before the other person has had a chance to really excavate and express the layers of their thoughts and feelings.

This way of listening is all about a quality of attention. It's about maintaining and expressing through eye contact and body language a keen interest in what the other is saying, whilst also imagining ourselves to be a blank canvas or an empty cauldron for them to cast their thoughts into in order to try them out. We cultivate a trust that the other person holds all the answers they need within them already, and we make our listening the container that gives them the time and space to discover those answers for themselves. When they get stuck, or pause, we breathe deeply, and keep listening for what we know they, at some level, already know.

The Bright Mirror

Otherwise known as Active Listening. A good one for drawing the speaker out, helping them to clarify their thoughts, and making it clear they're welcome to share them with you.

Give the speaker your full attention, and make it clear with your body language (leaning forward, nodding) and your facial expression that you're doing so. If thoughts or responses arise, gently set them aside, or imagine filing them away. You can always ask the person sharing whether they would like a response later. Instead of offering your own responses, reflect what they are sharing back to them occasionally if it seems like they're faltering or getting stuck. You can do this either by filling in sentences such as "What I'm hearing you say is …," or, if you're picking up on what they're feeling and empathising accordingly, expressing that with the occasional word or sentence like, "Wow, that sounds like a tough time."

By "mirroring" back what the other is sharing, you make it clear that they're being heard, which in turn reminds them they are worthy of being heard. This helps them not only to get clear on what their thoughts/feelings are, but also to know that those thoughts and feelings are valid and welcome.

~

If listening in ways like the above is not something you've done a lot of; if you often feel the need to respond to another person's sharing with one of your own, or to defend or justify yourself; or if communication has been an issue in relationships past or present, it can be worth practising some or all of the above, separately or in combination, before you embark on the communication tools for more difficult conversations below.

Some playful ways to practise listening with a friend, partner, or family member (these are all great practices to try with children if you're wanting to introduce more conscious communication into your family time) might include having them recite a poem they know by heart, read your horoscopes, or tell you a story you've heard them tell a couple of times before. In each instance, you can take it in turns to be speaker and listener, and decide which of the listening techniques above you're going to practice. After the speaker has finished, they can feed back on how heard they felt by the listener.

I cannot stress enough what a powerful experience it is to be listened to with someone's full attention and compassion. We often don't realise just how powerful until we go without it for a long stretch and then experience it for ourselves. As a therapist, as a facilitator of sharing circles, as a friend, and as a lover, I have been astounded again and again by the power of simply being heard.

If you're not convinced, then I suggest you find yourself a safe sharing space as soon as possible. Check out the Resources section for inspiration.

Clearing the space between us

Philosopher Martin Buber is quoted as saying: "Our relationship lives in the space between us and that space is sacred space."[18]

Sometimes that space needs a good old spring clean.

I am someone who has always wrestled with conditioning—from my upbringing and wider culture—around what we have come to perceive as so-called "negative" emotions. I resonate deeply with Susan David's assertion that "being positive has become a new form of moral correctness."[19] Because

18. Schleifer, "The Power of Connection."
19. David, "The Gift and Power of Emotional Courage."

of the moral weight that we have assigned to natural and necessary emotions, I can find it difficult to express or clear a difficult feeling that's arisen in the space between me and someone I am close to. And this is just one of countless reasons why I—and many of us—allow things to build up between us and those we love. Perhaps we weren't equipped with an emotional language growing up. Perhaps we're used to burying our emotions under who we think we "ought" to be, or how we think our relationships "ought" to feel. Perhaps the last time we tried to express a difficult feeling it wasn't well received by the person we needed to clear things with. Perhaps we just didn't really notice something building up until it felt too big to actually talk about. Perhaps our feelings seem like a betrayal of the other person. Perhaps we just haven't had the damn time to reflect and recognise what we feel between working our job(s), and/or caring for our dependents, and/or dealing with our physical/mental health, and so on.

My point is, in relationship, shit builds up. And the more we deepen our relationship with ourselves, and the more awareness we bring to our connections with others, the less possible it becomes to just leave it there.

It's not all that surprising that so few of us have the tools and the language to befriend and express our emotions when our cultural understanding of emotions is still in its infancy. Along with the moral judgment we place on different feelings, our cultural narratives, entertainment, and media offer a fairly monochromatic view of our emotional landscape. A person is either angry or kind, loving or sad, depressed or lustful, because that's what makes good drama—and that's still the simplistic view we have of these frightening and unpredictable urges we call feelings. There's little room for nuance, for complexity, for messiness, for being both. This can leave us ill equipped to address the inevitable mess of emotions that evolves in the space between two people.

A common misconception that arises from this monochromatic and fearful understanding of our emotional landscape is the idea that, if we're not feeling consistently loving toward our partner(s)—or alternately, if we're not in a constant fever of desire for them—we're no longer in love. But we are much more emotionally complex and multifaceted beings than this would imply. As much as we struggle to handle nuance and complexity as a culture—finding it difficult to see beyond binary and right/wrong viewpoints—

this is a good thing to take the time to understand, because it reminds us that we're capable of holding many feelings at once.

Some of these are transient—like my annoyance over my beloved's apparent refusal to close doors behind him—and some rest constantly within me, to be rediscovered time and again, such as my love for that same partner. Throughout our daily lives, we are in connection to the space between us, and we are consciously or unconsciously putting things into or projecting things onto that space: that thing one of us said when they were really tired, that moment when our partner wasn't paying attention, that crisis we had to handle together. So we can see how emotional detritus might pile up. I'm not saying that these emotions are somehow "less than" more constant feelings. Besides being valid in their own right, they can be important signposts to undercurrents than need to be resolved. What I am saying is that they do not make up the totality of the space between us, of our relationship. Instead, we can share and resolve them, in order to let our love breathe freely again.

As a psychosexual coach, I sense that many of the clients who approach me are hoping that I am going to furnish them with some magical love tool, some crucial quick fix that someone just forgot to hand them when they hit puberty/fell in love/got married. Nobody wishes this was the case more than I! Instead, there comes that inevitable point in our work together where a client's face falls because I have just broken it to them that they are going to have to actually talk to their partner. Because ultimately, the three magic words are almost always: Communicate, Communicate, Communicate.

At the beginning of 2017, my long-term partner and I did one of the best things we've ever done together. We made a pact, and every evening that found us at home together we talked for at least thirty to sixty minutes. We made lists of all the big subjects that we were feeling difficult or dissatisfied around, or that needed to change for us—sex, money, health, future plans—and we thrashed our way through them one tough conversation at a time. We didn't move on from a subject until we'd arrived at an intention or agreement that felt like a mutually satisfactory solution. It took us over a month to work through it all. As the year had turned, we'd been feeling distant, with unspoken or unresolved resentment running rife beneath the surface in the space between us. By the time we were done, we felt like we'd taken another step deeper into intimacy together, like we were ready for the next stage of our mutual adventure. Like I said, it was one of the best things we've ever done, an exercise I really cannot recommend enough for long-term partners.

Needless to say, during the Time of Big Talks, we covered a whole bunch of subjects that were thoroughly uncomfortable for one or both of us. And we continue to do so, as our relationship continues to teach us that nothing—nothing—is as effective at clearing the space between us as talking to one another, no matter how embarrassed, ashamed, afraid, or otherwise resistant we may feel about doing so. As with so much of what I've talked about so far, putting a structure on these conversations—making rituals of them—makes them somehow so much more possible and effective. Having something that holds us while we face down our together-demons, allowing for the possibility that there is something larger than us holding our love, can turn the tough stuff into relationship gold. But before I share with you some of my favourite communication magics, I want to take a moment to acknowledge the attitudes, the overriding intentions, that make it possible for those conversations we are most afraid of having to take us deeper into intimacy together.

Being your beloved's ally

This is something my long-term partner is particularly excellent at reminding me about when we're in conflict. "I'm with you, not against you," he tells me in pained tones when I'm a little too caught up in being "right." Ultimately, if both parties are willing to get down and messy with the painful stuff that's accumulated in the space between them, it's because they're both invested in the sustainability of the relationship. Acknowledging this about each other, and reminding ourselves and one another that we are allies as we traverse moments of conflict, gives us a better chance of acting like we're on a team, rather than in opposition. And that gives us a better shot at coming through those moments together.

This attitude takes on a new level of importance when we're talking about conversations relating to differences that are not just interpersonal, but also have sociopolitical weight or stigma attached to them. Conflicts that stem from our cultural, race, or class backgrounds, or that touch on our gender, or our physical or mental health, these are the moments when the personal really does become political. If we can develop the capacity to hold an awareness of each other's reality, and the strong intention to be our beloved's ally, even as we speak our own needs and desires, then it isn't just our interpersonal love that has a chance to evolve. Anne Geraghty writes: "The deeper the intimacy and the love, the deeper the level of conflict that can emerge because it is safe to do so. The journey of love takes every couple into cultural and collective conflicts as well as personal and familiar ones … Every loving relationship can be a homeopathic remedy for the planet." [20]

Being willing to stick it out

When my aforementioned beloved and I first started living together, our arguments would often lead to him storming out of the room. His previous experience had taught him that conflict was a bad sign, and in our early days he assumed many of ours were the beginning of the end. That doesn't happen very often anymore. Time has taught us that our difficult conversations are actually us turning toward each other, and trying to reconnect through all the crap that's built up between us. As such, we now have an understanding that arguments are also a healthy part of our togetherness, and an ongoing agreement to stick at those tough conversations until that minor miracle occurs and suddenly we're out the other side and deeper in connection with one another.

Make an agreement to stick conversations out; to keep making eye contact and coming back to your intention to work through it together; and to avoid making big decisions or taking statements made in anger, shame, or pain at face value. Your arguments are one way in which your desire for one another is expressed. If it didn't matter, you wouldn't fight for it.

Being mindful that you're both right

No one sets out to be the person in the difficult conversation who is wrong. Interpersonal conflict is rarely a case of facts versus fake news. Instead, it's the clash of two different viewpoints. Sometimes those are two different angles on a particular situation, and sometimes they are two different worldviews. Almost always, those two viewpoints have arisen from two different experiences. Each of those experiences is very real to the person whose experience it is, and each of them is valid. Therefore, both of the stories arising

---

20. Geraghty, *How Loving Relationships Work*, 54.

out of those experiences deserve to be heard—and each of those stories is right.

The magic happens when we can share our stories, and then fashion a new one, a rounder viewpoint and clearer picture, out of both. This is where reconciliation so often occurs, and this is where we take a step deeper into togetherness. But unless we're willing to have enough faith in one another and our relationship to hear both of those stories out, we're not going to get to make that magic together.

Being kind

It strikes me that, when it comes to difficult interpersonal discussion, kindness is about discernment. It's about knowing the difference between honesty and brutal honesty; between standing our ground, and refusing to comfort the other person; between the validity of our own experience or feelings or needs, and invalidating another's; between asking for change, and assuming the other person's malicious intent is behind those things that need to change. It's about knowing the difference, and it's about acting accordingly, whenever we can do so without unkindness to ourselves.

"Be a little kinder than you have to" is a quote from E. Lockhart's *We Were Liars* that I stumbled across whilst thinking about this.[21] It speaks to a kind of constant, choiceful kindness that is threaded through all of the attitudes above, and is a fundamental ingredient to sustainable relationships between happy hearts.

A note on triggers and abuse

The attitudes above are intended to work alongside your self-care and your safety, not to supersede or replace them. Needing a break or setting a boundary during conversations like the ones we're talking about here should not be looked on as a failure. If the conversation triggers a past trauma, and/or you find yourself going into fight, flight, freeze, or fawn, and/or you need a time out to process something that has come up in the conversation solo before you can process it together, you are allowed to call time on the conversation. If you have the capacity to agree to come back to it at a later date, perhaps with some extra safety provisions in place, that's great. But your well-being

---

21. Lockhart, *We Were Liars*, 101.

and safety are always paramount, so work out how you can re-establish that, together, separately, or both.

Likewise, if you find that your attempts at co-creative conversations seem to keep coming round to your failings, or you being in the wrong, or if you find yourself being used as a verbal punching bag, or if your partner just isn't willing or able to communicate in ways that feels safe for you, you are not obliged to stay in the conversation. You might want to look into getting professional help to find safer and more effective ways to communicate with each other. Having a neutral third party hold you while you traverse this stuff together can be incredibly helpful, and equip you with new skills for relating to each other. Alternately, it might be time to check out the reasons for letting go of a relationship on page 192, to see if any of them resonate with your experience.

~

I'm now going to introduce you to some of my favourite tools and rituals for having your own Big Talks. We've already explored listening in depth. We're now going to look at sharing in a similar way, as well as some ways to respond to sharing. And finally, I'll describe some of my favourite structures within which you might want to try bringing together these different components.

Imagining uncomfortable conversations or interpersonal conflict through the lens of the attitudes above, it becomes clear that, if we are to relate and communicate as kind and willing allies, many of our learned communication habits are just not going to cut it anymore. Since our primary purpose is to nurture our relationship and deepen intimacy, and we recognise that engaging in difficult conversations is one route to that, then using conflict as an opportunity to put down or take down our partner(s) as though they were our opponent(s) no longer serves us. We need to find ways to clear the air, to open up the space between us, that don't blame, shame, or hurt the other person, and send them further away from us. At the same time, each person's feelings and experiences need to be totally welcome, otherwise that space isn't going to get cleared.

There's a delicate balance to be struck—or at least striven for—in these conversations, between owning our feelings and recognising them as relational. The speaker needs to acknowledge that the feelings they are sharing are their own, stemming from their experiences—and the listener needs to hear those feelings without taking them personally, so as to be able to truly listen to them. At the same time, both parties need to be aware that feelings are relational—they arise in the space between us and because of the space between us (as opposed to the feelings we'd be having anyway, even if we weren't in relationship and had never even met). Because feelings are relational, both parties are to some degree responsible for them, and it is worth taking the time to explore them together. The more comfortable we can get with holding this balance, the kinder and more constructive our conversations can become.

I also want to preface this by saying that what follows are a series of tidy tools that are not necessarily meant to make relating a tidy experience. Rather, they are offered here as support systems to help you navigate the mess with the most grace, creativity, and open-heartedness you can. I meant what I said above about arguments being a healthy aspect of relating, and a way of expressing and stimulating our desire to relate. Sometimes we all need a good blow out. I've seen too many people use nonviolent communication techniques to try and avoid dealing with what really needed to be expressed to advocate too fiercely for tidy, orderly communication. Instead, I ask that you take what follows as a series of invitations to be kind, and also real, and to get comfortable with accompanying one another through the less comfortable—but nonetheless necessary—aspects of being in relationship.

The sharing checklist

Here's a handy list of approaches to bear in mind when you're getting ready to have a difficult conversation:

Get consent: When it comes to clearing the relational space, a great place to begin is with consent. It's the magic of "May I?" all over again. Getting the other person's consent for those trickier conversations, and giving them a heads-up about what you need to talk about and what you need from them as a listener, gives them a chance to get on your side. It's a shortcut to starting out on any difficult subject as allies. Of course there will be times when our beloveds, friends, or colleagues spot that something is amiss and invite us to share, but it's neither practical nor fair to wait for this to happen every time. When it comes to taking that first step, asking for the conversation you need, and allowing the other person to pick a time and space conducive to them hearing you, allows you to begin the conversation together, and gives you a good chance of getting out the other side together as well.

Ask for the listening you need: Hopefully by now you have a sense of the different ways in which we can listen to one another, and the ones that help you to feel particularly heard. Requesting these from your listener doesn't just create safer space for you to share, it also continues that sense of co-creating the conversation together as partners—rather than placing the other person in the position of being attacked. And it gives your listener a clear purpose, which gives them a better chance of staying focused on hearing you, rather than on their own responses to what you're saying. Have a look at page 106 for some ideas for how you might like to be listened to.

Set an intention: We've already explored how a clearly set intention can transform any activity into an effective piece of creativity, change-making, and/or magic. The same absolutely applies to communication. A stated intention can carry us through an apparent stalemate into co-created solutions. It focuses the individual parties on the purpose of the conversation, which is more likely to keep them kind and present through the tough parts. And having a common goal strengthens the sense that we're allies in the conversation, rather than opponents.

Keep it personal: Sharing is most effective when we share about ourselves. When we "speak from the I," when we talk about our own feelings, experiences, and perceptions, when we are aware of our own pasts, wounds, and biases, and how these affect us, then we have the best possible chance of

- Effectively expressing how we feel
- Stimulating compassion in the listener
- Helping them to understand our perspective
- Gaining their trust, rather than their resistance
- Remaining in alliance, rather than slipping into opposition

Some ways to keep it personal include using words that describe how you're feeling (sad, angry, afraid), rather than words that imply something is being done to you (neglected, betrayed); not conflating perceptions with feelings (for example, "I feel like you're not listening to me" is not a feeling, it's a perception); avoiding words that imply a judgment or criticism (it's often best to resist the urge to apply any adjectives to the other person or their behaviours, such as "you are being cruel to me" or "don't be so ungrateful"); and resisting the urge to make categorical statements (e.g., "everything is falling apart"). Instead, make it personal again (e.g., "I have a fear that we might be falling apart").

Sharing really is caring: In those moments when you are challenging yourself to share something particularly vulnerable, remember this: You are half of this relationship. Without you, the space between you and the other person—and everything it contains that each of you so value—would not exist. The more you bring of yourself to that space, the richer it becomes—and, correspondingly, the more you withhold of yourself, the poorer it gets. Furthermore, you deserve to have relationships that can hold as much of you as possible. The only way to experience those most precious of connections is to take the occasional leap of faith, and show yourself.

Keeping the above in mind, here are three of my favourite sharing tools for you to try when you're ready to tackle some difficult subjects.

⇒ PLAYTIME ⇐
Let's Have a Cup of TEA

This sharing structure was created by the terribly clever Andy Davice. His original intention was for it to be used in the corporate world as a way of giving feedback that would lead to empowering conversations and creative solutions, and I believe it can yield similar results in an intimate setting. Besides which, I do love a good acronym!

TEA represents a series of three sharing points, which should ideally follow one another in that order. They are:

- Talk about the problem: The problem in question might be an incident, or a recurring behaviour, or something that was said. The important thing is that you're able to quantify it. You need to be able to be as specific as you can about your experience of the situation—about the visible, audible, tangible facts of what happened. For example: "Last night, I heard you tell me that you would do the dishes if I put the kids to bed. This morning, I came downstairs to find that the dishes hadn't been done, and you had already left for work."

- Explain the impact: Having been as clear, factual, and detailed as you can be above, this is where you get to talk about the effect that the problem in question has had on you. Remember to keep it personal, and to be as open and heartfelt as you can under the circumstances. For example: "This delayed me making breakfast, which had a knock-on effect on the school run. I thought we had an agreement, and I feel hurt that you didn't stick to that agreement. I also felt stressed as a result of the delay to the school run, which meant I was a little shorter with the kids than I would have liked to be. The tension I was feeling carried through the rest of my day, and the kids are still a little grumpy with me as a result."

- Ask for help: This is the part of this model that helps us to make real change. Here, the sharer is encouraged to ask for the support that they need moving forward. Again, be as specific as possible. The more specific you are about the actions the other person can take to help you make the situation better, the easier it will be for them to do so. For example: "It would really help me in future if you would follow through on your stated intentions around housework. Specifically, I would really like it if we could alternate the dishes and the kids' bedtimes on weeknights, so that they both get done, and the kids get the full attention of whoever is on bedtime duty."

Now, depending on the kind of listening and responding the sharer has requested, this may evolve into a dialogue where it becomes clear why the dishes didn't get done on this occasion, and both parties get a clearer sense of what happened as a result. The important thing is that the sharer feels heard at the end of the conversation, and an agreement has been negotiated in response to their request for help that feels possible for both parties. It is also worth scheduling a time for further down the line when the two of you will check in to see how that agreement is going, and whether anything needs adjusting accordingly.

⇒ PLAYTIME ⇐
What's the Story?

This structure has some aspects in common with TEA, but it differs in two ways that I feel make it both a more vulnerable exercise, and also a more powerful container to get vulnerable in. I first came across it via Kate Napier, my wonderful mentor during my interfaith ministry training.

As with TEA, you begin by outlining the events that have led up to your wanting to have the conversation in as clear and as factual a way as possible. Then, as with TEA, you explain the emotional impact of the events, using phrases like "I feel" to help you speak from the I. Let's carry on with my benign(ish) example about the dishes, and assume the same sort of things that were said in Talk About the Problem and Explain the Impact above are said here.

With the above complete, the next step starts with the sentence "The story I'm telling myself about this is…" This is what makes this structure a particularly good one for those of us who tend to extrapolate things from the behaviour of those we love, and draw conclusions about whether or not they love us back accordingly. This part is where you get to talk about the conclusions you've drawn based on prior events or behaviours. Often the reason why conversations like these feel as edgy as they do is because we're afraid that, by having them, we'll discover that our fears are in fact true. The invitation here is to clear the relational space by sharing those fears that are building up from your side.

For example: "The story I'm telling myself is that our agreements are not important to you—which makes me worry that I'm not that important to you either. I'm also concerned that, on some level, you expect me to do the majority of the emotional and household labour that are needed to sustain our home and our family, and that scares me, because it makes me afraid that I don't have a partner in the face of all that work."

Notice that the emphasis is still on the speaker, and that each part of the story is named as the fear that it is. This structure emphasises that these fears are a story—a single side of a story—and this can open up the space for the other side(s) of that story to emerge.

The speaker has one more step to complete in this structure—which is to say what you would like to happen next. This is what you would like to happen in an ideal world, described as fully as possible, and shared with the understanding that you may not receive that, but it's your truth, and it's a part of your story, and so it's worth sharing.

Sticking with my dishes example, this might be something along the lines of: "In an ideal world, I want to be doing significantly less housework on weeknights, and getting some quality time in with the kids before they go to bed. And if that isn't something you have the capacity to support me with, then it would be great if we could have a conversation about how we can afford or barter for some help during the week, so that we can prioritise down time together as a family."

⇒ PLAYTIME ⇐
What's the Memory?

Another useful way to get to the bottom of the stories we're living—or, as the case may be, re-living—is to fill in the blanks in the following sentences:

When you _____ [insert action, e.g., don't stick to our agreements] _____ it reminds me of when my father/mother/guardian/sibling/previous partner _____ [insert memory] _____ and then I feel _____ [insert feeling] _____

Of course, finding the courage and a decent formula from which to share what's happening for us is only half the story. How we're received when we do so is crucial to our taking the risk to do so again.

Here are some ways we can show that we've heard the other person, and some ways that we can ask to be heard when we're the speaker.

What I heard you say is …

This is another active listening tool. It's also a great way to establish whether the speaker has managed to communicate what they were endeavouring to clearly, and whether the listener has managed to hear them. It offers an excellent opportunity to clarify what's been shared before moving on.

When the speaker requests it, feedback the key points of what you heard by filling in the sentence "What I heard you say is…" repeatedly until you feel you've covered all the points. Your speaker can gently clarify any time they feel you've misunderstood. If they do so, adjust that particular sentence until they feel fully heard.

May I respond?

Even if you established at the beginning of your conversation that the sharer is interested in hearing the listener's response to what they have to say, it's still great to get consent when you feel the speaker has finished sharing. This gives them a chance to share more if they're not in fact complete; it gives precedence to their feelings, which may be especially tender after sharing how they're feeling; and it represents a continuation of that intention to co-create and to be kind.

Assuming you do get consent to respond, resist the urge to do so out of anger or defensiveness. If you're feeling angry, or any other similarly strong emotion, share that fact in as nonviolent a way as possible (e.g., "I'm noticing some anger coming up in me in response to what you've just shared"). Then share your response, keeping it personal, and doing what you can to stay as open and heartfelt as you feel safe to. Ultimately, this part of the process is still about the person who has shared, so try and let compassion for them frame your response.

I hear you

Sometimes we just need to be heard. No responses, no discussion, just the knowledge that we've spoken and have been listened to. At times like these, the speaker can ask that the listener not respond to what they have said, and agree that nothing further is said on the matter for the time being. Instead, the listener can simply respond with the sentence "I hear you"—ideally with open eyes and an open heart. Offering a nonverbal response such as a hug may feel appropriate, but the speaker is of course under no obligation to accept.

If what has been shared is particularly emotionally stimulating for the listener, they may need to request the subject be revisited—in which case, set a date, e.g., in twenty-four hours, or in a week. Alternately, if the speaker has shared something personally painful that they would rather not revisit, the listener may need to get support and the chance to debrief elsewhere. The no-response option is best used for emotional emergencies. I don't recommend this option become your go-to, and do not, DO NOT, use it to verbally beat each other up. Seriously. I'm watching you.

~

It's great when we can use communication structures like the above to clear the space between us in ways that also take care of our relationship. And sometimes we just need to speak. Sometimes we're so entrenched in our stuff that we just need to pick a word, start there, and allow a stream of consciousness until we're done. The following communication rituals can be used with the structures above, and they can also support more spontaneous sharing. They work best when combined with the sharing checklist—but remember, the point of the checklist is to support you in sharing your truth as kindly as possible, not in continuing to conceal it.

≫ PLAYTIME ≪
The Talking Candle

This is a deceptively simple structure that I have repeatedly found to be profoundly effective. It uses a similar premise to a "talking stick," the idea being that when one person has the Talking Candle, they are the speaker, and may share without interruption for as long as they need to. It is the listener's task to hold space for them, and listen with as much presence and attention as they can muster. Listening styles like Ears in the Heart and Listening Tree work well for this, though a more active style like Bright Mirror could also be used in instances where the speaker is especially nervous to share.

The participants in the conversation sit opposite one another, with a candle between them. They take a moment to breathe together, perhaps to make eye contact, and to each state their intention for the conversation as they light the candle.

When one person is ready to share, that person draws the candle toward themselves. They are now the speaker, and may wish to clarify briefly the kind of listening they would like, and whether they want any response when they have finished. They then have as much time as they need to either use one of the structures above to express how they're feeling, or to simply breathe, place their awareness in their bodies, and speak what they find there. Having the Talking Candle can be particularly supportive for speakers who are experiencing intense emotional states, or otherwise struggling to share, as it means they will not be interrupted as long as they have it. This means there is time to sit, to breathe, to Listen In, to feel, to find the words, and then to share.

When the speaker feels replete, they can push the candle back to the centre. If they want any kind of response, or they want their listener to tell them what they heard, they can choose to have that next—but in this structure, you may wish to leave any response or discussion until after both people have shared. Once they have indicated their sharing is complete, the candle is once again available to be taken, and a new speaker designated. In this instance, it is vitally important that the new speaker does not respond to what has been said by the previous speaker during their sharing—unless they have gathered explicit consent to do so. Instead, the new speaker's task is to share as the first one did, speaking to what is present in them around whatever the topic of conversation is, and taking the time and space they need to do so until they feel complete.

It can be worth letting the candle move back and forth a few times before you either draw the structure to a close, or choose to move into a dialogue about what has been shared.

As with any ritual, make sure you give attention to closing, to giving thanks even if it's been tough, to blowing out the candle together, and to doing some aftercare, either together or individually.

⋛ PLAYTIME ⋚
Walk and Talk

For many, the prospect of sitting opposite the person they need to have a vulnerable and scary conversation with can feel overwhelming. The premise of structures like the Talking Candle can be adapted into an intentional walk. Walking side by side can feel less confrontational to many people, and movement often allows words to flow more freely. And if you're lucky enough to have somewhere beautiful to walk, the natural world also lends a gentle support, and a new perspective, to these tender moments where we make ourselves more known to one another.

Before or as you set out, set your individual or common intention(s) for the conversation. Once you're into your stride, decide who will share first. That person then gets to speak, perhaps using one of the options for sharing above, until they feel complete, with the listener offering them their full attention. Depending on what the speaker has asked for, the listener can then respond if that's welcome, or share in their turn.

Pass the invitation to share or respond back and forth as many times as you need to. Walks like these can take time, and as Brené Brown points out in her exquisite *Rising Strong*, you can't skip the messy middle.[22] These conversations will not be as effective if you're not willing to dive into their dark and difficult centres, to pick apart together what already belongs to each of you, what you need to take responsibility for, what you could do with forgiving, and what you're going to have to ask for help with. That messy middle— that second act as Dr. Brown calls it—is often the part of the conversation where we feel like this damn issue is never going to get resolved, where we're tempted to walk away. Stick with it, apply a little more kindness here, a little more truth there. Act two is often the darkest hour before the conversational dawn. If you wait long enough, the light usually reveals itself, sometimes in surprising ways.

At the end of the walk, give thanks to each other and yourself, and take a little time-out for some aftercare if you can.

In this chapter, you've experimented with looking deeper and letting yourself be seen; with taking the risks of being heard and listening more generously. You've travelled with me through what it takes to keep our relational space clean so that connection can flow freely. And you've practiced getting present, and being your beloved's ally. Well done. This part right here—this is the toughest part. So if you're still with me, please know I am a huge fan of you right now. Feel free to take a break, some deep breaths, and a moment to be kind to yourself, before we move on to building energy, pleasure, and magic together.

---

22. Brown, *Rising Strong*, 26.

Chapter 6

Union

You'll have noticed by now that a lot of what I'm doing with this playbook is offering you building blocks. From the ingredients of ritual magic, to the components of working through a difficult conversation, my aim is to supply you with the materials from which to build your own sex magical experiments in radical living and loving. To an extent, this necessitates starting with the basics—basics which are then built up to more complex experiences. Besides, there are always new treasures to be unearthed in the basics.

This section will be another box of erotic building blocks, and we'll be starting with the basics once again. I see you out there, rifling through the pages to find cool new ways to stimulate your lovers—and this section will most certainly touch on a few of those. However, that's not where we begin. This is partly because I believe there are more ways to commune with someone besides being physically intimate with them—and that physical intimacy is best when those other ways are also present. To which end, we'll begin by exploring tools to connect our breath, energy, and hearts—all of which will enhance our connection, intimacy, sensation, and capacity for pleasure later on.

I'm also starting with these other tools because right now we're being reminded just how much erotic touch needs and deserves to be approached with care, consciousness, and consent—so we'll be delving a little more deeply into those before we start getting our hands on one another.

The thing is, darlings, once you have all the building blocks in your sights, you can decide which ones to include when you build your pleasure palace, and which ones to set aside.

Breath and energy

In the previous section, we got curious and courageous enough to try making a little more eye contact, and also to experiment with aligning our breath and sending one another a little energy. We're going to dive more deeply into that now, and take some time to explore the relationship between breath and energy. In the exercises that follow, I'm going to be making use of the inhale as a route to receptivity, and the exhale as an active, projective, penetrative tool. Both will be used to move energy around—the former to receive/take it in, the latter to give/push it out. We're going to start with a few simple techniques for connecting to and manipulating our own energy.

A word of encouragement: How you experience so-called "energy" will vary from person to person. The trick is to stay curious, willing, and open to what is there, rather than concerning yourself with "getting it right." Some of you may experience energy as pretty colours, others as warmth, still others as waves of sound or motion, or a felt pulse or impulse. Welcome and work with what arises for you in the moment.

⇒ PLAYTIME ⇐
Energy Crafting (Solo)

Hold your hands in front of you, palms facing each other. Remember what we said about breathing out and giving energy, and breathing in and receiving energy. Begin to breathe fully and intentionally. Put your attention on the palms of your hands, and imagine you are breathing in and out of them. Once you're nice and focused, spend five to ten breaths imagining that, as you breathe out, you send heat from your right palm to your left; as you breathe in, you receive the heat into your left palm. Then five to ten breaths sending a pulsing beat between your palms. Then, spend five to ten breaths imagining sending lightning bolts from one palm to another. You may notice your breath getting more intense, especially on the out breath; that's great, keep going. Now try sending heat and lightning and musical crescendos between your palms all at once. And now just notice how your hands feel. See what happens when you move them closer together, move them farther apart, or move one closer or farther at a time.

Feel something? A warmth, a heaviness, a tingling, anything of that sort? What you're feeling is what, for the purpose of this playbook, we're referring to as energy. And even if you remain highly suspicious of the whole hippy-clappy, woowoo-energy-fluff stuff, what is important is that you're getting a sensation, however small that sensation may be when you're just starting out. Because if you're feeling something extra, then adding that something extra to anything you're doing—like, say, running your hands up and down your partner's spine—means that thing you're doing will feel "extra" something, right?

For those of you who have always secretly wondered if there wasn't "something more" to sex, I wholeheartedly recommend adding the "extra" ingredient of energy play.

⋙ PLAYTIME ⋘
Energy Crafting (Together)

Stand opposite a friend or beloved, and take some nice deep breaths together. Raise your palms out in front of you, parallel with your body, facing your partner's. Your arms can be relaxed and bent at the elbows. Notice that your hands are extensions of your arms, which flow all the way up to your shoulders, which connect to your chest and your heart.

Summon up some of the warmth you have for this person in your heart, and, when you're ready, breathe it down your arms, into your palms, and across the divide between your palms and theirs. Repeat for a few breaths— you might like to exchange breaths here for extra efficacy. Then imagine sending golden sparkles from your heart, down your arms, into your palms, and thence into your partner's. Then send what you imagine giggles might look like. Then the purest love you can muster. After a little while, very slowly move your palms backward and forward, closer to and then farther from your partner's, and just notice how that feels.

When you've finished, share your experience with each other, and see what each of you felt.

⋛ PLAYTIME ⋚
Heart/Heart Circuit Breath Revisited

What it's good for: Getting us out of our heads, with all their fears, judgments, and distractions, and getting us back in touch with our more tender, compassionate, loving selves. Opening us up to each other, and deepening our connection. Allowing us to feel more connected, intimate, loving, and/or in love.

How it's done: Stand or sit opposite your partner, at a distance that feels comfortable, from which you could reach up and place a hand on their chest if you needed to.

Take a moment to make eye contact, acknowledge each other, and take a few full, deep breaths together. When you're ready, start to synchronise your breathing, so that you're breathing out when your partner breathes in, and vice versa.

Begin to imagine that, as you breathe out, you send a little energy (whatever that feels/looks like to you), or a little love if you prefer, from your heart to theirs.

As you breathe in, you receive some energy or love from their hearts into yours.

Imagine that this energy, supported by your breath, becomes a circuit connecting your two hearts.

If you found it particularly helpful in the exercises above to get your hands involved, and if your partner is comfortable with this, place a hand on their chest, and imagine sending energy from your heart, down your arm, and through the palm of your hand into their chest.

If you find that your bodies begin to rock a little with your breath, or your breathing gets a little louder or more directed, go with it; sound and movement both help to build energy. Ideally, in exercises like these, there comes a moment when our imagination can take a step back—when we are no longing "doing" the energy, but rather the energy is "doing" us.

Feel free to pause and share, to see whether you felt anything, and what it felt like.

♥ *Messiness Alert!*

Structures like the ones we're exploring can lead to deep feelings of connection, trust, or steaminess—but they can also bring up unresolved stuff between you and your partner, and lead to tears and tough conversations. If this happens, be kind, be patient, and know that this is part of the process. Once you have talked through what came up, try to come back to the exercise for a few moments before completing.

⟫ PLAYTIME ⟪
Heart/Sex Circuit Together

What it's good for: As when done solo, this breath is a great one for connecting up heart and sex, love and desire. It's also a great way to build up erotic energy together, and can be a route toward energy orgasms, or energising physical sex and orgasms to make them more full-body and whole-being experiences.

Breathing the Heart/Sex Circuit together

How it's done: For this one, it's great to have not just your chest, but also your genitals aligned with your partner. Standing or lying opposite one another works, or finding a way to sit so that those parts of you face the other person—e.g., one person straddling the other on a chair, or cross legged on a surface such as a bed, or a semi-straddle (their right leg over your left, your left over their right).

Start with the Heart to Heart Circuit. When you're in a rhythm, make the circuit bigger by having Partner A imagine breathing in through their genitals while Partner B breathes out through the same, and then Partner A exhaling through their heart, while Partner B inhales through theirs. Again, it can be helpful to use your hands here—I often follow the circuit between us with mine, partly so we can keep track of where we are, and partly because I find it builds intensity.

When you have found a rhythm with the breathing, imagine you can add a little sparkle, a little heat, a little energy to light up that circuit.

Keep going. If your bodies start to rock, let it happen.

Feel free to share when (if) you feel like stopping. It's also most definitely worth switching the great circuit round, so that Partner A exhales through their genitals, and Partner B exhales through their heart, and so forth.

⁓

Hopefully the exercises above have given you a taste of something, a glimpse of what's possible with just breath, imagination, and curiosity. For some, with some, that is all it takes to go flying together; for some, with some, that's going to be more than enough to be going on with. And I'll be introducing you to some more radical energy experiments a little later on.

That being said, I know that some of you will already be wondering what this would feel like if you added touch. We'll be exploring that question very soon—but first, let's talk more about consent.

Consent

Consent, ultimately, is what allows us to enter into a state of union with another person.

When we have another person's full, enthusiastic, and sober consent, both of us can enter into connection, and any shared activity (and this includes breath and energy activities like those we've been exploring already), to the fullest extent possible, and be our fullest selves while we're there. Being in consent allows us to

- Be fully present—which, as we've already explored, is a key to intimacy
- Be more confident—both that what we're doing, and that what is done to us, will be something we enjoy
- Allow ourselves to be seen—which allows us to connect more deeply
- Be more embodied—which means more pleasure
- Surrender more deeply—which makes for much more ecstatic states

To practise consent is to negotiate to the point where our boundaries and our desires are no longer things that we are holding on to in our bodies in the form of tension, but rather are things that have been made welcome in the space between us. This allows our bodies to relax into what is happening, and allows us to have a more present and pleasurable experience.

When it comes to new or brief connections, practising consent lets us get intimate in ways that excite and nourish us both. It allows us to both feel empowered and welcome, and helps us get to know one another.

In a longer-term relationship, practising consent does all of the above, whilst also reminding us that our beloved is also a person—a separate individual worthy of our attention, respect, and ongoing curiosity. Remembering to see the other as an other, rather than another part of the furniture, makes for renewed and hot connection. Treating the other as an equal, who always has the right to choose, makes that connection sustainable.

So how do we practise the kind of active, enthusiastic consent I'm talking about here?

In my line of work, we often talk about a giver and a receiver—you'll have noticed these roles coming up in the exercises thus far. I want to acknowledge that, when it comes to our real-life interactions, things rarely feel as cut and dried as that. When we're being intimate with someone for the first time, and we don't know each other's preferences yet; or when we're in the full flow of intimacy, and we're both actively participating in what's happening; or when there are more than two of us involved in an interaction—these are just some of the moments where it may not be clear who the giver and who the receiver actually are. These roles may be in constant flux, continually passed back and forth. And of course there are times when we have enough of what is often referred to as "prior consent"—which is to say pre-negotiated and existing consent—to just throw ourselves into whatever our chosen activities might be. Note: prior consent is not the same as having been together for long enough to assume you know everything there is to know about the other person. It's always nice to be asked anew, and to be given a chance to discover or reveal new parts of our erotic selves.

Bearing the above in mind—as well as the work of consent pioneers like Betty Martin, which sheds new light on the roles of Giver and Receiver in other ways which we'll be exploring later on—for the purpose of exploring the building blocks of consent I'll be using the terms Active and Receptive. The Active partner is the one who is doing any given action, and the Receptive partner is the one being done to. Hopefully these two polarities will hold up well enough for us to explore consent together in this section.

Before we take a look at how each of these partners can be in consent, it's worth taking a moment to think about power, and the ways that power might intersect with and influence our ability to negotiate consent in any given moment.

Power and consent

The intersections between power and sex are incredibly complex and nuanced. The power balance (and imbalance) between two people will be impacted by a number of factors, including the following:

- Cultural, institutional, and societal structures of power
- Their respective histories and traumas
- Factors such as health, age, and body shape
- How their relationship unfolded, and what they each want from it moving forward
- Aspects of their relationship that they have negotiated (e.g., a Dominant/submissive dynamic), as well as aspects that they have not (e.g., habits around who does household chores)

Each of us brings a variety of visible and invisible factors to the power balance of any given encounter. When it comes to negotiating consent, if you have reason to suspect that you may hold more power than your partner (even if that is for reasons beyond your control, such as your assigned gender, profession, skin colour, etc.), you have a responsibility to be extra vigilant when it comes to making sure they are enthusiastically consenting to what you're doing—as opposed to yielding or pandering to the power imbalance between you. As the person with more power in the relationship, it is within your power to create greater space, opportunity, and encouragement for the other person to find their edges and express their boundaries.

If you suspect that you might hold less of the power in a particular connection or relationship, it's worth instigating conversations around that with the other person. Privilege does not come with a handbook, but it often comes with blind spots, so gently encouraging your partner to become aware of the power imbalance between you, and letting them know how they can be more mindful of it, can be good for everyone involved—especially the relationship. I would suggest being wary of anyone who is unwilling to have those conversations.

Being in consent as the Active partner
In order for the Active partner to be in consent, they need to have

- Self-consent
- Explicit and enthusiastic consent from their Receptive partner
- An exit strategy

If you're the Active partner, your first responsibility is to check in with yourself. Where is the activity you're about to embark on coming from? Is it arising from a sense of obligation or that there is a "right" or "sexy" way to do things? Is it coming from the knowledge that this is something your partner would enjoy? Or is it an impulse arising from your embodied flow and fuelled by curiosity and/or desire?

Later on, we'll be playing with the concepts of No, Maybe, and Yes, and as I write the above I notice I'm inclined to map those three options onto those three little words. You'll have a clear sense right now that this book is here to offer you a loving hand out of the rut of performance and into the land of permission—so if you find yourself about to do something for the sake of a "should," may I gently suggest that might not be a self-consensual activity to embark on, and encourage you to look for another way? If you do so, you'll likely find that, rather than it being a case of doing that thing or nothing, there will be a third way waiting to reveal itself to you if you just take the time to listen to yourself, and to the fertile space between you and your partner.

If you're about to embark on an activity because you know your partner will love it, it may be a Hell Yes for you (in which case, go for it!), or it may fit into the obligation category described above (in which case, rethink, communicate, look for that third way). Or, it could be in what my incandescent colleague Lola D. Houston calls your "OK Zone." Your OK Zone is the spectrum that stretches between your Hell Yes and your Hell No, and encompasses everything else—the myriad of moments where we might find ourselves saying "OK." Some of us—particularly those of us who were raised to please, appease, and perform for other people because of our gender, race, body type, or class—can spend a lifetime in the OK Zone, and not even in the half that's closer to the "Hell Yes" end. For those people, I recommend experimenting with only doing things that are a Hell Yes for a little while, to give yourself a head start on breaking down any habits that are coming between you and your self-consent. And whether or not that applies to you, I encourage you to keep consciously moving away from the nearer to No half of your OK Zone, and negotiating with your partner until you arrive at activities you know you can do for them and take pleasure in—or at least take real pleasure in their pleasure. As Lola says, unlearning OK is a lifelong process—start practising today!

If you're about to embark on an activity that already feels like an embodied Hell Yes for you, you can move straight on to phase two of negotiating consent.

Phase two is to find out whether your Receptive partner would like to receive the activity you're feeling to do. Even if this person is someone you have prior consent from, checking in can make people feel seen, respected, and cared for, and make activities we've done together countless times feel new again.

The first step is to enquire verbally as to whether the activity is welcome. This is where the magic of "May I?" comes in again, as it's a simple tool that is great in both the heat of the moment, and as a way into more elaborate pre-negotiation. When gaining consent, you might find yourself doing any of the following:

- Asking a simple closed question about a specific action in the moment —e.g., "May I kiss your tummy?"
- Enquiring whether a particular activity would be of interest to the other person(s), and setting out the parameters within which you'd like to do so—e.g., "I would like to undress you, lay you out in front of the fire, and explore the tattoos on your tummy with my mouth. Is that something you would enjoy right now?"
- Exploring the possibility of indulging in an activity together with open questions that leave plenty of room for conversation and negotiation —e.g., "I would love to cover those scars on your tummy with kisses sometime. Does that sound like something you might enjoy? What would you need for that to feel like a safe and pleasurable experience? When shall we do it?"

Having asked for verbal consent, make sure you give your partner the space and time they need to process your question, listen in, and respond.

The answer you're looking for is a clear and enthusiastic Yes, or equivalent.

If you get a Maybe, you'll need to go through the same process you did with yourself earlier, and find out where the Maybe is coming from. Is it the product of someone having been conditioned to say Yes, or denied their No? If so, the Maybe may be a mask for a No, and the best thing you can do for your partner is support them in accessing that No, and celebrate them finding it. At the time of writing, No feels like a profoundly important word personally and culturally. Having the confidence and freedom to say No to something is a measure of how safe we feel, which in turn is often a measure of how safe we are. And the safer your partner is, the more they will be able to surrender when you do find that activity that is a Hell Yes for you both.

If you're receiving a Maybe because the activity in question requires negotiation or new parameters to become a Yes, see if you can find your way toward those parameters together.

If you receive a No or equivalent, give thanks for it, and move on to something else.

Along with verbal consent, we can also look out for physical consent. What does the Receptive partner's body language tell us about how they're feeling in response to an expression of something we'd like to do to them, or in response to what we are doing to them? How are they breathing, moving, and positioning their limbs? Are they making eye contact? Are they making any sound?

Some signs that your partner means the Yes they are saying, and/or is enjoying what you're offering them, might include visible or audible breathing, an open body (rather than a closed posture, which might include crossed arms/legs, heavy or stiff limbs, etc.), eye contact, and, of course, affirming words or happy noises. Downcast eyes, a closed stance, moving away, hesitancy in the voice, these are some of the signs that should encourage you to check in again with your receiver, and perhaps give them some space to check in with themselves.

Note: these are some signs I might interpret as nonverbal Yeses or Nos in someone coming from the same culture as me. They may vary culturally as well as from person to person. While time will educate you in a particular partner's nonverbal signals, you can also have a conversation about what those might be, as many of us will be able to pin down and describe at least one or two of our nonverbal Yes Please or warning signs.

An extra way to check that you have consent is to Listen In to the space between you. Does it feel like there's flow, ease, comfort between you, and in your heart and belly—or do things feel tight, tense, resistant, or in some way "off"? If the latter, check in.

Try not to think of gaining consent as a one-off event or a quick win, and especially avoid the assumption that getting consent for one activity means you have consent for another. Instead, let consent be an ongoing dialogue between you and the person you're being intimate with. Keep listening for their Yes in their words and body language, and in the flow between you.

Finally, it can be really helpful to have an exit strategy if things don't go as you were hoping they would—which, when we are in the habit of taking erotic risks, is guaranteed to happen eventually. Common exit strategies that are unlikely to support your intimacy or pleasure include blaming your Receptive partner for not enjoying what's you're doing; beating yourself up for "getting it wrong"; slamming doors; rolling over and turning the light out; pretending nothing happened and everything is fine, and never trying that activity again. Some possible alternatives include stopping what you're doing, making eye-contact, checking in to find out what's happening; using one of the options offered previously for tough conversations if something comes up that feels like it's likely to be a big topic for one or both of you; asking for direction so that you can do the activity in a way they would enjoy more, or asking what would feel good instead of what you were doing; taking a time out to do something that's mutually relaxing or soothing before coming back to being physical.

Being in consent as the Receptive partner

- Listen In for self-consent
- Translate for your Active partner
- Celebrate your No, and establish a safe word

When an activity is offered or initiated by an Active partner, your role as the recipient is one of translator. Your task is to Listen In, and translate the responses from your head, heart, and body for your partner. There will be times when you feel in flow together, and this is a relatively organic and easy thing to do—but it's also OK to take all the time you need to work out how you're feeling about any given activity. In fact, if you've not actively practised consent much before, it's recommended.

If you have an enthusiastic Yes for what has been suggested or instigated, remember to clarify whether that Yes comes with caveats or with particular boundaries.

If you find you're feeling a Maybe, check in with your OK Zone as described above. Where does this activity sit in that Zone? Is there something that could turn it into a Yes for this particular situation? Or would it actually be a No, if No was a thing you felt allowed to say?

And, of course, there will be times when your belly tightens or feels nauseated, when your skin seems to withdraw, when you can feel your feelings and/or body pulling away, when you feel suddenly drained, or when your thoughts simply say "Fuck No"—and it's time to draw a line.

Being able to say No is such a vital part of intimacy. Without it, we cannot have true connection. We cannot fully let another in if we don't also have a door we can close on them if we so choose. We cannot really let a beautiful caress into our skin if we cannot also ask not to be touched. We cannot surrender to bliss if we do not have a safe foundation and container within which to surrender. Our ability to set boundaries, to state our edges, to speak our No, is vital to our reaching a place of ecstatic Yes.

All of this is not to say that saying No is easy in our culture. It is to say that practising your ability to say No is a gift you give not only to yourself, but also to your relationships. You never have to justify or apologise for saying No to any kind of touch. If you want to be polite, if you want to be kind, say No Thank You. And of course there may be times when you wish to explore and explain why you've arrived at a No, as doing so will help you to remain connected and build greater understanding—and hopefully lead to your trying things together that are more of a Hell Yes. But it is not your job to explain your No. It's your job to practise it, to strengthen it like a muscle; to treasure and to celebrate its existence—and to find ways to articulate it. In the event that your No—or other expressions of nonconsent—is not respected, your duty is not to the disrespect, but first and foremost to your No, and to yourself.

It can also be useful to have a "safe word" in place. This is a word, or a physical signal, that lets the Active partner know that what they or we are doing needs to stop—for a moment, or completely—and that you need to check in. It's best to choose a word that doesn't come up in intimacy very often, and that both people recognise as a signal to stop—e.g., "Hyacinth." You can also have a safe word gradient—a common one being the stoplight signal, where Red means stop, Green means yes please keep going, and Yellow means we need to slow down, check in, and maybe change direction. If for whatever reason you're unlikely to be able to speak during any given activity, you can agree on a "safe signal," such as tapping the bed or floor three times to indicate you need a time out, or holding a ball which you drop if things don't feel okay. Safe words are useful because they let us communicate that something isn't working for us in a way that isn't loaded or shaming. They also allow us to play at our edges, so if we want to agree that "no" won't mean No while, e.g., our three play-partners tickle us mercilessly, we can say "bananas" instead if we're actually hyperventilating and need a moment!

As the Receptive partner, it's important to get into the habit of practising ongoing consent rather than thinking of it as a one-off event, or as a contract set in stone. Communicating with your partner about how they are touching you, and the activities you're enjoying together, helps them to learn what works for you and what doesn't, which makes for more positive and pleasurable experiences all round. It also means that, if you consent to something, and then discover it's not in fact what you want in the moment, that ongoing communication allows you to express that. You always have the right to change your mind. Experiences that end up feeling nonconsensual, even if they began with consent, are not ultimately good for either party. You do not owe anyone your consent.

~

I want to pause here, and acknowledge that for some of you that last section may have been a lot to take in. You may be experiencing niggling discomfort or waves of intense emotions as you become aware of times or areas of your life where consent has been lacking. If that is the case, I invite you to breathe, and to resist the temptation to berate your past selves for not having the power, language, or skills to change that.

Consent is radical stuff, because we do not live in a consensual culture. We live in a culture where human beings are allowed agency and value based on factors beyond their control, such as their gender, age, and ability to be productive according to Western standards. Nonconsensual behaviour is expected of us every day, in one direction or another. All we can do is start where we are, and use what we have to create consent culture in our own lives. Not just in sex, and not just in our relationships, but in all our interactions with others.

⪼ PLAYTIME ⪻
Yes, No, Maybe—a Consent Game

This is a game that has been doing the rounds in the conscious sexuality world for years—and yet each time I come to it I learn something different about myself, and my relationship to those words. You can try it with friends, as a teaching tool for consent within families, and, of course, with partners. If you're in a long-term sexual/romantic relationship, I recommend revisiting it as a way to reconnect, do consent as an ongoing practice, find out more about each other, and have some fun.

Decide who will be Partner A and Partner B. Partner A is the Active Partner, and Partner B is the Receptive Partner. Partner A has the ability to move, and to choose whether and how to touch Partner B. Partner B has three words at their disposal—Yes, No, and Maybe. Hopefully, we've already explored what these mean enough above for you to have a clear sense of when to use them. Partner A, when you hear a Yes, you may proceed with whatever you're doing for as long as you choose. When you hear a Maybe, slow down, pause, or try something new until you hear a Yes or a No. When you hear a No, stop what you're doing, and try something else. Be curious, be playful, and try and get at least one clear No from your partner—because we all need the practice!

Start a little distance apart (at least five paces). Begin by making eye contact, and taking some deep, full breaths together. When you're ready, Partner A, you can start to walk toward Partner B. Partner B, you want to be saying either Yes, No, or Maybe every three to five seconds, depending on how you're feeling, and how you want Partner A to proceed. For instance, if you're happy with them walking toward you, you might say Yes; if you wanted more time just breathing and eye gazing, or you don't want them to come any closer, you might say No; if you want them to come closer, but not so fast, it might be a Maybe. Your responses are likely to change moment to moment, which is a great reminder of why ongoing consent is such a vital thing to practice.

Partner A, if you get closer to Partner B, you might want to offer them some touch. Move slowly enough to give them a chance to respond to each kind of touch you offer, and the different parts of their body you decide to touch them on. Continue to touch them in whatever way you feel drawn, paying careful attention to their responses, and adjusting what you're doing accordingly.

Do this for five to ten minutes. Once your time is up, Partner A step back to where you began. Take a few deep breaths, thank each other, and then switch roles. Feel free to share about your experiences afterward—or to just keep switching!

Once you've gotten practised at this game, you may wish to try incorporating it into other activities. For examples, you could try it in a massage, with Partner A giving the massage, and Partner B receiving and responding, or during sex, taking it in turns being A and B.

Touch

For those of you who have skimmed other sections of this book in your eagerness to get this far, I'm going to come straight out with it: the greatest transformer of how we touch ourselves and each other is Presence. Specifically, how present we are able to be with a person, and even more specifically, with their skin. We played with getting present with our own skin a little in the Loving Hands exercise in the Making Love with Self section of this book, and this might be a good time to revisit that exercise, to remind yourself how it is to be touched by hands that are truly "listening."

To get present with another person's skin, we need to do three things: breathe, listen to our hands, and give ourselves permission to slow down.

Try the following experiment with a friend or partner: With your partner's permission, take their hand in both of yours. Without thinking about it a whole lot, touch their hand in a way you would assume would feel good for them. Do that for a minute.

Then pause. Simply hold their hand in yours. Take some deep, full breaths. Imagine that you can put your ears, or your eyes, or all of your senses in your fingertips. When you feel more focused in your hands, get curious about how the skin you are touching wants to be touched. As you feel guided to, begin to caress or massage or squeeze your friend's hand again, this time guided by what you can "hear" through your fingers. Do that for a minute.

Then slow down a little more; breathe a little deeper; keep going for another minute.

Then ask your partner which of the three felt best to them, and notice which one felt best to give.

Chances are that you and your partner noticed a marked difference between the quality of touch when you made an assumption about how to touch the other person, and when you got present with their skin. Let's look at how getting present like this changes the way we touch:

- Breathing helps us to be more present in the moment, and in our own bodies—which means the more breathfully we touch another, the more aware we will be of what we're doing. Breathing mindfully also reminds our receiver to breathe, which in turn helps them to be more present in their bodies, and helps spread the sensations of our touch around.
- Listening to the other person's skin helps us to stop focusing on our fears or assumptions about touching them, and start focusing on how their body feels, and how it wants to be touched. Putting our attention on the receiver like this also helps us track their pleasure responses— whether verbal or physical—and find out what they are most enjoying.
- Giving ourselves permission to slow down makes our touch more exquisite. It also means that, if we lose the flow of what we're doing, we can simply pause, breathe, bring our attention back and listen to the skin again for however long it takes for us to find that thread once more. We tend to assume that touch should be all go; in fact, holding our hands still on the receiver can give them a chance to savour how their skin feels from the touch we've given them so far, as well as having the potential to make them feel held.

Practising bringing that level of exquisite presence into your hands is the single best thing you can do to enhance the way you touch other people. If touch is an area you feel unskilled in, start there—and then try adding any of the following to what you're doing, and see what your recipients enjoy. Top tip: this will be different for each recipient, which is why getting used to listening to the skin, and paying attention to physical as well as verbal feedback, is the place to start!

Gliding strokes

Place your palm on your recipient's skin, and let your fingers wrap lightly around that part of their body. Listen to their skin, and then glide your palm over it as you feel drawn to. Make sure it feels like you're flowing over the skin; if you feel like you're dragging your palm you may be applying too much pressure, and if you're just grazing the skin it may be too little. Don't be afraid to make full, firm contact with your palm, and allow your fingers to keep gently wrapping round the body as you go. This touch works especially well on the limbs, the torso, and the planes of the body.

Feather strokes

Not to everyone's taste, but certainly one of my personal favourites, this involves shifting this awareness from the palm to the fingers, and gliding just the tips of them over the surface of the skin. Some recipients will enjoy this with your fingertips making full contact with the skin, and others will enjoy just the very tips of them, gliding so lightly that they're only just making contact. For people who like this type of touch, this can be great place to begin touch with. It works particularly well on areas of the body with a lot of nerve endings, such as erogenous zones like the nape of the neck, the scalp, the nipples, and also along the spine.

Kneading strokes

A relaxing stroke featured in most kinds of massage, kneading squeezes and releases the muscles, helping to release tension and soothe body and mind. On slimmer parts of the limbs, wrap your hand around the fleshier part, and knead by rhythmically squeezing and releasing, moving up or down the limb. On fleshier parts of the body, knead the flesh handful by handful, as you might knead dough, or as a kitten might knead its mother in search of milk. Kneading strokes work particularly well when relaxation is needed, or when assisting someone to feel grounded and present in their body. They feel especially good on muscular parts of the body like the butt, thighs, upper arms, and back.

Squeezing strokes

Like kneading, squeezing strokes are great for releasing tension, and helping your recipient to feel relaxed and present. They involve squeezing a part of the body, holding for a few seconds, and then releasing. You can then move your hands to an adjacent part of the body, and repeat the process. Again, this works well on muscular parts of the body, so you might start by squeezing and releasing the shoulders, then squeezing and releasing down the upper arms, then working on the back, down to the glutes, and so on.

Intense sensation strokes

I am casually mentioning what is in fact a whole world of possibilities here. They are laid out in much greater detail in a plethora of excellent kink 101 manuals (check out the Resources section for some of these). Many of those possibilities should ideally be learned from someone who knows what they're doing. However, you can up the sensation levels in your touch with plenty of less complicated options. Intense sensations mostly fall under the thuddy/throbby variety, or the stingy variety. Some people like both, some like one or the other (and some don't like either, and that's totally wonderful too). Thuddy or throbby sensations can be produced with cupped palm tapping/slapping, gentle thumping, or more intense kneading or squeezing, or with deep biting. Like kneading and squeezing, they help the receiver get grounded into their body and release tension. Stingy sensations can be produced with nails, pinching, nipping, and slapping. They tend to sensitise the skin and raise energy rather than ground it. Since these are potentially more intense options than the ones mentioned so far, if you haven't explored them previously with someone, proceed slowly, and keep checking in with the three levels of consent we looked at earlier.

Holding

Simply holding someone, whether it's cradling a part of their body, or cradling the whole person, can provide a surprisingly powerful experience. Whether you're interspersing other touch with moments of stillness and holding, or doing nothing else but enfolding someone and breathing with them, do not underestimate the power of taking the time to be present with their body, and all that it holds. Holding makes space for inner movement and release, supports relaxation and rest, and allows for integration.

～

Along with getting present in your hands, and getting more confident with your touch techniques, one of my favourite ways to add that "something more" factor to touch is to incorporate energy. This can add another level of intensity—and, like more intense sensations, will require an extra level of consent at least the first time you try it with someone. For some people, this is the only way they like to play—but for others it can feel too overwhelming or vulnerable, so they will want to have choice around if and when it happens.

Here's a little experiment to get you started.

⋟ PLAYTIME ⋞
Electric Touch

Take this one in turns, with one partner giving, and one receiving. The giver stands behind the receiver. Giver, stroke your dominant hand down your partner's back a few times to start. Then come back into your own space, still standing behind them.

Giver, get some energy building up in your belly—with, for example, a little Breath of Fire.

When you've got a nice bellyful of the stuff, start imagining that as you breathe in, it flows up to your heart—and as you breathe out, it flows down your dominant arm and out of your fingertips. Once you've taken a few of those breaths, you can build on them by using your nondominant hand to encourage the energy from your heart, running your hand from your chest, over your shoulder, and down your arm on the outbreath. When you get to the tips of your fingers, imagine they extend a little further than they actually do, and run your nondominant hand along them, drawing the energy with you, until your hand slides off the imaginary finger extensions.

Repeat a few times, breathing energy up from your core to your heart, and then out from your heart, down your arm, and into your extended fingers. Keep using your other hand to encourage the energy along, and in your mind's eye, see those extended fingers becoming more and more real, bright, buzzing, and energised.

When your dominant hand feels nice and "full" of energy, stroke it down your partner's back a few times. Ask them if your touch feels any different to before.

Then repeat the energising process in your own space again, drawing a few deep, full breaths of energy up from your belly, down into your hand, extending your fingers… And then run those extended fingers down your partner's back, without physically touching their skin. See if they can feel the touch.

Share about the experience, then switch over.

⌒

If you take the time to get practised in manipulating your erotic energy with breath, imagination, and intention, you will find you can add it to most kinds of touch and physical intimacy. Depending on how receptive to energy your partners are, doing so can add a new level of psychospiritual depth and bliss to physical intimacy.

The kinky cats among you may already have started to wonder whether it's possible to add this stuff into your pain and power play—or indeed, in reading some of the above, identified something you're already doing. So without further ado, yes, you can do this energy stuff with toys as well. An adaptation of the technique above works wonderfully for handheld impact toys like floggers, fingers extensions like talons or scratchy mitts, or even vibrators.

⇶ PLAYTIME ⇴
Electric Toys

Having selected your toy of choice, take it in your dominant hand, and give yourself or your partner a few simple strokes with it.

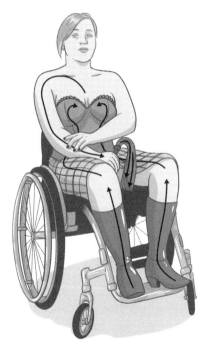

Charging up your toys with energy

Now it's time to energise your toy. This is basically another version of the exercise above—but for this one, especially if you're playing with intense sensation, I want to invite you to bring your awareness back to the soles of your feet, and drop some imaginary roots down into the Earth. I find when it comes to dealing in impact and pain, the Earth has a surprising amount of gleeful, fiery energy available to lend her kinky devotees.

So, get some of that rolling up your spine and into your belly, then up and into your heart—and then, as we did above, breathe it out of your heart, and down your dominant arms and into your toy. This time, you're envisioning your energy extending into your toy of choice until it becomes an extension of your arm. Use breath, use visualisation, use your other hand to "push" energy out of your heart and down your arm, "pulling" it into the toy, and extending all the way to the end.

Once you can feel your own awareness at the tip of the toy, do a few experimental strokes, and see what you and your recipient notice. This is an exercise where I find I really notice a difference in the experience of giving as well as that of receiving, so remember to take a mental note of whether you as the giver of sensation feel any different before and after energising your toy of choice.

⩔ PLAYTIME ⩕
Dermal Rites

If the Electric Toys exercise had you feeling left out because your personal perverted preferences lean toward more precise play—piercing for example—fear not. Anything can be played with intentionally—indeed, when it comes to playthings such as needles, intention is the keyword. You might use breathing and visualisation like those described above to get you focused and build energy. But as something like a play needle or a clamp is going to stay in/on the skin, rather than focus your energies on making it an extension of yourself, you can instead focus on infusing it with a specific intention.

For example, during a co-created magical ritual, I invited myself and my partner to focus on the purpose for which the ritual was being done, and imagine the energy or feeling of that intention or wish infusing the needle that I then pierced his third eye (the skin between the eyebrows) with. By doing this, I was quite literally putting the new intention into his body. We suspect this is also a rather effective method of planting the seed of that wish in the subconscious.

~

Before we stray into the marvellous realms of genital touch and play, I want to dive a little more deeply into this whole giving and receiving thing that crops up in so many of the exercises in my field, and in this book. Of course, this is not to say that the giver/receiver model is the best or only way to do conscious intimacy. Rather, I cover it because including giving and receiving in your erotic practices can have the following effects:

- It invites us more fully into presence with one another since we are putting our complete focus on either the doing of the action in question if we're the Active Partner, or the experience of receiving the action if we're the Receptive Partner. As such, if getting present is something we struggle with or just want more of—whether it's being present with each other, or present in our bodies, or present during sex and pleasure—giving/receiving structures are a great way to expand our capacity for that.

- Giving/receiving structures also allow us to hone our capacity to touch one another. Rather than both trying to touch each other in pleasing ways at the same time, in these scenarios one person gets to practise giving pleasure to the other, with the other perhaps giving the kind of generous feedback that supports their partner to touch them in more and more pleasurable ways. Thus, these structures become a way for us to learn each other's sweet spots and turn-ons with much greater accuracy than we might otherwise.

- Exercises that invite a giving/receiving structure also expand our repertoire. So many possibilities for intimacy—from a good massage to a power exchange dynamic—rely on our ability to give and receive fully. Practising these skills gives us a wider range of possibilities for pleasure.

Something else that giving and receiving structures can do is show us what lies underneath the way we habitually touch one another. This in turn allows us to be more choiceful about how we touch, and what our intentions are in doing so—whilst it also allows us to be more choiceful about the touch that we receive. Betty Martin created an exquisite system to illustrate this called the Wheel of Consent. The Wheel is divided by two axes—the axis of Doing and Done To, and the axis of Give and Receive. These split the Wheel into four quadrants—Serve (giving whilst doing) and Receive (receiving whilst being done to), and Take (receiving whilst doing) and Allow (giving whilst being done to).

The best way to understand the nuances of these quadrants, and to get a sense of what they can tell us about how we touch, is to do the following exercise that Betty commonly uses to teach them. It's an exercise called the Three-Minute Game, originally invented by Harry Faddis, and I cannot recommend strongly enough that you try it, and you try it multiple times. It will teach you volumes about how you tend to touch and how you'd like to touch, as well as how you prefer to be touched. It can also pinpoint with great accuracy the aspects of being intimate that we most struggle with, and give us a chance to practice them.

⤜ PLAYTIME ⤛
The Three-Minute Game

To play the Three-Minute Game you will need a timer and a partner. The game consists of two questions, and each partner takes a turn at asking, or at being asked, those two questions. The questions are:

For the next three minutes, how would you like me to touch you?

and

For the next three minutes, how would you like to touch me?

In both cases, the person who is being asked the question should take some time to Listen In and notice what would feel particularly good for them in terms of touch in that moment (and there is no right answer here, people; you can ask for anything on the spectrum of just sitting in the same room through to the wildest sensual activity you can possibly imagine doing with someone for three minutes), and then ask for that as clearly and specifically as they can. The person who asked the question then needs to do their own Listening In, and decide whether they can offer what's been asked with a full and happy heart. If they can, set the timer for three minutes, and off you go. If not, negotiate until you arrive at an activity that feels close enough to what was asked for to be pleasurable for the receiver, but which the giver is fully comfortable and happy to give—and then set the timer, and off you go.

The first of these questions invites us to sink fully into the respective roles of serve and receive. It's all about what would feel good to the receiver, and about the giver facilitating that unfolding to the best of their capacity. The clearer the Receptive partner states what they desire, the better this exercise works—which makes it a wonderful practice for those of us who have grown a little too comfortable with giving, or who are haunted by previous experiences of unwelcome or invasive touch, to develop our capacity to state what we want, and to receive it. It's also a great opportunity for Active partners who are uncertain about how to touch, or have developed habitual ways of touching, to get clear direction, and a fresh opportunity to meet the other person's desires.

The second question introduces us to the roles of taking and allowing. The receiver is still the one getting pleasure, but in terms of the direction of touch, they are now the Active partner, taking their pleasure from the giver—who is allowing them to do so, always within the limits of what feels comfortable. This can feel like less familiar territory to some people, but it actually helps us get clarity around ways that we already touch each other—while also showing us how we most enjoy touching others, and how we can allow others to touch us in ways that are not especially pleasurable for us, but are for them.

As the giver in the first question, we discover—or remember—what it is to be giving touch that is a gift for our partner alone. When we take our turn as the receiver, and become the Active partner for the second question, we get to discover—or remember—how it is to touch another person purely for our own pleasure. Many of us when we give touch are actually doing a combination of both these things. Experiencing them separately like this helps us to be more intentional with how we touch on a daily basis, as well as giving us language to describe the kind of touch we'd like to receive. There are times when it's wonderful to get caught up in a mutual flow of switching roles and types of touch back and forth; but there are also times when we want to take or be taken, and there are times when we want touch to be a gift that is just for us. And for many people, it takes being firmly in one of the quadrants of the Wheel of Consent to really get them fired up, turned on, and tuned into their erotic energy.

Genital touch

I want to begin this section with notes of reassurance.

Genital touch is not a requirement for being sexual. The majority of the sexual experiences we see in the media emphasise genital touch—specifically genital penetration—as the goal of sexual activity. However, genitals neither are, nor need to be, everyone's go to sexual organs of choice, and both pleasure and orgasm-like experiences can and do occur independently of genitals that do or don't like to be touched.

You do not have to receive touch on your genitals in order to include them in your erotic life, and indeed in your erotic life with other people. Whether you're squeezing your PC muscle to heighten your awareness of your body and your arousal, or whether you're experimenting with mutual masturbation as a genital-inclusive way to enjoy each other without touching, there is a spectrum of scrumptious ways to be sexual with genitals that are not open to being touched by someone else.

All genitals are different, and genital touch is an area where no one size fits all. What works wonders for one person may leave another feeling ticklish or disinterested or hurt. Despite the prevalent but unspoken belief that, on reaching puberty, we should somehow be miraculously imbued with the knowledge of how to touch not only our own genitals, but also other people's, I give you my word as a sexuality professional that this is not the case for anyone. When it comes to touching each other's genitals, the best thing we can do is look for active consent, communicate clearly with one another, and resist the impulse to lose heart or beat ourselves up if things go wrong.

Offering good genital touch, particularly to someone whose body is unfamiliar to us or traversing change, is a delicate balance of two things: dropping our assumptions, whilst leaning into some basic truths about touch.

We need to drop our assumptions because, as I mentioned above, genitals are as diverse as the people they belong to. Our understanding of genitals as fitting into two types is thankfully becoming outdated as we become increasingly aware that they in fact span a spectrum of shape, size, and accompanying chromosomal make-up. Meanwhile, their capacity to receive touch and experience pleasure is shaped not only by their physiology, but also by our previous experiences of pleasure and pain, by our erotic practices and our erotic habits, and by our mental and emotional states, and our relationship to the person offering us said touch.

As we realise that genitals don't in fact fit into one of two "jello moulds,"[23] we're also becoming aware that particular genitals do not equate to specific genders.[24] At the same time, as we discover the changeability and fluidity of gender, we're also discovering a complementary fluidity and capacity to shape-shift in our genitals. While for some of us, that fluidity requires hormonal or surgical support to feel physically manifest, others of us discover the mutability and possibility of not only our visible genitals, but also their invisible, energetic, but not necessarily less tangible counterparts.

With so many of our cultural narratives about romance and being a "good lover" tied up in spontaneity, effortless mastery, and natural talent, it's all too easy to reach for cultural assumptions around types of genitals, and the types of touch they enjoy, to steady ourselves as we silently strive to "get it right." However, as the above demonstrates, these will only get us so far. Better to release our assumptions and turn our attention away from what worked before, or what worked for someone else, and onto our partners. Being attentive is sexy, and we can apply that attentiveness to our partner's body language, and to the tips of our fingers, and allow these to guide us in what's feeling good.

And we can, and must, talk to each other. Everything we explored in the consent exercises above can be applied to genital touch, from "May I?" through "How would you like me to touch you for the next three minutes?", to checking in regularly to find out how what you're doing is feeling for your partner. I was recently playing with a lover's genitals for the first time, and reached for Yes, No, Maybe as a way for her to let me know what was feeling good at regular intervals. For those of you out there who are assuming that incorporating this kind of structure and clarity into your erotic interactions would make them stilted and unsexy, let me assure you that the symphony of Yeses that tumbled forth in whispers and moans was unutterably hot. And it was super reassuring to know I would get a Maybe or No if she needed me to

---

23. Darnell, "The Atlas of Erotic Anatomy and Arousal."
24. Howitt, "Genitals Do Not Equal Gender."

pause or change direction, as the last thing I wanted to do was interrupt that flow of pleasure.

That being said, here are a few things that do seem to be fairly consistently true of genital touch, at least for people who like that sort of thing:

- Breath focuses us on and expands pleasure. Breathing into the touch we are receiving helps us feel that touch more fully. It also gets more of our body involved in the sensation, which allows any pleasure we get from it to become more of a full-body experience.

- Another way of bringing our awareness more fully into our genitals, and expanding the sensation happening therein, is using our PC (pubococcygeus) muscle. This is the muscle that contracts during orgasm, and that we use to stop the flow of urine. Gently squeezing this muscle, perhaps in time with our breath, whilst receiving genital touch helps to build and expand our pleasure.

- Genitals tell us when they're ready to be touched, and when they're enjoying the touch they're receiving. They do this with the results of blood flow to the area (engorgement, erection), with the secretion of fluids, and through signs we talked about in the consent section such as pushing up or opening up to meet our hands, while the person they belong to makes sounds of pleasure and moves their body. With genital touch it becomes even more crucial to watch out for these secondary and tertiary levels of consent, as well as checking in for verbal consent, as this is a part of our body that can end up holding fear or trauma from unwelcome or unskillful touch, as well as unwanted habits around pleasure and arousal.

When it comes to giving genital touch, it's worth knowing that all genitals start out the same, and are made of similar tissue. The work of pioneering sexologists like Cindy Darnell[25] shows us that all genitals begin as the same little buds in utero, which then blossom into a variety of shapes, ranging from external erectile tissue (often referred to as penises), to internal erectile tissue (often referred to as vulvas), with many more variations in between

---

25. Darnell, "The Atlas of Erotic Anatomy and Arousal."

than our limited cultural representations of such things would have us believe. Almost all these different shapes are made up of:

- The glans—often referred to as either the clitoris, or the head of the penis
- The shaft—familiar to us as either the stalk or stem of the clitoris, or the shaft of the penis
- The inner labia/penile raphe—external erectile tissue closes and fuses together in utero, creating the line extending from the scrotum to the underside of the penis; on internal genitals this same tissue forms the inner labia
- The bulbs—otherwise known as the outer labia or scrotum
- The legs—the roots of the genitals as they extend into the body

From this knowledge we can glean the following information:

- Erectile tissue is of a comparable size for everyone, regardless of whether it is internal or external. This means that the clitoris is far from the total extent of the erectile tissue on internal genitals. It extends into the inner and outer labia, as well as under and around these through the "legs" of the clitoris. Put simply, this opens up a much greater spectrum of sensation, pleasure, and relaxation that is available for internal genitals. It is, in short, an invitation to broaden the area and variety of touch. For many people with internal erectile tissue, this wider area is a much more pleasurable and relaxing place to begin than direct clitoral stimulation.
- A similar invitation extends to external erectile tissue—because even here we cannot see the full extent of that tissue. Including the scrotum, perineum, and surrounds in erotic touch for external genitals can also build pleasure, and expand the horizons of sensation.
- If we're all made up of the same types of tissue, then regardless of the shape of the genitals we're touching, we can know a little bit about what each element of them might potentially enjoy. For example, glans often like friction rather than pressure, and some can only take very light friction if any. Many shafts on the other hand enjoy pressure as well as friction. Long gliding strokes can work well for shafts, whereas many glans prefer circular strokes. Gentle kneading and/or caressing often work well for bulbs—and so on.

- Likewise, if we're all made up of the same types of tissue, there's nothing to stop us from finding ways to treat the genitals in front of us as the owner of those genitals feels them to be, rather than as our genitals and gender-equating cultural habits might lead us to. If, for example, the person we're touching experiences their mostly internal erectile tissue as a cock, there is nothing to stop us adjusting our touch to treat the parts of their genitals that are external as just that.

Some extra tips to bear in mind when touching genitals:

- To build, prolong, and expand pleasure (and orgasm), remember to intersperse genital touch with touch that moves around the rest of the body. Stroke or squeeze the pleasure into your partner's thighs; draw it up into the belly, and roll it round the chest or into the nipples; brush or pull it down the arms; caress it into their face and hair. Then come back to the genitals, and build it up again. Resist the temptation to think of pleasure as a straight line toward a goal; no one wants their bits treated like a football (well, OK, some kinky folks do, but that's beside this particular point). Instead, think about pleasure as an infinite ocean, and yourself as the tide pulling it through your partner's body, one wave at a time.

- Lubrication is a lovely thing. Some people have it in abundance all by themselves, but even then a generous handful of warm coconut oil (not to be combined with latex), or a favourite water-based lube (fine with latex), can make a surprising amount of difference.

- Stillness and movement are equally important. As arousing as the right sequence of repetitive strokes can be, moments of still contact can feel everything from warm and soothing, through to profoundly holding and healing. For example, if you're penetrating your partner's genitals or anus with your fingers, holding still at the entrance can give the body a chance to invite you in. Taking the time to cradle or hold the genitals after orgasm can also support a longer basking period, and give your partner a chance to fully surrender to the aftershocks of pleasure.

~

Having experimented with adding breath, energy, and imagination, plus consent, to touch and toys and genital play, we can hardly leave out penetration—and for those of you for whom penetration of one sort or another is a desirable thing, I promise you, you won't want to. I'm going to touch on physical penetration first, and then close with one of my favourite pieces of this whole sex magic thing—energetic genitals, or energyfuckery as I fondly term it.

You have probably gathered by now that incorporating more breath and awareness into any erotic activity will build sensation and expand pleasure. The more we move away from the "quick and quiet" habits so many of us learn around our pleasure as teenagers, and the more we find the courage and focus to incorporate breath, sound, and movement (particularly of the pelvis, hips, and spine if we can) into our lovemaking, the more freely our erotic energy can move around our system, and the bigger our erotic experiences become.

The connective breath practices we've already looked at can be adapted beautifully to penetrative sex.

Breathing in harmony with each other helps us to find a common rhythm, and connect with our mutual flow. It never fails to amaze me how much closer such a simple thing as matching my breathing pattern to a lover's can make us feel, nor how effectively it builds the energy between us.

Exchanging breath helps us to build not only our mutual flow, but also our mutual fire. Try interspersing breath exchange with kissing as a way to kindle that flame.

Use your breath, combined with energised/electric fingers, to move sensation and energy around your beloved's body—running it up the spine from the genitals to the heart, or to the crown of the head, for example, or encouraging it down the limbs. Draw the energy with your fingers and inhale, or push it along with your palms and exhale, imagining that energy stuff, whatever that looks or feels like to you, flowing as you direct it.

During penetration, experiment with the Heart/Sex Circuit. As the penetrative party, try breathing out through your genitals (or whatever part of you you're using) as you push into your partner, sending energy with your breath. As the receptive partner, breathe in through your genitals as your partner breathes out, and then exhale through your heart into theirs. Penetrative partner, breathe in the through the heart as you pull back, and so on.

Alternately, you can switch that flow, so that even though physically one of you is penetrating the other, the receptive party is pushing energy into their partner's genitals. When it works well, this can feel like two-way fucking!

Energy genitals

As I mentioned above, the fine art of energyfuckery is one of my favourite pieces of the pie that is sex magic. I love it as much as I do because it opens up new horizons of possibilities for connection, pleasure, and sex; because it gives us new ways to queer the fuck out of our sex lives by building funky new genitals to fit our felt gender or our momentary whim; and because it really does prove that all you need in order to have an ecstatic sex life is breath, and a willing imagination.

Needless to say, I won't be going down the cunts and cocks route with this. Not just out of respect for those readers who don't think of their genitals in terms of "one or the other," but also because I personally do not shapeshift only between the genital options we're told are available to us. Sometimes I grow a tail or open up a portal to infinity—so I wouldn't dream of limiting you, dear readers, to the options available in first-year medical textbooks.

Instead, I'll be talking in terms very similar to those I've been using for energy. We'll be experimenting with Active and Receptive genitalshifting—and you're welcome to try on whatever suits you in the moment. I know there may be some of you who are working hard to ensure that you never have to either penetrate or be penetrated in your erotic encounters, and you are oh so welcome to pick and choose what you want to play with from the experiments below. As a general principle, I would encourage all of you to try embodying both sides of the equation at least once. Both penetrating and being penetrated have their own unique vulnerabilities and potencies; experimenting with them not only expands our capacity for play and pleasure, it also deepens our capacity for compassion and understanding for those who usually inhabit other points of that spectrum to us.

I offer you two ways of building your energetic genitals in the exercise below; personally, I usually use a combination of the two.

⇒ PLAYTIME ⇐
Erotic Shapeshifting

With intention: If you've never done this before, I recommend at least beginning by yourself, even if you're planning to take this into partnered play imminently. Decide whether you're going to play with being a penetrator (Active) or penetratee (Receptive)—and remember to negotiate accordingly with anyone else involved. Then, come back to the Heart/Sex Circuit; if you're planning to be the Receptive party, breathe in through your genitals, and out through your heart, and get some of that energy stuff, whatever it looks like to you, flowing in time with your breath. If you're planning on being the Active party, get that circuit flowing by breathing out through your genitals and in through your heart.

Close your eyes, and focus on that circuit of breath and energy for a moment. When you're feeling energised, perhaps even a little turned on, invite your genitals to become more Active/Receptive, depending on what you're choosing to experiment with right now. If you're planning to energetically penetrate your partner, you might imagine your genitals energetically extending in some way as you breathe out, and taking on a form that will allow you to do so (a cock, a tail, a tentacle, a lightsaber—whatever gets you off/feels natural in the moment). If you're anticipating being penetrated, you might feel your genitals opening, softening, juicing up, unfolding, expanding (a cave, a cauldron, a cunt, a heart, a cherry blossom, etc.).

Use your breath, imagination, and anything else that helps—movement, sound, using your hands to "sculpt" the energy or touch yourself—to make this as real, sensational, and juicy an experience as you can. When you're ready, you can either explore what self-pleasuring might look like in this state, or go and find your partner. Remember to keep using your breath—solo or together—to enhance the experience, and get you high on erotic energy!

With attention: With so many strands of philosophy, spirituality, and gender theory arguing that we all have both active and receptive energies and characteristics within each of us, why shouldn't the same apply to genitals? Perhaps we don't need to "create" our energy genitals; perhaps they're already there, just waiting to be discovered.

Once you're juiced up on breath and energy, begin to breathe your awareness deeper and deeper into your body. When you have moved down from the mind into the belly, breathe your attention into your genitals, and "look" for your active or receptive erotic and energetic bits. Invite them to make themselves known to you. See what impressions arise automatically, and, if they appeal to you/turn you on, build them up with breath, energy, sound, movement, and anything else you fancy, and proceed as above!

~

If you're trying out the exercise above with a partner, start by having a play with just your energy genitals together. Use your breath, sound, and movement to heighten the experience. If one of you has built penetrative genitals, and the other penetrable genitals, start breathing the Heart/Sex Circuit together, and see where you're drawn to go from there. The more you can find the courage to suspend disbelief, follow the flow between you, and get creative with this one, the better it will feel. Don't be afraid to take risks, try different ways of connecting and different positions, and feel free to be playful.

Crafting your energy genitals

This exercise can also be added to penetrative sex, either as a way to build on the existing flow—or as a way to switch up the dynamics associated with penetrative sex, and penetrate the penetrator. It also works particularly well as a way to extend our energy, and even our capacity for sensation, into prosthetics like strap-ons and packers.

Finally, while the exercises above focus on manifesting energy genitals in place of, or in combination with, our existing ones, don't be surprised if you find them rocking up on different parts of the body. Some of the best sex of my life has involved hands that morphed unexpectedly into energy cocks—just saying!

Sex magic, together

Hopefully some of the experiments, or building blocks, that I've covered in this section have left you feeling energised, inspired, and ready to make some magic together. So let's take a look at how we might build some of these into a co-created sex magic ritual.

By now, you're familiar with the components of ritual:

- Creating Space
- Invocation
- Setting Intention
- Raising Energy
- Release
- Surrender
- Giving Thanks

In the introduction to this book, I talked about the gifts that each of these has to offer our erotic lives. From getting into the habit of carving out designated space and time to be sensual or sexual, to practising fully letting go into the aftershocks of pleasure and connection, the fact is that treating our sex lives as sacred has the potential to radically change the quality, and in many cases the quantity, of the sex we're having. And one way of doing that is to simply treat sex itself as a ritual: a ritual where the intention is to be sexual with each other, whatever you wish that to look like, and with whatever outcome your favourite sexual experiences tend to lead to—embodiment, connectedness, relaxation, orgasm, transcendence, etc. In such a case, you might create space based on what you find mutually conducive to pleasure; set an erotic intention together, and agree upon the practices that are likely to get you there; raise energy with them, following the flow between you, building and extending your pleasure with some of the tools we've been looking at; attain whatever release you had intended; and surrender into the aftermath together.

That would be one way to use ritual as an erotic tool. Another approach is of course to use sex as a ritual tool in order to raise energy for a particular vision or change you're wanting to manifest or make. The distinction is in the intention or focus; in the example above, sex is the intention, and ritual enhances and supports that. In the following section, a vision or change is the intention, and sex enhances and supports the ritual.

Here are some of the reasons you might co-create a sex magic ritual:

- To raise energy for a quality you want more of in your life together—such as more passion, abundance, or peace
- To raise energy for a common goal, or the next chapter of your lives together—such as a major move or creative project, a new lover for you both, or calling in a child
- To support one of you with a change they are wanting to make—whether that's an external change like a promotion, or internal transformation like feeling more confident
- For the benefit and/or evolution of your relationship
- For the purpose of healing, whether that's healing for one of you, for both of you, for your relationship, or for the planet

When it comes to co-creating sex magic rituals together, the key ingredients you will need to negotiate in advance are as follows:

- What is the intention of the ritual? Is it a mutual desire, or one person's wish that the other person or people involved can really get behind and support? Is the intention clear to everyone involved?
- How are you going to balance raising energy and staying focused on the intention of the ritual? What will you use to raise energy that will be erotically charged, but not so complex that you can't concentrate on anything else?

- What will release look like? Will all parties involved be building up pleasure in their bodies, either through breath or self-pleasuring or mutual touch or intense sensation or fucking, or will one or more parties focus on one individual as the "vessel" for the energy raising and release?
- What is everyone's ideal surrender scenario? What aftercare might be needed? What do we need to have to hand?

One way to answer some of these questions is through the use of sigil magic. While there are all kinds of wonderful ways to encapsulate your chosen intention that leave you free to focus on building your ritual—including single words or sentences; images or objects; things that can be set on fire, such as candles or flash paper—what is often referred to as a sigil remains a personal favourite of mine. A sigil is a simple image that has been created to sum up and hold a magical intention, ideally an image that can be easily brought to mind when needed.

If what you are calling in with your ritual is a situation, experience, person, or thing with an abundance of different known qualities, two good ways to create a sigil might be:

- To draw a picture of the thing in question, or draw all its many qualities, and then find a way to bring all those elements together into one interconnected image. Once you've done that, start to simplify. Take out details. Strengthen the main lines. Allow each individual image to fall away into a simpler single sigil, made up of a few key lines. Keep simplifying, until you have something you can easily bring to mind, or at least something simple enough that you could draw it on your lover's skin in five to ten seconds.
- To write down all the different qualities, and then use the first letter of each word in much the same way as above. Connect those letters up into an abstract image, and then simplify until you have something that can easily be visualised.

If, on the other hand, what you are calling in is more of a feeling or experience, then see if there is an image that comes to mind that encapsulates that experience. Once you have one, simplify again if you need to; for example, if what came to mind was a single red heart, you have your sigil—but if what came to mind was a magician in full robes and a pointy hat waving a magical wand about, maybe just use the outline of the hat!

As you're probably gathering by now, it is not important that the sigil look like the thing it's representing; if anything, some would argue it will speak more effectively to your deep mind if it doesn't. What is important is that you have a sense of your sigil being imbued with the qualities or feelings you associate with what you're hoping to call in.

When it comes to working out when to put your attention on your sigil, and when to simply focus on raising energy, my personal favourite is to bring the sigil to mind at the start of your ritual, and again at the moment of release.

You might begin your ritual by sitting and breathing together, and focusing on the sigil, either bringing it to your mind's eye, or looking at a drawing of it. You can imagine breathing energy into it, and see it getting bigger and brighter. You can send it your love, or whisper Yes to it. Or you can trace it on one or both of your bodies in a substance that will have come off by the time you've reached whatever release it was you were aiming for (e.g., chocolate body paint, or ochre powder, or menstrual blood).

Sex Magic Ritual—raising pleasure in the vessel

As you approach whatever moment of release you have agreed on, bring your sigil to mind again. Imagine it filling up with all the energy you've raised. As you release, let your sigil go: you can imagine it floating away into the cosmos, or being buried in the ground, being placed in the hands of a loving divine being—whatever works for you. The important thing is to release it, and know that your work is done, and that which you have been praying for is in the hands of something greater than yourself.

The surrender phase then becomes an extension of that letting go, a leaning back into the knowing that there is nothing more for you to do. Rest, receive, and give thanks—for it is being taken care of.

Sex Magic Ritual—raising pleasure together

Like solo sex magic, partnered ritual can also pack a punch as a regular erotic practice. Having looked at the kinds of things we might use sex to power occasional ritual for, let's explore what regular erotic ritual can do for us.

When it comes to creating a ritual container for our erotic activities, creating that container on a regular basis can help us to:

Sustain mutual desire: In the early stages of attraction, we often allow ourselves to be consumed by our desire for each other. This tends to take the shape of giving each other the lion's share of our attention, carving out time to spend with each other, and not being able to keep our hands off each other. As a new relationship becomes integrated into our daily lives, as we make a habit of the other person, we often allow our schedules to consume us once more. However, desire is as reliant on being that intensely present and engaged with one another as it is spontaneous, and the erotic is a force that builds when fed, and diminishes when ignored. Having a regular slot carved out in the calendar, dedicated to an activity or series of activities that are shaped by the particular flavour of desire that you share with your partner(s), can keep you connected with that desire, and continue to fan its flames.

Rekindle desire: When we're in a long-term relationship and trying to find our way "back" to being sensual and/or sexual with one another after a time of disconnection, it's all too tempting to try to get straight back to where we remember being before, and to be disappointed when that doesn't happen. Whether it's because our desires or our bodies have changed over time, or because there's simply so much built up between us that we need time to work through, it's unlikely we will be able to go straight from struggling to be sexual with one another to having sex that rivals what we remember from our erotic heyday. One way we can begin to integrate the sensual back into our relationship is to choose an activity that feels both desirable and accessible for us to share on a regular basis. Ideas might include anything from eye gazing and breathing together, through to sharing massage or touch; from making out on the sofa like teenagers, through to a flogging or spanking; from simultaneous masturbation, through to taking a regular walk together while holding hands. The important thing is to pick something that feels manageable to you both, and is something you can give and receive with an open and happy heart. Something that will invite you into the moment together and give you small victories to celebrate, but will also help you build toward the sex life you're longing to have together again.

Support one or both of you through an emotional or physical transition:
When life throws us curveballs, it's easy to let the erotic slip in the face of everything else that's happening. In doing so, we're often depriving ourselves of a fantastic source of comfort, integration, healing, pleasure, and a way of staying in our body, and getting used to challenges or changes therein. Agreeing on an erotic practice with a partner or partners that gives one or all of us what we need during a big change can help us to stay present, to process, and to know that we're worthy, welcome, supported, and loved through that change. This is especially recommended in the case of physical/surgical change due to illness and/or surgery, or cases of emotional or physical trauma, since these particularly result in dissociation from the body, and a carefully chosen and fully consensual erotic practice can help us get back in our skins.

On the other hand, when it comes to using the erotic to power magic for transformation or manifestation, if your intention is one you feel will need a big energetic punch to power it, or one you know will take time due to changes that need to happen in you or in your life to allow for it, or a project or change that of its own nature takes time to unfold, then you can use regular miniature sex magic rituals to keep sending your energy, your welcome, your love toward that intention—drawing it tenderly and collaboratively into your lives together.

Practical Magic: *You and I have been struggling to be sexual this year. It seems as if all the reasons why you find acting on desire so difficult, and all the reasons that I have had to be angry with you about that, are up in the space between us. And while I think this is happening in part because the container of our relationship is strong enough to take it, it hasn't made for much in the way of easy erotic moments between us of late.*

But it's Beltane, our favourite point on the Wheel of the Year—and one that, for us, is as inextricably bound up with sex as it is with fire and the coming of the summer sun. We have a date planned for tonight, and even though we're coming out of tough and tearful conversations, we're determined to find a way to make some magic together.

It takes extensive negotiating. Finally, we alight on three components that feel possible, and meet the themes of the festival for us: Breath, Fire, and Self-Pleasure. We set our Intention as we light the candle on our shared altar, an intention that speaks to what we wish for our relationship going forward. We take the time to breathe together, to connect, and we use the What's Here Now structure to help us process some of what is in the space between us. At last, we're feeling close enough to begin to raise energy together.

I light my fireplay sticks, and caress both our bodies with the flames, warming up our bellies and hearts, and encouraging the energy down into our hands. We make eye contact as we self-pleasure. At first I feel wary and reserved, but I commit to the breath, and to looking deeper and seeing you more clearly. I breathe the energy of the fire around inside me, and my heart softens, and expands. The contracted feeling is replaced by a sense of capacity, and I'm reminded of the way that everything about our lives right now is inviting me to open up, to love bigger. I dedicate the pleasure that's building in my body to our Intention, to a vision of us moving forward together with greater intimacy and joy.

When we climax, it's almost as though the orgasm doesn't happen in my body. Instead I feel the energy being sucked into the space between us, revitalising our connection, strengthening our togetherness.

The next morning, we get up early, go up to a high place, toast the rising sun, and sing in the dawn together. We smile at each other. It's the first time we've ever managed to sing in harmony.

$\sim$

From getting consent to giving erotic touch, from energyfuckery to sex magic ritual, this chapter should have filled your burgeoning sex magician skills cup to overflowing. And while I do hope you've paused to enjoy yourselves along the way, I hope the story above may serve as reassurance that this stuff works even when things are tough between you and your beloveds. Remember to hang on to those principles of practice and playfulness in your experiments together, and give yourselves permission to try things out, take risks, and have fun!

Chapter 7

Being Together

When we go the distance with someone, whether that person is our only partner, or one of many, or indeed a close friend or other family member, there comes a time when loving that person ceases to be a matter of falling in love (if it ever was). Staying in love is less about falling—though it is certainly possible to fall in love with our long-term people again and again—and more about choosing: choosing to turn toward that person with love on a daily basis, and choosing to let them in and let them love us anew.

Done consciously, done kindly, this kind of choiceful relationship can show us what is possible in terms of collaboration, commitment, courage, kindness, and personal growth. As easy as it is to become consumed or constrained by long-term relationships, it is also my experience that conscious relating over time can help us to access and become more of ourselves than we would have otherwise. Taking on the challenge of "loving through"— through changes and challenges, through fear and anger and hurt, through life's curveballs, and through the moments that make life worth living— makes for human beings with a depth of wisdom, a gift for creativity, and a wealth of love to share.

In honour of this, I'd like to take a moment to explore some ways we can make relationships more sustainable using the principles of sex magic we've been exploring up until now. I'll be referring mostly to romantic and/or sexual relationships, but many of the ideas that follow are ones that can be applied in other kinds of long-term connection.

Creating Sacred Space—making time

One of the primary ways in which we demonstrate the meaning and value that something has for us is to make time and space for it. Right now, the things our culture values most are progress, productivity, and profit. Accordingly, the majority of our time as children is spent in institutions that have the twofold purpose of teaching us skills to achieve progress, productivity, and profit, whilst keeping us out of the way of our guardians so as to prevent us distracting them from maximising the progress, productivity, and profit they need to achieve in order to keep us all alive (staying alive being something we're expected to achieve as individuals, rather than something we take responsibility for as a collective). When we reach adulthood, we're expected to take over where our parents left off—and do better than them at amassing status and stuff. What this demonstrates is a cultural perception that we're only as valuable as the profit we're able to produce. This perception not only fails to take into account the fact that we do not all start from an equal playing field, and that the institutions we're expected to be productive and profitable within are rife with structural inequalities—it also encourages us to place profit above people, which is inherently damaging to our relationships with ourselves, each other, and our communities.

OK. Rant over. My point is, we are taught to value productivity and profit, and so the majority of us in the West dedicate the majority of our time to these values, because we have learned to treat them as important.

So what would it look like if we were to treat our relationships as equally important?

How would it be to dedicate to intimacy the kind of time we might give to mastering a skillset, taking forward an important project, or nurturing a career?

As I type this, I am in three intimate relationships—one with a long-term partner whom I share a home with, one with a new partner, and one with a long-term friend recently turned girlfriend. Observing the amount of time and quality of space necessary for me to achieve the level of intimacy with each of them that I most enjoy is providing me with fascinating insights into just how necessary the gift of time is for sustaining intimacy. My new partner and I can sink into our loved-up bubble the minute they get through the door, and hit a bunch of peak moments of pleasure and intimacy during their visits—which often last around twenty-four hours. We're mindful of the clean slate we currently have in the space between us, and put in a lot of communication time to keep it that way. By contrast, it takes my long-term partner and me around three to five hours of quality one-to-one time to wade through the stuff that inevitably builds up through living together day after day—to open up, relax, and get back to the level of loved-up that I associate with "us." Meanwhile, my girlfriend and I have known each other for seven years, and have spent a lot of that time repressing or struggling with our feelings for each other. Accordingly, we have developed a bunch of bad habits between us that are proving hard to shake. At the moment, it takes spending time together, and sleeping in the same bed, before we wake up the next morning feeling fully reconnected.

Now it's your turn.

How long does it take you and your partner(s) to get (back) to the kind of connection you really value sharing with them? What qualities does your environment need to have to support that happening? (Follow the flowchart on the next page with your answers to this question.)

Time is a magical thing. As someone who tends to be solution and action focused, it's easy for me to forget the vital role time plays in my relationships with myself and others. That time is a great healer is something of a cliché, and yet time can heal hurts we never imagined we'd make it through; open us up to trusting anew or even for the first time; and help us to forgive where we had given up on forgiving. Sometimes conflicts that seem insurmountable, and certain to tear our love apart, are gently unravelled in the hands of time, revealing themselves to be entirely surmountable after all.

Carving out quality time to get present with our beloveds helps us to see and hear each other anew; to reconnect with the living person who is doing the best they can on the other side of our projections and assumptions; to remember why we loved them, and to discover why we love them now. Make the time and the space to be together, and allow yourself to be surprised by the minor miracles that unfold in the space between you.

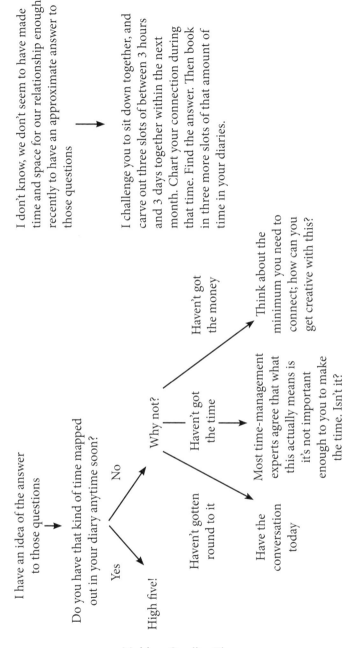

Making Quality Time

Setting an Intention—choiceful relating

We've established that doing something with intention can transform a mundane activity, or apparently random sequence of actions, or even something we've been putting off because we're nervous of doing it, into a creative, magical, loving experience.

In long-term relationships of any kind, we tend to get into habits. Activities that might have been carefully chosen or negotiated when we first got together become either go-to ways of being together, or fall by the wayside because they require more effort or resources than we're inclined to expend on a daily basis. Hopefully most of us have experienced that feeling of "profound interest,"[26] of wanting to know the other person inside out, that comes with some new relationships. Yet as time passes, that curiosity can all too easily give way to those three most dangerous words in the English language: "I know that." When we move from the precious process of getting to know someone into knowing them, knowing can all too easily devolve into assumptions, expectations, and, worst of all, silence.

When we stop asking our beloved about themselves, we are in danger of ceasing to acknowledge them as an ever-changing human being. And when we stop negotiating our time together, we stop being co-creative, and we are in danger of ceasing to be choiceful about how we spend that time. Particularly if we see each other on a day-to-day basis, it can be all too easy for choiceful quality time to give way to habitual quantity time.

Some of the symptoms of habitual time include the following:

- Spending more time together on passive activities—such as watching TV, or reading the newspaper—than on co-creative activities—such as going outside, working on a project together, or having a conversation or sex

- Noticing that hours are passing by while you're with your beloved, but finding you're not sure quite how they were spent, and not feeling particularly nourished or connected by them

- Not getting round to sharing something that is important to you, and then not getting round to sharing it again, and then again, until you

---

26. Michaels and Johnson, *Partners in Passion*, 51.

realise you're living a whole story that your partner has no part in, because you just haven't had a proper conversation in so long

- realising that you have allowed your habitual time with your partner to take over all your free time, and that you can't remember the last occasion on which you spent choiceful quality time with yourself
- descending into bad communication habits with each other—one or both of you being regularly critical or snappish or passive aggressive, because stuff is building up between you that you're not talking about

You may already be noticing, when they're put down on paper like that, that a lot of the symptoms above require the medicine of communication. One of my favourite stand-up comics, DeAnne Smith, does a great line in tipping straight men on pleasing their partners. "As much as you're going down on your lady right now, double it, triple it—you're welcome. That's all you need to know." [27] I feel much the same about communication—not just for straight men, but for all of us.

In order to relate Intentionally, we need to talk to each other: from discussing what we might want from an evening spent together, to negotiating a playdate or ritual, to exploring what our respective visions for relationship are, and whether they can be woven together. In order to shift from habitual time to quality time, we have to be willing to show up, and be real about our feelings, desires, and preferences. We need to communicate in order to co-create a life well-lived.

♥ Messiness Alert!

Relational habits take time to break—and the effort required to shift any given habit is likely to reflect the amount of time for which that habit has been in place. Breaking habits is a practice rather than a single action—a practice that takes patience, the willingness to give each other not just second, but third and fourth chances, and, above all, kindness: kindness to each other, and kindness to yourselves, as you work together to make the changes you desire.

27. Smith, "DeAnne Smith Melbourne International Comedy Festival Gala 2017."

Raising Energy—renewing the flow

Perhaps one of the hardest things to do in long-term relationship—especially if we are painfully aware that our togetherness is crying out for a change—is to resist the temptation to reach for quick fixes, and instead to be present with what is.

One of the reasons that stepping out of the kind of habitual time we talked about above, and coming back into presence with each other, is so scary is our fear of the unknown. When we're first falling in love we want to know everything there is to know about the other. The unknown is enticing. But once we believe we have come to know someone, the unknown can seem like a source of uncertainty, and very frightening. Whether it's not understanding what our partner is feeling, or what we are feeling for them; whether it's the uncharted territory of a new relationship chapter, loss, or life transition; or whether it's not knowing how we are going to get out of a habit we've ended up in … it can be tempting to take one look at the unknown and move as quickly as we can in the opposite direction. However, we need to be willing to be present with what is under the surface if we are truly committed to going deeper with each other.

This is because relying on what we think we know in our relating holds the twofold danger of our losing contact with what is actually alive between us, and of holding the new at bay. And we need to balance Flow and Creativity if we are to dive deeper into intimacy, and move forward together.

By making time to get present with one another, and to listen with openness and curiosity to the space between us, we give ourselves a chance of finding that flow that is unique to our love. Our love that has a plan, that knows where it's taking us and how to get us there—if we would just trust it. If we would just stand still long enough to hear what it has to say.

Concurrently, by allowing for the possibility that our love, and the person we love, still have the capacity to surprise us; by embarking on new adventures together, taking new risks, and trying new things in co-creative and consensual ways; by engaging with and sharing our erotic selves, and seeking out new ways to be intimate; and by being willing and enthusiastic participants in our relationship—by adopting these attitudes and actions, we find the Creativity that is the essential counterpart to our Flow.

Flow and Creativity. Deep Listening and Right Action. Trust and Will. This is the delicate balance we seek to strike in order to keep the space between us alive, in order to let our love blossom season after season.

Rising to the challenge of that balance is no easy feat. Its paradoxical nature guarantees that any attempts to "get it right" will only set us up to fail. Instead of grasping for it, or giving up on it, we need to stay present to both possibilities—Flow and Creativity. And, as we tread the path of relationship, we must intuit when to lean gently in the direction of one or the other, and when to simply keep walking, keep choosing, and trust to the love to carry us through.

In need of inspiration? Revisit the Threefold Attention exercise, and the exercises that follow it in the Connecting section to help you reconnect with your flow, and search the Erotic Checklist in the Resources section for new erotic adventures.

Release—letting each other in

As important as it is to make things new, it's also vitally important to be open with each other about what is. Being open with each other can look a lot of different ways. Sometimes it's tender, beautiful, spontaneous. At other times, it looks more like cracking open, or falling apart. It can be hard to believe that both of these can bring value to a relationship. Certainly both of them can feel like taking a risk since both require an element of vulnerability. When we reveal ourselves to one another, we feel vulnerable to rejection or attack in a way that we might not when we're playing a role for someone else, or sticking to the status quo of the relationship.

And yet, when we can and do take those risks, we discover new possibilities for building trust, and rebuilding connection. By allowing ourselves to be seen at our most vulnerable, we both demonstrate and practise trust in our partners. By receiving and meeting each other in our vulnerability, we show ourselves to be trustworthy. By allowing ourselves to be heard, we open ourselves not just to rejection, but also to compassion. By listening deeply to each other, we allow the seeds of compassion to blossom in our hearts. With the building blocks of compassion and trust, our love is able to build bridges across the space between us.

The process of revealing ourselves to each other also reminds us that we are none of us static, and so allows for not just reconnection, but also rediscovery. Our partners don't become uninteresting to us because they're unchanging—but rather because, in assuming we know them, we disengage our profound interest from them. We cease to see one another as the ever-changing worlds that we are. We become like continents, drifting quietly apart, unaware of the extraordinary landscapes unfolding just across the straits. So look up, listen up, open up, and go adventuring for favourite kingdoms and uncharted territories in the landscapes of your beloved(s).

Surrender—letting in the mystery

One of the things that can be problematic about the concept of "working" on our relationship is that it can get us thinking that it's all down to us. Whether you tend to take on the majority of the emotional labour in a relationship, or expect the other person to step up and fix things all the time; or whether it's that you spend a lot of time together "trying"—"trying" to connect, or "trying" to get back to how things used to be—the danger of trying to "work it out" is that we end up working so hard we leave no space for the love between us to just do its thing.

I love the way psycho-spiritual therapist Anne Geraghty writes about Love as the third entity in a relationship, an entity with its own agenda—which is to make more love by helping us to grow into ourselves so that we can love bigger. Anne suggests, "Love brings to the relationship only what can be handled, and provides what is needed even when the individuals themselves do not know what to do."[28] Sometimes, the best thing we can do is show up, and then get out of the way; make time and space, and then be still and wait for love to do its thing.

We need to allow mystery to work in the space between us. A great way to do this is to treat relationship as a spiritual practice, and trust that wherever it takes us, that's where we need to go. That's where we need to grow.

---

28. Geraghty, *How Loving Relationships Work*, 57.

Giving Thanks—expressing appreciation

I know, I know. You'd be rich if you had a penny for every time someone told you life would get better if you were just more grateful for what you already have. It's a new-ageism that can smack of such privilege, when it takes a basic foundation of well-being to summon up the energy to feel grateful. But if you do have that energy, and something between you and your partner lights that spark of gratitude, even if just for a moment—use it.

Appreciation is the fuel love runs on. Introduced at the right moment, it can even be self-generating. Most of us love to feel some flavour of

- Valuable
- Useful
- Appreciated
- Important
- Acknowledged
- Seen

And when we do, we often feel thankful as a result, which can spark a sweet loop of mutual appreciation between us and our beloved(s). As Tantra teachers and authors Patricia Johnson and Mark Michaels write, "consistently turning toward each other, and receiving and acknowledging the bids for connection whenever possible, will create a positive feedback loop that reinforces the mutuality of your profound interest." [29]

Appreciating one another is a practice that can become an art form. You can make a study of how your partner most effectively receives appreciation. Using a tool such as Gary Chapman's Five Love Languages[30] can be useful here to work out how to express your appreciation of your partner to maximum effect. For example, finding out whether your partner receives love most effectively through words, touch, gifts, quality time, or acts of service can help you pinpoint the best way to show them how precious they are to you. We often resort to showing our appreciation in the way in which we, ourselves, feel most appreciated, but that won't necessarily be the most effective route to communicating our gratitude to our partners. Taking the time

29. Michaels and Johnson, *Partners in Passion*, 53.

30. Chapman, *The Five Love Languages*.

to learn what they most wish to be acknowledged for, and how to best express your appreciation, can make them feel truly valued, and sow seeds of sweetness, openness, and intimacy in the space between you.

Commitment ceremonies

It became abundantly clear to me from my first forays into being a celebrant that there are few things I love to do more than create and facilitate commitment ceremonies. There is something both deeply romantic and profoundly radical about two people who know the score when it comes to relationship choosing to bind themselves to one another through ritual—choosing faith in each other and the love they share, and often choosing to celebrate that love bravely, brazenly, beautifully with their people. I concur wholeheartedly with the quote ascribed to Tina Modotti in the film *Frida*: "But when two people know that, and they decide with eyes wide open to face each other and get married anyway, then I don't think it's conservative or delusional. I think it's radical and courageous and very romantic." [31]

I also think there can be value in creating ceremonies like these for other kinds of significant relationships where we wish to affirm our commitment and celebrate what we share.

So why might you opt for a commitment ceremony with your beloved? Some great reasons include the following:

- Practising relationship as a spiritual path, and treating the commitment ceremony as a container for that practice
- Wanting to clarify, deepen, and consecrate an existing commitment
- Wanting to celebrate and share the love between you with the people around you, and/or your personal pantheons
- The desire to underpin the challenges of your day-to-day relating with a strong commitment made not only to each other, but also to yourselves, and/or your community, and/or your personal pantheons
- Wanting to create a support network for the third entity that is your relationship, made up of the people who witness your ceremony and celebrate your love

31. Taymor (dir.), *Frida* (DVD).

If you are considering a commitment ceremony for any of the following reasons, I strongly advise you to have a rethink, or perhaps find a celebrant who can do some pre-ceremony coaching with you and your partner to check in around your intentions, before going ahead:

- One person is not getting their needs met, or is feeling insecure in the relationship, and the other wants to "give" them a ceremony in an attempt to change or appease that. In this instance, I recommend looking at your needs, expectations, and values around relationship, and negotiating around your communication and treatment of each other, before or instead of opting for a ceremony.

- You think it's the logical next step in your relationship escalator. Ceremony is something to opt for when you feel a strong, whole-person pull toward it, when you feel moved by the knowledge that this is the right thing for you and your love right now—not when you think you "should" give it a go.

- Someone else—family, peers, other couples—is encouraging or pushing you to do it. Ritual is a powerful force that requires an open and willing heart. Doing ceremony that pushes your heart to appease other people doesn't just water it down for you, it waters it down for all of us.

- Cultural status. Embarking on a legally recognised commitment ceremony can bestow status, acceptance, gifts, and tax breaks upon us. If you need to embark on a legally recognised bond for your well-being, or the well-being of your children, you can still be choiceful within that, and use it as an invitation to reflect: Do we want to make this about our love? Do we want to use this as an invitation to reflect on our commitment? Do we want to consecrate the spiritual, emotional, and erotic space between us, as well as sign some paperwork? If the answer is no, I recommend sticking to signing the paperwork.

The above can be summarised simply by saying that the word "should" is best left out of rituals of the heart.

～

All "shoulds" hopefully set aside, I want to share with you some of the ways you can use the ritual structure that's threaded through everything else we've been doing to create commitment ceremonies that speak to your intentions around commitment, reflect your unique relationship, and amplify the love between you.

Creating Space—calling in witnesses

One of the key ingredients when it comes to a commitment ceremony, besides finding a time that suits you both and a location that makes your hearts sing, is deciding who you want to be witnessed by. Witnessing is a vital aspect of commitment ceremonies. Making a commitment to each other in sight of those you love can deepen that commitment. Adding others' love and intention to your own can make the bond between you feel more tangible, solid, and strong. The right witnesses can also provide a support network for your love in the future.

This doesn't mean you can't have a private commitment ceremony. You can be witnessed by just one or two close heartkin, or by the gods of your understanding, or by the tree you love to stop and kiss under. The point is to choose witnesses whose love can hold your love accountable when it falters, raise it up when it stumbles, and remind you of it when you are in danger of forgetting—at least for as long as you stated you would like your commitment to last.

⩒ PLAYTIME ⩓
Co-creating Ceremony I

Where will you have the ceremony? Make sure it's somewhere that speaks to your love, is appropriate to the season, and has capacity and accessibility for the witnesses, seen or unseen, that you would like present. As well as its availability, you may also want to check legalities if those are important to you, or if the space is privately or publicly owned.

When will you have it? If you want other people involved, you'll need to give them fair warning. And again, you may want to think about the season, and factor in the relevance of the date or time of day to your relationship and intentions.

Who will witness you? How will you invoke the unseen witnesses (e.g., deities, ancestors, guides, spirits) of your choice at the start of the ceremony? How will you welcome the earthly ones (e.g., friends and family)?

Who will marry you? Do you want to involve a celebrant? Do you want them to be able to bind you legally as well? Having the right person to hold you through the process of planning the ceremony, and officiating on the day, can allow you to lean even more deeply into the magic taking place in the moment.

Intention—negotiating commitment

Planning a commitment ceremony is a wonderful invitation to unpack and explore your hopes, fears, expectations, and needs around commitment—from inherited familial and cultural assumptions around partnership, through to those little things you spotted in this movie or that friend's marriage that spoke to you—and to get choiceful around what you do and don't want to weave into yours. As with any ritual, this is really the most important piece of work, which all too often in conventional commitment ceremonies gets swept away in a tide of colour swatches and seating plans.

Some useful questions to ask yourselves, and share with each other:

- What is my/our intention for the ceremony? Why are we doing this?
- What does commitment mean to me/us? What are my/our values, hopes, and dreams for committed relationship?
- How long do we want to make this commitment for? A year and a day? As long as love lasts? For the rest of our lives? How can we care for our relationship and check in around our commitment during that time?
- What do I/we hope will change after the ceremony? What do I/we hope will stay the same? Are there any agreements or actions we can put in place to support both of these?
- What is my commitment to you/us?
- What gifts do I hope to bring to you/our relationship?
- What commitments would I like from you?
- What would I like to receive?
- Is there anything I/we want to be different in our relationship before the ceremony? Is there anything we'd like to change in the longer term?
- How would we like to grow together? What can we put in place to support our individual and relational growth?

- What would we like to build together? How can this ceremony be a beginning for that?
- How do we hope to love each other in the future? How can we best show one another love? How can we nurture the love between us?

As well as exploring the strengths, gifts, and love that you bring to your relationship, it's also worth taking the time at this point to explore the things that you wish you weren't bringing with you to the relationship, but that will be coming with you anyway. The parts of you you find harder to love in yourselves and each other. The parts of you that feel like threats to your relationship. The parts of you that behave in ways you wish you didn't. These too are part of you, these too participate in your togetherness, and it's worth including these in your commitment ceremony accordingly. This should be done with compassion, kindness, and—if possible—humour. Only by practising accepting and loving ourselves as we are can we hope to be fully present with each other.

Apart from including the parts of you that you find harder to love in your pre-ceremony sharing, you may wish to acknowledge them on the day—in your vows, in your speeches, in the questions from your celebrant—however feels appropriate to you. Alternately, you can do what is sometimes referred to as a "shadow wedding," a ceremony held before the official commitment ceremony, in which you take the time to show your beloved(s) your whole selves—fears, tears, scars, warts, and all. To see the same in your betrothed. And to pledge all that you are to them, and receive the same in return.

Incorporating the parts of you that you find harder to love into the conscious commitment process allows you to enter into it in the knowledge that you have revealed yourself, and been found lovable—and that you and your beloved(s) have already practised doing some deep and vulnerable relating, skills which will serve you well if you plan to stay with them for any length of time.

⇒ PLAYTIME ⇐
Co-creating Ceremony II

Include a statement of intent at the start of your ceremony. This helps those making the commitment to get present and aligned, and those witnessing them to get their love behind the intention being stated.

Raising Energy—opening to love

Having arrived at your time and place of choice, invoked/welcomed your witnesses, and stated the intention for your ceremony, this next piece is all about speaking to the unique love that is between you. It's about finding ways to express your love that will help the two of you to sink more deeply into connection as you approach the crucial moment of making your commitments to one another, and also touch the hearts of those present, so that their love can amplify yours. Whether it's sharing your memories or stories, listening to particular poetry or music, or simply facing each other in silence, breathing together, and gazing into each other's eyes until you're ready to make your vows, this section should raise the love energy in the room as you head toward the peak moment of your promises to one another.

⇒ PLAYTIME ⇐
Co-creating Ceremony III

Think about the love that you share, and the characteristics, quirks, behaviours, and shared passions that make it unique. What are your shared love languages? What music or memories speak to the journey that has brought you to this point? Which chapters of your story are still the most significant to you, and how can you weave those into your ceremony? Are there activities you particularly love to share, and can they be shared with your witnesses? Have you come across songs, words, images in your time together that spoke to your love, and could they be incorporated into its celebration?

Don't be afraid to be creative—and more than that, don't be afraid to let your love be seen. Being visible and vulnerable in this most powerful act of loving each other doesn't just allow others to witness and bless our love—it allows our love to bless and inspire them.

Release—making promises you want to keep

Making your promises to one another generally takes one or more of the following forms:

- Questions and answers (with your celebrant asking the questions if you have one)
- Vows
- A binding

Personally, I like to include all three, since I see them as having a distinct purpose.

The questions are my way, as the officiant, of both challenging and affirming the commitment of those I'm holding the ceremony for. They are the way I invite the recipients to really step forward for one another, and also a way to ready them for the challenges, as well as the joys, of partnership. If the ceremony is happening in sight of the partners' community, I will often also ask that community to make a commitment to cherish and nurture the love between the people being wed. In a way, this is the interpersonal seal of their love.

The vows are the beloveds' way of affirming each other, and their love for one another; of naming those qualities that are especially theirs, those gifts that they each bring to the love between them, and celebrating those; of building the love energy to its crescendo. Sometimes these vows will include not only those being wed or bound to one another, but will also be made to children who are included in the family unit that is being made, or other biological or logical family members. This is the personal seal the partners place on their love.

The binding, whether it's done with ribbons and ropes, with garlands, or with rings, is where Mystery, divinity, a greater love comes in to bind and seal the love between the lovers.

⋙ PLAYTIME ⋘
Co-creating Ceremony IV

How would you like to be bound to one another? Do you want your celebrant to ask you questions based on your religious tradition, or on the intentions that you agreed with them when planning the ceremony? Do you want to write vows that speak to the unique qualities of your relationship, and what you plan to bring to it—or are there traditional vows that already speak to you? And do you want a physical binding—e.g., rings, a handfasting—and do you also want that to be a spiritual binding?

Surrender—receiving blessings

One of the reasons why some of our last remaining rituals in the West centre around relationships—and why we need more rituals that do—is that commitment is a tall order. Indeed, the more solid a committed relationship is, the more likely it is that it will become a container for our "stuff"—our old wounds, our greatest fears, the patterns of behaviour we most need to let go of. The longer we spend together, the more the romantic ideals we projected onto one another fall away, and we come to really see each other. If we're lucky, in time we come to see each other with a clarity and depth that makes for more intimacy. But many of us go through a period of seeing everything that disappoints and hurts us about the other person before we get there, and that period is a tough one to stick around for.

Besides this, we place a lot of expectations on romantic and partner love these days. We look to our beloveds to be our "other halves"—everything from our confidants and friends, to our family, co-habitants, co-parents, business partners … the list goes on. Society encourages us to isolate ourselves, often with just one other person, in small units, whilst simultaneously demanding that we be perfect partners, and productive members of our "community." And isolated is often how our love ends up. We buy into a romantic ideal of "us against the world"—but what happens on those days when it's us against each other?

All of this speaks to why we need to let our love receive, why we need the blessings of support from family and friends, of guidance from experts and elders, and of miracles from the unseen. Commitment ceremonies make space for us to receive some of these blessings, which can be administered by the celebrant if you have one, by the circle of community if you choose to have one of those present, and by a greater love if you're willing to allow for that presence. Once you've made your promises to one another, and been bound to each other, allow space for those promises, that binding, to be blessed.

⇒ PLAYTIME ⇐
Co-creating Ceremony V

Some ways to let your love be blessed include the following:

- A blessing from your celebrant
- Asking for a blessing from your unseen ancestors, guides or guardians, or the god(s) of your understanding

- Walking among your witnesses, or inviting them to come up to you, and allowing them each to bless you with their own wishes
- Being still in nature, and receiving the blessing of the land beneath you, the sky above you, and the elements

Giving Thanks—celebrating your love

The aftermath of a commitment ceremony is an ideal time to bask in the love that has been consecrated, and to share it with each other and those that you love. In a culture that is so focused on competition, choosing to take time away from the rush of our daily lives to celebrate the mystery of finding someone we want to share those lives with can be not just romantic, but radical. Whether you are planning on sharing the abundance of your love with your community, or consummating it privately together, think about the qualities that make this love the love you're wanting to stick around for, and how your celebrations can reflect and amplify those. This will lead you much more accurately to the shape of celebration you really want than any wedding catalogue.

Don't just be romantic. Be radical.

Revisiting commitment

One of my favourite things about the neo-pagan reimagining of the hand-fasting tradition, which most of the ceremonies I officiate at are based on, is the option to commit to one another for a year and a day. Not because I hope that the commitments I bless will only last that long, but rather because I see therein an invitation to revisit the commitments made at annual intervals. Instead of making an assumption about the longevity of the relationship, or the unchanging nature of the commitments made on the day, these ceremonies invite partners to re-examine those commitments on a regular basis. This doesn't just mean those commitments can change and adapt as the relationship requires; it also invites the beloveds to actively choose one another anew, with all that they now know that entails. This allows the relationship to grow in company with the partners, and also guards against some of the assumptions, expectations, habits, and tendencies to take each other for granted that can be so dangerous in long term commitment. It is, in short, an invitation into conscious, choiceful, intimacy.

If you make—or have made—any kind of formal or ceremonial commitment to your beloved, I strongly suggest revisiting that commitment together on a regular basis, such as once per year. You may find that all you wish to do is celebrate that commitment, and affirm it in its original form. Or, you may find that it needs to change or expand to accommodate the new knowledge you have from loving one another for the last year. Either way, taking the time to check in, recommit, and choose one another anew, definitely falls for me into the "romantic, and also radical" category of relating.

I hope this chapter has awakened you to the possibilities that more intentional, magical, and radical relating hold for long-term loving. Having explored the ways that ritualising our relating, and creating ceremony for our commitments, can enrich and sustain our love, it's now time to look at how those same principles and practices can help us to let go, if a time comes when we choose to say goodbye.

Chapter 8

Letting Go

Another of the places I believe we are currently in need of the compassionate container of ritual in our culture is endings. While we do still have some—albeit heavily commercialised—remnants of ceremony for beginnings (namings, birthdays, graduations, weddings), our understanding of our comparative needs when it comes to closure is profoundly lacking. In a recent funeral I was asked to officiate at, I was given a twenty-five-minute slot in the crematorium to celebrate ninety years of life—and a life richly lived at that. With our focus so squarely on performance, productivity, and progress, we don't only struggle to know how to rest, how to feel unhappy emotions, and how to say no—many of us also have no idea how to make an ending that is conscious, compassionate, and that honours what is coming to an end.

This is all the more true with relationships, for a number of reasons:

- We are still haunted by the ideal of "happily ever after," and, despite the profound differences between our lives now, and the lives of the first readers of the Grimm fairy tales, we still judge a relationship that comes to an end as a failed one.

- We live in a culture that has its psychospiritual roots embedded in Abrahamic religions, and in the judgments the majority of those religions hold against anything that is not married monogamy. Ending a relationship is not smiled upon in those narratives.

- As we've already touched upon, we've been taught to place value judgments on our feelings, prizing certain feelings over others, and being encouraged to see some of them as "positive," and some as "negative"—the latter to be passed over, avoided, or clamped down on, so that we can carry on being pleasant and productive members of society. This means we have to fight for our right to carve out the time and space required to feel, process, share, and make choices around our so-called "negative" feelings, which often abound during times of ending and separation.

- As a result of the above, we receive little to no education around how to sit with, express, and process difficult emotions, never mind sitting with and untangling the difficult emotions of two people. And while we're shown how to do things, we're not often taught how to undo things. In a culture that prizes being right, and being the best, crucial skills like apologising, admitting we don't know, and acknowledging that we can't do something—skills vital for creating an ending—are denied us.

All of this impacts our capacity to create endings, and therefore impacts our capacity to relate, since endings are a necessary part of doing so. Indeed, our nonromantic relationships are sometimes hit the hardest by this. The fact that we have some language at least around romantic endings—albeit language that is often harsh and abrupt, such as "breaking up" or "being dumped"—indicates that we have at least some collective experience to draw from in relation to those endings. However, we're sorely lacking in language or models that address the tailing off of friendships, or drawing a line under toxic family connections.

Having dedicated so much of this section to coming together, and staying together, it feels important to also talk about those moments when it is necessary and healthy to come apart. The skills we've been looking at can also be applied here, allowing us to relate differently—and more creatively—to endings, and to each other.

When to let go

Let's begin by exploring some of the reasons we might consider letting go of a relationship—romantic or otherwise:

- An imbalance emerges between our intrinsic worth as a human being, and the way we are being treated. Of course, we all mess up in relationship; loving and being loved can be a vulnerable, scary, or just downright difficult task. However, if a hurtful pattern of behaviour is repeatedly discussed, and still persists, there may come a time when we need to consider that perhaps actions speak louder than words, and start treating ourselves as we would wish to be treated. This in turn may lead to letting go of the relationship in question.

- We discover a fundamental difference in values. This may appear early on, or develop further down the line. As we've discussed, rather than a difference in taste, this is a difference in the fundamental beliefs that underlie the way we move through the world and the way we relate, as well as what we want from our lives and the future. What are our priorities in life? What is our vision for relationship? How do we each treat the balance between work and love, rationality and feeling, the physical and the spiritual? What are our respective feelings and behaviours around gender, race, equality, ecology, human rights? Having fundamentally different answers to these questions can make for an unsustainable connection.

- Love is asking more of us than we can give. Anne Geraghty reminds us that "love keeps trying to teach us how to love, and we don't realise how much we have to learn."[32] Sometimes one or both of us doesn't have the resources (time, energy, health, wealth, support), or the will, to learn the lessons love is asking of us through our conflicts or struggles. These are often those endings that feel like "a waste." We know there was more potential in the connection than we were able to glean, but we realise that gleaning isn't going to happen anytime soon, and we need to value ourselves enough to move on. Never fear. Love is a patient teacher, and will find its way back to you in a different guise, carrying on your lessons at a more conducive date.

- It becomes clear that the other person no longer cares for us, or in the case of intimate sexual relationships, desires us, as we do them. These are some of the hardest endings, the ones that seem not of our own

32. Geraghty, *How Loving Relationships Work*, 30.

choosing. And yet, to choose to be with someone who does not choose us back is not really a choice in favour of ourselves—and ultimately, abandoning ourselves serves none of our relationships.

As valid as these reasons for letting go are, there can be no question that bidding farewell is no small feat. As time goes on, it becomes increasingly clear to me that, when we lose a person, we do not just lose an individual. Instead, we lose access to the microcosm that person was, each of us being a whole little world moving through the larger one we share. And the space they leave behind is not just that of a small world, but also of all the things we shared, the needs we felt were met by them, the hopes and dreams we built together, and the fantasies we imagined them fulfilling.

Sometimes, when we have shared a life with someone, letting go of that life can feel like a kind of death in its own right. Here are some useful things to remember when you're considering looking death in the eye:

The fine line between "understandable" and "acceptable"

When we have known another person intimately, as a friend or partner, it is likely that we gain some understanding of their inner world. We know a little of their history, how they have suffered, how life has marked them. This helps us to be compassionate when they struggle, or if they make mistakes in relationship with us. It is however very easy to slip from being understanding toward our beloved, to accepting behaviours from them that are in fact hurtful or indeed abusive, just because we recognise that they are struggling. Understandable does not always equal acceptable, and just because you can empathise with the source of a behaviour, it does not mean you should simply stand there and take it. Another person's struggles do not negate your rights as a human being and a partner.

All of you is needed for you to live

When in relationship, we inevitably reveal different parts of ourselves at different times. Often, we will inhabit more of certain aspects of ourselves with one person than we do with another. This is not only natural and appropriate, it's also one of the many reasons why we need a network of different relationships in our lives. However, if we are being required to show only certain aspects of who we are in a particular relationship, and encouraged either subtly or directly to repress or be rid of other aspects, then we might rightly start hearing alarm bells. There's a difference between relationship inviting us to grow, and only receiving love when we limit ourselves to being a particular type of person. This risks stifling both our multiplicity and our creativity—along with all the things those contribute to, such as personal growth, self-acceptance, fulfilling our purpose, a sense of integration and wholeness, self-actualisation, our very aliveness. The list goes on.

The gut always knows

When in doubt, ask your gut. If you can summon up the courage to breathe deep into your belly, past whatever other feelings are roiling around in you, and ask your wise belly whether it is in your best interests, and will lead to your best self and life, to stay in this connection or let it go, you are likely to find some wisdom therein. As we've discussed before, if a connection is not sustainable, your gut will usually have had an inkling about that right from the start.

There will be an after

It's tempting to stave off an ending we know in our heart of hearts needs to happen because we are afraid of the loss that will follow. It is moments like these when knowing we can call on those practices of sitting with the uncomfortable within can help us steer toward our best lives. The pain will pass, one way or another. This is one of the hardest things to imagine when we are on the edge of the ending abyss, looking into the unknown. It can seem as if all we will ever know again will be the loss of this dear person, this dear world. But often, if we look back on previous experiences of endings, it's likely we'll recall that they were, eventually, followed by meaningful life experiences, and joy-bringing connections we could not have imagined before we exited stage left, pursued by grief.

The suggestions that follow are designed to support you in meeting endings in new, more creative ways—ways that honour the realities of your loss and contain opportunities for healing from beginning to end. If the ending you're facing is in fact not the end of the relationship, but rather the end of one part of it, and the transition into another (e.g., moving from being romantic partners to being co-parents), what follows will hopefully support you in traversing it more kindly and collaboratively in order to pave the way for your next chapter together. The majority of these practices can also be called upon to support you with losses that are not the endings of intimate relationships, such as bereavement.

So let's have a look at some of our options when it comes to letting go …

Letting go alone

This is the route most of us are used to taking when it comes to traversing relationship endings. It's also the route that fits most comfortably with the way our culture treats grief—as something to be kept apart, dealt with in private, and moved on from as quickly as possible. I can't speak to whether this is the easier or the harder route to follow. Both this, and the possibilities explored in the Letting Go Together section, come with their challenges and blessings.

I will say that both require a fierce ally, willing to strike a balance between doing the work, and tending to the pain. In this first scenario, that ally is you. Hopefully you will find yourself supported by other allies too—friends, lovers, family, community—but endings can be tricky times. Sometimes their finality bleeds into other connections, and we find ourselves losing not just one person, but several, or groups of people, or even beloved places or animals. Loss invites us to take tenacious and tender action on our own behalf, sometimes in the face of what others would have us do, and certainly in the face of our feeling-phobic culture.

Here are some ways of being a fierce ally to yourself during end times that I can thoroughly recommend:

Treating grief as a treasured guest

Like any feeling, grief asks us to be present with it. The best way I have found of doing this is treating Grief as an honoured guest. Imagine: a dear friend, whom you have not seen in far too long, contacts you out of the blue to announce they are coming to stay. Their visit feels long overdue, and very precious. Some of the things you might do for them, which can also support you in your journey with grief, include:

- Preparing your space: Wherever an ending finds you, do what you can to make that space a safe container for you to sit with your grief. The physical act of tidying will help you order your thoughts. It will give your body a chance to move, which will help your emotions move more freely too. It will give you a chance to put away anything that might exacerbate your grief in ways that don't feel kind, and it will help you to create a blank canvas to express your grief upon as you need to. Small victories such as a made bed can feel like big wins at times like these.
- Taking time off: When Grief the Friend arrives, you may wish, if you can, to take a day or two off to honour their visit. To give yourself a chance to listen deeply, to hear what they have to tell you about where they've been, where they are coming from, what they are in need of, what you are in need of. A chance to share in your turn, to tell your story, to remember and process together.

Grief the Friend

- Sitting together: Inevitably, even though you have a treasured guest in the house, you will need at some point to tend to other obligations—work, studies, caring roles, and so on. However, because your guest is still with you, it's worth carving out time each day to sit together, share how the day has gone, discuss what is arising on your journey together at present. Time to breathe. Time to feel.

- Trusting things to run their course: Like any guest, you can trust that, at some point, their visit will be complete, the two of you will have shared all there is to share, and Grief the Friend will depart. Because you can trust this, you can make the most of your time together: talking late into the night, taking long walks, jumping about to favourite songs you haven't enjoyed for a while. Many of us fear that, if we once risk feeling a big emotion like grief, we won't be able to find our way out. But in fact, the more present you get with Grief the Friend, the sooner you're likely to find them packing their bags, and moving out to make room for new feelings to arise, and new days to dawn.

Small is beautiful—and you're also worth the Big Time

Try to strike a balance in your radical self-care between small actions that you can take regularly throughout the day—my favourite being tea and toast, with other options ranging from taking ten breaths of your choice, to dancing to your favourite track for five minutes, to reminding yourself you're rocking this whole keeping going thing—and some bigger actions that acknowledge the size and shape of what you're experiencing.

Let these bigger actions be inspired by the parts of you that have been hit the hardest by what's happened, or been happening. If your heart feels broken, what can you gift it with to help it feel and heal? If your inner kid feels abandoned, how can you take care of and coddle and remind that inner kid that they are perfect, and perfectly lovable? If your artist self has been lying dormant during the relationship, can you provide yourself with colours and permission to get messy with them? If you've been making yourself small for someone else, what can you do that will help you burst forth from that chrysalis and feel big and shiny? What parts of you were not being met in this connection, and how can you joyously celebrate them now?

Give yourself the gift of daily practice

The practices that have really stuck with me over the years are the ones I began during times of grief. This is because these are the times when having a reflective practice that we spend time with every day can reveal itself to be truly life-saving, as well as life changing. Find a way to ritualise the process of coming back to yourself for a part of every day, of paying yourself some compassionate attention, and finding out how you're feeling, what you're thinking, how the process is unfolding within you. Check out the daily practices on page 54 for further inspiration. When it comes to grief, processes which may prove particularly supportive include writing, breathing, and feeling.

In the first section of this book, we also touched on the way ritual can hold and help us process grief. Ritual can also support us in letting go. What follows is a practice often referred to as Cutting the Ties. It's designed to disentangle us, emotionally and spiritually, from the connection we are saying goodbye to. I have found this to be a useful practice, not only for connections that were indeed coming to a close, but also for connections that then carried on in other forms. By consciously releasing the relationship that is dying, we make space for the connection to evolve into something new, if and when that is appropriate.

⋙ PLAYTIME ⋘
Cutting the Ties That Bind

Begin by carving out some time and space, getting comfortable in a seated position, and taking some deep, full breaths to support you in letting go of your day and your surroundings, and in paying attention to your body and your inner landscape.

Now, in your mind's eye, it's time to choose a safe space. This needs to be somewhere where you can invite the other person or people in the connection to come and sit with you "in spirit," so to speak. It could be an imaginary space—a beautiful cosy room that feels really safe and welcoming, or a gorgeous natural landscape—or it could be somewhere you associate with this person or the relationship.

Choose your place, and imagine yourself there.

Take your time to get as clear a sense of the space as you can—to get comfortable there, so to speak. Use all your senses to bring you present there. How does the air taste and smell? What sounds can you hear if any? What are the textures beneath your fingertips and feet? What colours and shapes fill the space, what do you see?

You can also call in support if you need it—a guide, an ancestor, a guardian, a friendly protective creature—whatever you need to feel supported in your working.

When you're ready, invite the person(s) you're saying goodbye to to join you in this space. Feel them arrive, taking your time to get as clear a vision of them as possible, and greet them however feels comfortable to you.

You can now take some time to say anything that needs to be said to this person. If you need to really let rip, this is a safe space to do so. If you simply want to have a conversation with them, you can allow that to unfold. If there are things about the connection you will miss/feel thankful for, you can reflect and share on those.

Take your time. Say what needs to be said. Allow them to respond if that feels welcome and appropriate. When that feels complete, move on to the next stage.

Become aware of the ties that connect you to this person, that have built up between you over time. You may feel them as strings of energy connecting different parts of your bodies, or see them as threads bridging the space between you. These threads are woven of hopes, fears, projections, desires; moments of pain, and moments of joy. They are pieces of your shared history that cling to you and bind you together—and so they are part of what makes it hard to let go. When the time feels right, invite a being to join you who can lovingly sever them for you. It could be the archangel Michael with his sword of light, or Okoye with her Sonic Spear—whatever works for you. Ask for the ties between you and your guest to be severed for the purpose of closure and mutual healing.

See the threads between you severed. Say goodbye to the person you're bidding farewell to. And then sit and welcome some healing for the places in your body that once held the threads, and for the parts of you that are grieving, before you come back.

～

The final thing I want to say about letting go solo is that you will need to speak your grief, and it's worth being discerning about how you do that—or rather, whom you do it with. To share our grief is to allow a very vulnerable piece of ourselves to be seen, and since our culture doesn't have a whole lot of time for those parts of us, not everyone has learned how to see the beauty in them, or realised what a privilege it is to be allowed to see them at all. And yet when we are in the throes of loss, our need to share is sometimes so acute as to cause us to misplace our sharing. For example, we might:

- Share with people who have not yet demonstrated their capacity to hear and hold us when we're cracking open.
- Share more than we meant to, in terms of the detail or depth to which we share, or how long we share for.
- Form new bonds that are based on sharing our grief, which then either keep us entrenched in our grief, or fall away as it shifts.

And yet, grief needs to be witnessed.

We've already touched on some of the ways we might witness ourselves: Creating ritual containers for grief or offering ourselves the gift of deep listening on a daily basis. Using the automatic writing techniques from page 26 to allow the parts of us that are hurting to speak. Cutting the Ties that Bind. And writing letters: letters that don't hold back, letters that move the pain from our heart to our hand to the pen to the page; letters that we do not send, letters that are pure processing, letters that get cast into the fire or a flowing river to be let go of. Letters like these can also be a powerful tool for grief.

And what about other people? Who can we turn to during loss? Brené Brown asks the question "who has earned the right to hear my story?" [33] I might rephrase it as, "Who knows your unique power, purpose, and gifts intimately enough, that getting to know your pain and your shame will not shake their knowledge of the former, but rather deepen their love for you? Who sees you clearly enough to be worthy of seeing your pain?" I would also ask the question, "Who is here? Who is taking action on your behalf?"

I have found that there is nothing like loss to show me who my people are. Experiences of both loss of love, and loss of means and stability, sit at the heart of some of my most treasured experiences as a friend and partner, and at the foundation of my most lasting relationships. I have found it's not always the "first wave" of listeners I need to share deeply with; our grief

33. Brown, *The Gifts of Imperfection*, 47.

can attract both spectators and rescuers, but these first responders are rarely the last on the scene. Here are some characteristics I look for in the people I share my losses with:

- A history of holding: People whom I have experienced as being able to hear and hold my feelings, without judging, or making it about them, or trying to fix it, or applying relentless positivity to get me to look on the bright side before I've fully processed what I'm feeling. People whom I have that history with are the people who have really earned the right to hear my story.

- Compassion born of experience: I find this to be both an excellent foundation for sharing, and also profoundly sexy. It's something I seek out in all my close connections. It is what is left after someone has had a painful life experience, chosen to let themselves to be fully cracked open and transformed by it, and developed a deep compassion for the pain of others as a result. Sharing with people who have had similar experiences can be profoundly affirming, healing, and reassuring.

- Taking direct action on my behalf: A memory that remains one of my most precious and healing is that of my friend Miranda picking me up from work the day after a significant breakup. My manager had exercised wisdom and kindness in finding me a series of manual tasks to do in the back office, which I could sit and cry over out of sight of the customers. He also elected to hand me over to Miranda a couple of hours before my shift would normally have ended. She took me by the hand, bought me a large bag of cookies, and then took me to the public library, where she sat and read stories about dragons to me while I let the tears flow, pausing occasionally in her reading to let me share things as they came up. Before putting me on the bus home, she took me to a fancy supermarket (I was very poor at the time) and filled a bag with fruit, juice, and sweet treats to send me home with. That combination of compassion and practicality is a key ingredient in the glue that has kept us fast friends through all manner of tough and terrific times ever since. Words come easy to many people, but direct action is such a hallmark for trust.

All that being said, there have most certainly been times of loss in my life where I didn't yet have connections with the qualities I describe above. I know from those times that friendships like these are a great gift and a privilege, even as I now know them to be a vital component of an emotionally sustaining life. Those are the times when I made mistakes like the ones I listed earlier—oversharing with new connections that couldn't bear the weight of that, or sharing with people who couldn't see me clearly enough to know that I was more than the sum total of the grief I was experiencing. If you're traversing such a time, I urge you to consider accessing the support of a fellowship or professional. And you certainly don't have to wait for grief to come knocking to seek out that support.

Professional support is not just for

- People with more "serious" mental health problems than you
- People with more "real" problems than you
- People with more money than you

In order to live as our most whole, most integrated, most actualised, and most real selves, we will all need professional support of one sort or another at some point in our lives. If there's a particular image you associate with the concept of professional support that you don't like, please know that it can look like a lot of different things:

- Fellowships (e.g., twelve-step groups), sharing circles (e.g., women's peace circles), heart circles—many of these are often free or donation-based
- Pastoral support/counselling (linked to a particular faith, or interfaith, or humanist), religious buildings, services and meetings—these can often be accessed for free, or on a sliding scale
- Personal development workshops, meditation groups, spiritual gatherings—sometimes available on a sliding scale or donation basis, or with bursary or assistant spaces
- One-to-one or group therapy—again, hold any assumptions or preconceptions about this option lightly, and don't be afraid to look around for a modality or approach that speaks to you. If you can't afford the practitioner of your dreams, contact them anyway and find out if they have

a sliding scale or low-income slots, or look around for any local clinics and voluntary centres offering affordable counselling

- Bodywork, or coaching and therapy based around movement or creativity, or walking groups, or movement classes. Getting into the body is vital for processing grief of any kind. Again, these are sometimes available on a sliding scale, donation, or voluntary basis

Your grief needs, and deserves, to be witnessed. This is a vital part of letting go.

Letting go together

As with every other aspect of relating, doing things consciously, choicefully, and magically can allow us to transform how we part ways. If we can find within ourselves the willingness to be allies in our ending, then we can chart new territory in togetherness that extends beyond the timeline of our official "relationship."

In exploring how this might be possible, I gathered stories from friends and colleagues who had dared to do separation and divorce together, rather than in opposition—often with the intention of shifting from one form of relationship to another, rather than ending their connection. Looking through these stories for the common threads that tie them together, I find that the key ingredients for co-creating closure are very similar to the ingredients required by the aspects of conscious relating we've looked at so far:

Being willing to stay present

The stories I gathered described how important it was, in order for the relationship to end and transition into something else, to make the time for all the parties involved to express what they were feeling, and be fully heard. While these are some of the moments that most test our ability to sit with one another's pain, without striving to fix it or backing away, they allow each person to feel fully, and to feel seen in what they are feeling. Thus, the space between us is gradually cleared of debris, and made ready for the seeds of a different kind of connection to be planted.

Being kind to self and other

Another thread that kept coming up in the stories was that of kindness. Kindness to the self in the form of boundaries set, lines drawn. One person mentions having to ask for more time before agreeing to co-create a closing ritual; another talks about how being friendly wasn't always possible during the process. But also kindness to the other, in the form of compassionate listening; generous gestures of love and friendship; and, ultimately, the willingness to keep on putting those guards down, in order to reconnect, and work out how to move forward together.

Daring to get creative

Creativity featured prominently in all of the stories—in small gestures like heartfelt letters and meaningful gifts, but also in the commitment to doing things differently exhibited by those involved. Conscious endings seem to be made up of a series of radical acts, whether those are small acts of kindness to one another, or big acts of co-created opposition to our cultural and/or legal narratives that call for acrimony and righteousness at the end of intimate relationships.

Letting things be messy

It's clear that co-created endings are not easy. It's often so much easier to shut down than to stay open. Succumbing to disconnection, defensiveness, and acrimony, pandered to as they often are by our environment and the people who love us, can look a lot more attractive than getting in a room with the person who is breaking our heart, or whose heart is breaking. This is a process that asks of us a delicate balance of patience and perseverance, care and self-containedness, holding what is and taking action to move forward—and no one is always going to get that balance right. It is, by its very nature, a messy process. We must be willing to apologise, and to accept an apology; to keep coming back to kindness, and to our intention to move forward as allies; to let things be what they are sometimes, even if that is untidy or unknown; and to write the rules of engagement as we go.

Letting time work its magic

When it comes to ending one kind of connection with the intention of moving forward into another, time is your friend. Time is the third person in the picture, the companion in the process, the extra factor that allows you to move from wanting to punch the person who was once your beloved, to you being the top candidate for godparent to the kid they had with the person they left you for. Do not underestimate what time can do, and make sure that you give yourselves and your connection plenty of it, particularly early on in the process. You cannot truly start a new relationship without ending the old one, and you may struggle to integrate that ending if you continue to spend the same amount of time together that you did originally. At some point, you may well need to pick an amount of time and agree to spend it out of contact with one another. When you come back into contact, have a discussion about how much and what kind of contact feels healthy, and supportive to the new kind of connection you're hoping to build.

Co-creating rituals of letting go

The following is one of the stories that was shared with me when I was doing the research for this section. I think it illustrates both the potency of ritual containers for holding endings, and the breadth of possibilities available to us in terms of what those endings look like:

Practical Magic: *Two months after our break up we attended a Hook Pull ritual. We had booked onto it months before and had intended to attend together. Somehow, we managed to both attend despite how bad we were feeling at the time. A hook pull ritual is an ordeal rite where steel hooks are pierced through the flesh (usually on the chest). Cords are attached to the hooks and one can pull on the hooks, on one's own, attached to stationary points, or with one or more other people.*

One effect of hook pulls (and in my opinion, one of the main reasons to do such an ordeal rite) is that it opens the heart. In my experience it's impossible to do without feeling intense love for everyone you're sharing the rite with. There came a moment in the ritual where C and I (having had the armour around our hearts torn apart) found ourselves face to face, feeling raw and holding our own cords.

A moment passed between our eyes. Without speaking we offered our cords to each other. Holding each other's hearts in our hands, we slowly pulled back against each other. As the flesh stretched and the sensation intensified, we kept eye contact, both of us crying soft tears. For me, the tears felt clean. As we pulled harder we gently allowed each other's cords to slip through our fingers, inch by inch. We cried and we consciously let each other go. It was exquisitely, beautifully, sad. And somehow felt right.—B

The sharing above hopefully gives you a sense of the infinite possibilities available to you when it comes to creating rituals to release a relationship. As familiar as you now are with the components of ritual, you can assemble those components out of anything that feels meaningful to you both, and anything that feels like it will allow you to collaboratively and cleanly cut the outdated ties between you. Here are some key ingredients to include:

- Establish a foundation of consent, kindness, and a common intention everyone involved can get behind.
- Make sure there is space for everyone's feelings to be present, to be seen/heard, and, where possible, to be released.
- Give back and release what is theirs; receive and take back what is yours.
- Include an activity that feels to your body, as well as your mind, like letting go with love.
- And if you can get to the point where you're able to honestly and openly share gratitude for what has been, go for it!

Having travelled together through parting company with the ones we love, and explored how intention, communication, and ritual can bring kindness, creativity, and new possibility to loss and letting go, we are now two thirds of the way through this sex magical odyssey—and on the other side of a whole segment dedicated to one of the hardest things we can do as human beings: be in relationship with one another.

Thank you for sticking with me, and for exercising courage and curiosity in trying out some new possibilities for opening, connecting, and communing with one another.

In the next section we'll be looking at how we can do that with life, the Universe, and everything!

No biggie. You've totally got this. Here we go …

Part III

Making Love with All That Is

This third and final chapter of your sex magical odyssey is a guide to taking your place in what poet Mary Oliver terms "the family of things."[34] In it, I seek to offer you a new vision of intimacy, one that extends beyond the islands of ourselves and our chosen people to include Nature, divinity, and All That Is. From the fine art of ecosexuality to erotic encounters with the gods, I'll be introducing you to new ways to let the love that is waiting for you in, and inciting you to share the love that you have in more compassionate and creative ways. The practices in this section expand the experience of radical relationship beyond the confines of the self, and also hold the keys to personal ecstasy. Finally, we'll be looking at sex magic rituals for creating the change we want to see in the world—but also at how living more magically can change our worlds from within.

---

34. Oliver, *Dream Work*, 14.

Chapter 9

Making Love with Earth

So by now we're all blossoming sex magicians, burgeoning experts in the craft of conscious and creative pleasure. When faced with one of the most beautiful, generous, and mysterious lovers we can ever hope to encounter—to wit, Nature—we are naturally tempted to get down to some magical business or other as soon as we get out onto her rolling riotous body. Or we feel like we ought to come up with some sweet act of adoration on the spot to express our wonderment at her glory.

I say that there's no better time to take a break from all that doing, all that getting it right, than when you have at last escaped your busy Western existential crisis long enough to find your way to a field, forest, or fjord, and encountered Nature in all her tender and tempestuous splendour.

Of course, it's worth saying hello. It's worth taking a moment, as you step through the portal of the gate into the meadow or between the first two trees in the forest, to be aware of the privilege of what you are about to experience, and extending a silent or spoken greeting to the spirits of the place that is enfolding you with open arms dripping with moss or blossom.

However, before you get your sex witch on, I recommend you take a moment to receive …

Receiving Nature

"All that you are seeking is also seeking you ... If you lie still, sit still, it will find you. It has been waiting for you a long time,"[35] writes storyteller Clarissa Pinkola Estés. Nowhere is this more true than in the natural world. If you go outside and be still, Nature will come to you. The scurryings and flutterings that ceased with your alien arrival will gradually be renewed; your breath will begin to come and go with greater ease from your body; and you'll begin to notice things. You don't even need to try. Stay still for long enough, breathe easily for long enough, you will find there's nothing that you need to do about it; the magic unfolds all of its own accord.

Nature will come and make love to you.

Her light will warm your skin. Her gales will wipe clean the cobwebs from your mind. The sight of Her will kiss your eyes. The cool waters of Her will cleanse your body, and wash away the burdens from your heavy heart.

We've touched already upon the vital component of magic, of living magically, that is surrendering and receiving. There are few better chances to practice this than to go out into Nature, and to allow Her to meet you there.

Go outside. Be still. Breathe. Be loved.

⇌ PLAYTIME ⇋
Ecosensual Awakening

This is a more interactive, and more intimate, take on receiving nature.

Go outside in whatever way is accessible to you. Slow your pace. Begin to have a sense of moving on the Earth with the same awareness, the same care, with which you might enter the room in which a lover was sleeping. After a while, allow your eyes or hands to wander, and see if you're drawn by any particular shapes or objects—ideally things you can pick up and carry with you without doing harm. Once you have a small collection, find a place that feels beautiful to you to sit, and place the objects you've gathered within reach.

Begin by looking around you, if you're a sighted person. Slow the pace of your gaze. Let your eyes rest, here, then here, then here. Let them drink in each detail of each place they rest. Take your time. Receive slowly through

---

35. Estés, *Women Who Run with the Wolves*, 152.

your eyes. After a while, see if one of the objects you gathered draws your gaze. Pick up it. Examine it. Allow yourself the luxury of curiosity, of the possibility that you've never seen anything like this before. Take at least three to five minutes for your looking.

Then close your eyes. Inhale the air around you. Let your breath expand and relax your body. Breathe into any parts of you that feel tense; expand them as you breathe in, and invite them to relax as you breathe out. Once your body is sitting a little more softly, begin to notice the scents of the air. What can you smell? What aromas infuse the air around you? How is the weather making the land smell? If you can smell one thing, can you catch the scent of other things beneath or intertwined with that? Are you drawn to smell one of the objects you collected? Give your breathing and scenting three to five minutes.

Now listen, if you're able to hear. Let your breathing deepen, and quieten, and make space for your attention to focus fully on what you can hear. Listen outward for the noises that are calling for your attention. Listen downward for the softer, subtler sounds that are under them. And listen inward, for the voices that are whispering in you. Receive with your outer and your inner listening. Take another three to five minutes with this.

Bring your attention to your taste buds. What can they tell you? What can you sense with your mouth closed, and what aromas are made available if you allow your mouth to open and breathe through there? Is one of your objects something you would like to try tasting? Is there something in the natural world around you—a blade of grass, a flower, a fruit—that could awaken your taste buds? How can you allow Nature to kiss you on the mouth in this moment? Give this another three to five minutes.

Finally, pick up whichever of your objects you are most drawn to touch. Inspired by Betty Martin's awakening of the hands again,[36] rest your hands in your lap, and allow them to explore the object. Slow down your touch. Give each millimetre its own time; each change in texture its own pause; each shift in angle its own moment of intimacy. Receive through your fingers. Ask yourself how much pleasure you can get from this touch. After a while, if you feel drawn to, you can explore the object with other parts of your body:

---

36. Martin, "The Pleasure in Your Hands."

stroke it up your arm, run it over your lips, roll it along your thigh. Let this small gift from the natural world be a direct invitation for you to come into your own skin, and enjoy being there to the max.

⋙ PLAYTIME ⋘
Refill and Restore

A more energy-focused way to receive the natural world, this fantastic tool allows the cosmos to give you more resources when you're in need. I also rely on elements of this exercise for the energy I use in many of my sex-magical workings. It can be done inside or out, making it more versatile than the exercise above—but doing it in nature is particularly sublime.

This one is best done standing, with your feet shoulder-width apart, and your knees relaxed. But feel free to do whatever works for you. Begin—you guessed it—by taking some deep, full breaths. When you're feeling more centred and present, drop your awareness down to your feet. Imagine that you can extend roots through your feet, and feel them wriggling down through the surface beneath, and into the Earth. Keep breathing, and wriggle your roots through the layers of mud, silt, and stone, until you come to the fiery core at the centre of the Earth. Now, as you breathe in, let some of the energy from that core flow up through your roots. Feel it rise up into your body. Keep breathing, and let that molten heat flow up your legs, into your pelvis and belly, up your spine, down your arms, into your heart. Have a sense that you're filling up your tank, and keep going until you feel warmed and energised.

Now take a few more centring breaths, and then reach your awareness in the other direction, up toward the sky. Reach past the place you're standing, past clouds, past the atmosphere, and into the stars. Whether you reach for the sun shining down on you, a heaven or divine realm, or for the starlight coming from other solar systems, it doesn't matter. Once you have a sense of a benevolent brightness, begin to breathe it in, back down the thread of your awareness, until it flows into your body. Let it pour through you like soft summer rain, flowing through your crown into your head, down your neck into your shoulders, down your arms and spine, into your torso and pelvis, down your legs. Let it flood your system. Breathe. Fill up.

Finally, bring your attention to your heart. Notice the two energies—the one from above, and the one from below—coming together there. Here you are, betwixt the two, perfectly earthly, perfectly heavenly, perfectly human—and perfectly restored.

⪫ PLAYTIME ⪪
Sit Spot

Sit Spot turns receiving nature into a daily practice. To establish a Sit Spot—a spot from which you can encounter nature where you sit for ten to thirty minutes each day—is to enter into an intimacy with the natural world that is not the fleeting glimpse, the rare weekend away, the dalliance with nature that many of us occasionally indulge in. Rather, it is a daily relationship, a committed partnership, a marriage of two mirrors.

To enter into this unique union, you must first establish your Sit Spot. It should be somewhere near your home, easily accessed and safe for you to sit in. A garden serves as well as a forest, or a rooftop with pots on it will do if there is no green space to be had nearby. And it should also be somewhere you find a pleasure to be, somewhere that draws you enough to keep coming back. Next, you must go and sit in your spot on a regular basis—ideally daily—and let your senses take in the nature around you. Breathe deeply. Try not to do much of anything else. And repeat.

Over time, having a Sit Spot allows us to release the illusion that we are a tourist in the natural world. After stripping away some of the weight from our shoulders, the tension from our bellies, the worry from our minds, our surroundings begin to gently blur our sense of separation, until it is less a case of inside and outside, until what we see in the natural world is ourselves. A daily practice like this reminds us of the family of things which we are part of, reconnects us to that family, and in time teaches us how to live as a member of that family.

We learn that all things start from small struggles and humble beginnings: the shoot pushing up, the fledgling tumbling from the ncst. We learn that all things must close if they are to open, rest if they are to blossom, let go if they are to be renewed. The fox teaches us how to be present to life. The fallen oak sprouting moss and mushrooms teaches us how to gracefully let go of the same. A Sit Spot shows us that all things that live are beautiful. And so are we.

~

Entering into these kinds of connections with the natural world can feel like the beginning—or the rekindling—of an intimate relationship. Like a new lover, nature can awaken our senses, make us catch our breath, and remind us of our beauty and aliveness.

Some of you may already be wondering how you can take this new intimacy toward the realm of the erotic. So let's take our first foray into the sweet and sensual world of ecosexuality—staying, for the moment, with this focus on letting the natural world in.

Ecosexuality is a spectrum of practices that all, in some way, combine our individual eroticism and our natural environment. I believe the magic of ecosexuality is two-fold. Like any consciously chosen intimate relationship, it holds gifts for both parties. On the one hand, as you may have begun to get a taste of via the exercises above, the natural world has unique ways of inviting us into our senses, encouraging us into our own skins, grounding us in the present moment, and reconnecting us to our capacity for pleasure. Nature has a cornucopia of ways to support and enhance our spiritual, sensory, and sensual experience.

The other transformation that entering into intimacy with the natural world can evoke in us is one of compassion. And compassion is the seed of change. Just as when we enter into relationship with another person, we embark on a process of understanding them, learning their story, and allowing their experiences, needs, and desires to touch us, and move us to action—just so, when we take the Earth as our Lover, we experience a shift in how we relate to them. I'm shifting to a gender-neutral pronoun for the Earth here with a purpose. Perhaps like some of you, I very much think of the Earth as a she, but this could be argued to be part and parcel of the way we have treated the Earth in recent centuries.

Our cultural conceptions of the Earth as a mother hold certain implications in a society that has little respect or appreciation for women, or for parents and elders. If we think about our archetypal images of mothers—the Earth mother, the Empress in the tarot, Mary—we see that they are unconditional, ever-present, always available, always with more to give their end-lessly demanding offspring. Think about how we treat mothers in the West right now. As we emphasise single-unit families and individual achievements more and more, mothers find themselves isolated, expected to naturally possess the wide range of skills and interests that will allow them to meet the full spectrum of diverse physical, psychological, emotional, and spiritual needs of their children, whilst simultaneously being fantastic partners and/or providers, and loving the whole experience the whole time—because mother-hood is still considered the peak experience that women can have.

If we think about how Western cultures have treated the Earth in the last couple of centuries, it is not dissimilar. We look to our planet to provide for us unconditionally. We expect to be able to simply keep on taking, without Earth requiring anything back of us—after all, "she" is our Mother Earth, and we are her children, and that's what children get to do. Except that we're not children. We're a supposedly advanced civilisation, with an abundance of data in our possession about the impact we're having on our planet, and the sophistication to be able to process and understand that data, as well as the means to do something about it. And our faculties are telling us loudly and clearly what dire straits we're in. The term "ecological grief" is gaining ground as a way to describe the mental health impact of "climate-related losses to valued species, ecosystems and landscapes." [37] The risk of feeling this grief too acutely is one of the reasons why it's so much easier to lose ourselves in virtual escape mechanisms than it is to go outside and let the world in.

Entering into intimacies with the natural world invites us to become more conscious and choiceful in our behaviour toward it. As in any long-term re-lationship, there naturally comes a time where we experience a call to make a commitment to the beloved—in this case, in the form of the environment. Annie Sprinkle and Beth Stephens' marriage to the Appalachian Mountains wasn't just about their love of the mountains, or the pleasure they derived from being in proximity to that piece of geography.[38] It was also about stating their commitment to honour and treasure an entity that they loved, and to

37. Cunsolo and Ellis, "Ecological grief as a mental health response to climate change-related loss."

38. Stephens and Sprinkle, *Goodbye Gauley Mountain* (DVD).

take action against the mountain top removal that continues to devastate the area.

As you continue to explore ways to allow the natural world to get under your skin, and into your senses, loins, and hearts, allow yourself to be moved by the world around you. As Joanna Macy says in her book *Coming Back to Life* about repressing what she calls our Pain for the World: "If we won't feel pain, we won't feel much else either—loves and losses are less intense, the sky less vivid, pleasures muted."[39] Allowing ourselves to be touched by the natural world opens us up to new depths and breadths of feeling and pleasure, while also inviting us to become better lovers of the extraordinary living system we are all part of.

⇒ PLAYTIME ⇐
Sun Breathing

Unsurprisingly, this works best when you have access to some direct sunlight, and ideally a safe space to lie on the Earth. But it can also be done in any patch of daylight, with the remembrance that the sun is always somewhere up there above the clouds.

Find yourself a sun-soaked spot on the Earth, or equivalent.

Adopt your pussycat-caught-in-sunbeam posture of choice, and get comfortable. Get some of delicious full breaths happening, and notice how solidly the Earth beneath you carries and supports you. Begin to invite your body to sink into that holding. If it's been a particularly rough day/week/life, you may want to do this piece by piece, bringing your attention to each part of your body in turn—from the plates of your skull and the muscles of your face, to the softening soles of your feet—breathing into each one, and then imagining it melting into the ground as you breathe out. Notice if you can feel a heartbeat—first in yourself, then in the Earth below you.

Breathe. Release. Surrender. Sink into that embrace. And perhaps take a moment to give profound thanks for the way the Earth keeps carrying you on every step of your journey, no matter what.

Once you've settled into the ground, and are really receiving that embrace, start to notice the sun on your skin. Become aware of receiving that

---

39. Macy, *Coming Back to Life*, 31.

warm caress—of your cells responding to that life-giving heat—and relax deeper. We're now going to start playing with the Heart/Sex circuit breath we've done before, but this time, we'll be adding sunlight to it.

As you inhale, imagine that you inhale the sunshine, that sensual pulsing heat. Breathe it in through your sex, up your spine, and into your heart. Pause for a moment to savour as it pools there, golden, warm, pulsing … and then breathe out through your heart, allowing the light to cascade down your arms, through your abdomen and stomach, warming and releasing each part of your body, before arriving back into your sex. Repeat for as long as you wish.

Once you and the sunlight have a good groove going, you could also add self-pleasuring to this practice if you wished. Or have a cat nap. Or you can simply bring the practice to a close when you feel replenished.

However you choose—receive the sunlight. Allow it to fill your reserves—energising, healing, relighting your fire.

This breath can be adapted for whichever of the elements you feel especially drawn to. You can do it while lying on your bed listening to the rain, while floating on your back in the ocean, or standing on a mountain top in a gale!

⇒ PLAYTIME ⇐
Sun-Soaked Sauciness

This is another take on the above, for those of you who are a little more fantasy orientated—or stuck indoors during the darker months of the year! It can be lovely to do in a sunbeam, but it can also be done in a pillow fort.

Begin, once again, with full deep breaths—breaths that allow you to let go of your surroundings, and get centred and settled in your own body.

Close your eyes, and open your mind's eye to a sun-soaked spot somewhere else: somewhere beautiful such as a dappled woodland or the banks of a mountain stream. Take your time to look around you, to get as clear an impression as possible of the place where you find yourself to be. Once you have a sense of your surroundings, look for a path in this new, inner landscape, and follow it. Follow it until you come to a bower, a resting place formed by nature: moss covered tree-roots curling round to make a perfect nest, or a soft grassy riverbank, or a flower-strewn clearing. Settle yourself here, check in to make sure you're still breathing, and then invite the sun to come and visit you in a form you can enjoy.

Because the roots of my spirituality are decidedly pagan in nature, for me this would look like Pan, the Lord of the Forest. For you, it might be a being made of light, a particular sun deity you're connected to, or perhaps a group of fire nymphs. Receive this being in whatever way delights you both. Allow the sun to come to you in a form that arouses you. If it's your kind of thing, you can allow the sun to penetrate you in your vision, just as you allowed the sunlight to penetrate you during the breathing above.

Add self-pleasuring how, if, and when you wish, and enjoy…

When this feels complete, give thanks, and allow the sun to bestow any guidance or gifts it has for you before departing. If you're doing this in bed at the end of the day, you can fall asleep in this beautiful place. Alternately, in your mind's eye, walk back along the path to where you started, and from there breathe yourself back into your body and your physical surroundings. Take some time to ground before moving on to other activities.

⋛ PLAYTIME ⋚
Erotic Shapeshifting, Take II

I now want to introduce you to another tributary of the erotic shapeshifting journey we set out on with the genital shapeshifting in the Making Love with Each Other section, which also happens to be a further way of inviting the natural world into our erotic experiences.

One of the great gifts modern spirituality has been blessed enough to inherit—or, perhaps more accurately, appropriate—is that of the concept of spirit guides. Working with unseen guardians or helpers is a feature of almost all religious and spiritual traditions the world over. However, the spirit guides I'm primarily referring to when I talk about allies in this section are drawn from neo-shamanic and modern pagan traditions, which in turns owe much of their core material to Indigenous American and Eastern European shamanic practices. These allies are often intrinsically connected to the natural world, and communicate with us in the forms of wild creatures, or beasts from myths and legends, that are recognisable to us.

Having worked with guides since the very early days of my spiritual path, I found myself falling in love with a heathen spirit-worker. After he introduced me to the concept and experience of "aspecting" guides—which is to say, inviting them to come and inhabit my body with me—inevitably I got curious about the possibilities this practice might hold for sexual encounters.

Not long after that, a new guide revealed himself to me, and made it very clear that this was a piece of work he was up for helping me with. Since then, that same guide has transformed my experiences of both the shamanic journeying techniques described below, and sex. He has been tattooed on my skin, and has brought a new sexual partner—who also happens to have such a creature tattooed in the same place on the same arm—into my life. In this section I'll be sharing ways to encounter your own erotic allies, and see what transformations they can bring about for you.

One way to meet your allies is through techniques commonly referred to in modern Western spirituality as shamanic journeying. The version I offer below is the one that my aforementioned spirit-worker beloved teaches.

So, where will you be journeying to exactly? For the purpose of meeting an erotic ally, we recommend the Lower World/Underworld: the realm connected with the Earth, with animal spirits, and, correspondingly, with our more carnal and embodied selves.

And how will you be getting there? To journey in this fashion, you'll need three things:

A clear intention. In this case, your intention will be to meet with an erotic ally who is willing and able to support you in your own sexual (r)evolution.

A way in. This can be a doorway of your choosing, ideally one that already exists in this world—the Middle Realm—and that you're fairly familiar with. Somewhere that holds special significance for you perhaps, or that you experience as particularly magical. Mine is an opening in the roots of a particular tree I spent one moonlit night camped under. My beloved's is a waterfall he's been visiting since he was a small child. Yours might be a similarly natural portal, or might be somewhere more urban—a door, an alleyway, a train you've wondered idly about jumping on. Pick a place you love that you can imagine might lead down into the ground, and visualise it clearly.

A drumbeat. This may seem distracting at first, but it will provide you with extra support on your journey, and we find we're much more focused with that support than without it. If you're as fortunate as me in having someone in your household who is willing and able to provide you with a simple monotonous drumbeat to follow, great—but a recording will do just fine.

Once these three things are present to you, get comfortable in a position you won't fall asleep in, and take some deep, full breaths. The kind of breaths that are going to support you in letting go of your immediate environment, relaxing, and turning your attention inward.

Once you feel fairly focused, bring your portal to mind, and walk toward it, holding your intention clearly in your mind and heart. Walk through the portal. The rest is up to you. Trust what arises, allow yourself to be surprised, and keep an eye out for an erotic ally. At this point, you're just popping in to meet them, have a conversation, and then come back again. Make sure to retrace your steps when coming back, come back through the portal, and then back to the room you're sitting in. Take your time coming back to your body and opening your eyes.

$\sim$

Some things to be aware of for the exercise above:

Many people are put off the concept of journeying because they imagine that, in order for it to "work," they need to be very visual people—i.e. to see pretty pictures—and they don't feel adequate to the task. However, just like energy, journeying can manifest itself in harmony with your primary senses—it's about giving yourself permission to have a go, to practice, and to trust the impressions that arise for you, whatever those may look/feel/sound like.

You are in control. Our experience of these realms is that they are inherently benevolent. You have set the intention to meet an ally, and we hope that is all you will encounter. However, if you have an encounter that doesn't feel right to you, while you can certainly reflect on it later, it is within your power and right to thank it for showing itself to you, say goodbye, and keep looking—or indeed just to open your eyes and come straight back to this world.

I'm repeating myself here, but this is important: allow yourself to be surprised. If you're a seasoned journeyer, or trying this for the first time, resist the temptation to censor yourself, trust your vision and your gut, and allow what arises to arise. Remember, your ally is likely to be a being that has some "medicine" for you, that has something fresh to bring to how you already relate erotically—so their form, manner, or gifts may be unexpected. Be curious, be willing, be respectful. Allow your connection and conversation to unfold, ask them what they have to bring to you, and what you can offer them—and always remember to say thank you!

~

So, you've hopefully been on some sort of journey, and perhaps you've already met an erotic ally. But how do you bridge the gap between you in this realm, and the magic they're holding for you in that realm?

Your ally may have other answers to that question to offer you, but here's one we love to play with. It's the shapeshifting side of Erotic Shapeshifting, also known as aspecting, or a mild form of consensual spirit possession.

⪼ PLAYTIME ⪻
Erotic Shapeshifting, Take III

Aspecting involves inviting your new friend to come and play in your body. This allows them to have fun being in physical form as we know it—and it allows you to literally embody some of the qualities they have to bring to your erotic explorations and expansion. To clarify, we're not talking about handing over complete control to another being—we're talking about creatively cohabiting your body together. You welcome your new friend in, you lend them as much control as you like, and then you thank them and say goodbye. You can even have a chat with them about the boundaries you're willing to play within before you start if you so wish.

If you're trying this for the first time, a good place to start is one very like the place you began when you were preparing to journey. Get comfortable. Put on some steady drum music. Take a few deep, full breaths, and begin to let go of your surroundings.

However, this time, instead of bringing a portal to mind, you're invited to simply take your focus deeper into your physical self. Breathe deeply, and allow your attention to follow the breath, until you feel settled in your own skin, and centred in your core. When you have found a place of stillness and groundedness, and you feel ready and receptive, you can invite your new friend to come and join you in your body.

How this feels will likely be different for each of you. My erotic ally tends to feel like it's wriggling up my spine and over my skull initially, while my beloved describes the sensation of being "put on" from the inside like a coat, and being filled up and stretched out. I encourage you to listen to what is happening in your body, to allow your new friend to arrive without censoring the impulses that come with that, and to give yourself permission to move and shift your body and your breath as feels necessary, in order for them to more fully inhabit you.

What you do once the two of you have found a way to coexist in your skin is up to you. If you're alone, allow your friend to explore your physical environs as they wish. Find ways to enjoy being in physical form together. This may look like a fresh take on self-pleasuring, or something more playful than sensuous. They may have advice to offer you, and they will likely have some attributes to lend you that you could use to your advantage.

If you're with a lover—hopefully someone willing to explore the above exercise as well—then take your time coming back to the space you're in, and allowing your new friend to adjust to your body and environment, as you to adjust to them. When you're ready, make eye contact with your beloved, and see what manner of creature is peering out of their eyes. Allow your new friends to greet each other, and explore, slowly, with great attention to your inner guide, how they wish to interact, and, hopefully, play together. Let this be within both your consent and the consent of your new friend—don't force either of you.

When your play is over, remember to thank your ally, and release them, knowing you can reconnect with one another, in your world or theirs, anytime you wish. Sitting or lying on the ground, breathe and imagine that with each exhale you release your ally into the Earth below, and with each inhale you invite yourself more fully into your body.

∿

With a little practise, it is likely that your relationship with your ally will become more fluid. As my beloved says, the more we travel to Them, and the more we invite Them to visit us, the shorter the distance between us becomes. You may find you can call upon them in a moment when you feel the need for those qualities that enhance your capacity for pleasure or presence or play—or simply because you're experiencing something you'd like to share with them. Treat them with the honour and respect they deserve, make time to nurture your connection with them, and know that you can look to them for guidance at those times when love-making feels too scary, or too much like hard work.

Relating to Nature

We're now going to shift our focus away from the ways in which the natural world can be an ally in our erotic explorations and expansions, and toward the ways in which our relational and sexual selves can make us better allies for our planet.

Practical Magic: *It's the last night of the retreat I've been assisting on. As per tradition, we're wrapping up the week with a play party. It's been a sexy, playful, profoundly queer, and thoroughly magical evening. Since we're in a stunning location in the Swedish woodland at midsummer, I've promised an ecowank as the final event of the night. Wrapped in blankets, alternately giggling and grumbling, the group follows me out onto the grass. It's ten or eleven at night, but the midnight sun is still giving the impression of a twilit evening. We arrange ourselves on blankets in a circle round the midsummer pole we erected earlier in the week. I hand out the lube, and state the intention: to self-pleasure, whatever that means for each of us, and to offer the resulting orgasmic energy to the ground. If we want to add in a circular breath with the Earth, so much the better.*

I've loved ecowanks since my colleague Belle and I ran one at the UK's first queer sacred sexuality festival four years before this story takes place. Their premise is so simple, and yet they are such inexplicably magical and ecstatic happenings. Sure enough, pretty soon we're all breathing in time with one another, our sighs and giggles rising and falling in unison. Our collective pleasure moves in waves. A few of us will climax, and the effects ripple round the circle, a murmuration of breath quickening in sympathy. Then there is a lull, until someone else starts to sigh a little louder, and we're off again. We finish with a collective Clench and Hold (from the Genital- and Gender-Free Orgasm you'll be meeting in the next chapter) which catapults the group into a cacophony of ecstatic moans and laughter.

~

While my colleagues and I initially conceived of ecowanks as a way to commune with nature, and to receive stimulus from our exquisite surroundings, I've now added the intention of giving the energy raised back to the Earth in an act of love and gratitude. This has meant that, as well as being ecstatic erotic community experiences, they have also become a way to directly link the erotic and the ecological. The ritual itself acknowledges that our pleasure is supported by the Earth below us, which carries and nourishes the bodies and minds from which we derive pleasure, and which brings us into being through a sexual act. As a ritualist, I believe that there's intrinsic value in offering the Earth our love in the form of a wave of orgasmic energy. But even if I'm wrong about that, in holding an ecowank, I'm still facilitating a reconnection with the natural world. By inviting those participating into an intimate relationship with the Earth, by reminding them of the connection between the Earth's existence and their pleasure and well-being, I hope to remind them to treat our planet accordingly.

⇒ PLAYTIME ⇐
What's Your Eco-relating Style?

We're all intimately connected to this planet. A vital part of us moving forward sustainably is the realisation that we're not separate parasitical entities indefinitely feeding off the Earth, but rather that we're part of one big orgasmic organism. There are no real lines between us and our planet. At no point are we not reliant on gravity, breathing oxygen, and using materials harvested from the Earth. We need to see through the illusion of the independent individual that our capitalist culture thrives off, and become aware of our interconnectedness. We are never not in relationship to our planet.

So what's your relationship style when it comes to that connection?

How attentive a partner are you to our planet?

How much time do you make for that relationship?

What acts of service or gifts do you bring to our earthly beloved?

How much do you allow that relationship into your daily life?

For example, I would say my current relationship style is a little too much conversation, and not enough action. I can talk about the importance of caring for our planet, but I struggle to find time amidst a multitude of different projects to actually go out into nature and spend some quality time there. I'm not as attentive as I'd like to be, and I'm not making as much time for the relationship as I want. At the same time, I make sure we have regular conversations as a household about how we can raise our environmental game, which means that we have, for example, reduced our plastic waste so much that we only fill a bin bag once every three months or so. So we're doing pretty well in terms of incorporating that relationship into our daily lives. And because I talk about those strategies to others, I have inspired other people to adopt some of them as well.

Now ask yourself:

What kind of partner would you like to be to our planet? If you were the Earth, how would you like to be treated?

What are your top love languages when it comes to giving, and how could you offer those to this particular beloved?

For example, I would like to be more attentive to the land around me, and spend more quality time replenishing, learning, and volunteering there. If I were the Earth, I think I'd like to be listened to more carefully, in all the little and large ways I'm crying out for help, so I guess I want to pay more attention to those cries as they reach me, as painful as it can be to do so. And, as I'm pretty good at giving words, I could raise my game in terms of my online activism, and sharing inspiration for more ethical living with others.

Of course, listening to the calls for aid from the Earth, from the people and creatures and landscapes that populate the surface of our planet, can be profoundly overwhelming. When we turn toward our Ecological Grief, it can be hard to know how to sit with the emotions it stirs in us, let alone how to respond. We can apply the same practices of breath and attention to this grief that seems to come from outside of us that we applied to other forms of grief in earlier chapters. By allowing it to crack us open, by fully welcoming and embodying it, by treating it as a treasured guest bringing valuable information, we let that grief move through us, and move us to action. As author and environmental activist Joanna Macy says: "Our experience of pain for the world springs from our connectivity with all beings, from which also arise our powers to act on their behalf. When we deny or repress our pain for the world, or treat it as a private pathology, our power to take part in the self-healing of our world is diminished.[40]

But what are our options for action? What can we do besides shutting back down in the face of all that we see happening through our current wide-screen view of our world?

One way to answer this is what I think of as "tending our patch." Our patch is the place where our skillset, biases, and passions meet the needs of the world. It's the cottage garden of activism. Just as no one person can try to grow all vegetables and fruits in their own garden, and must instead play to their strengths, to the way their garden is positioned in relation to the sun and the quality of its soil—so we cannot any one of us take on all the woes of the world. We need to pick our battles, and the best way to do this is play to our existing passions and skill set.

In tending our patch, we make creative use of our personal biases, and allow the things that already move us to do so for the benefit of our environment. The anti-fracking movement in the UK called the Nanas springs to mind: a group of grandmothers from diverse backgrounds and walks of life who became activists in response to the impact of fracking on their local villages, and in defence of the environment in which they were raising their children and grandchildren. Instead of leaving what needs to be done to others more radical than themselves, they take over fracking sites with dusters and cake stands, and use their standing with their local communities to start conversations and stir up trouble. In short, they allow things they already cared about to move them into more active relationship with their environment, and utilise their existing skills, tools, and privilege to make change.

⇒ PLAYTIME ⇐
Tending Your Patch

Think of five skills you possess that you can call upon with ease, and perhaps that you wish you were getting to do more of than you are. Make a note of them.

---

40. Macy, *Coming Back to Life*, 66.

Then think about the moments when you have felt cracked open by the pain of the world. For me, it's the animal cruelty I witnessed growing up. For my best friend, it's the growing homeless population in her city, which reflects her own experiences of homelessness as a teenager. How are you moved by the call of the world around you? Again, make some notes.

Now take a look at your two sets of notes, and think about how they might fit together. Got admin skills? Most charities these days have email addresses and websites as well as phone lines that need administrating. Want to spend more time outdoors? Start a litter picking scheme. Really good with kids? Many conservation projects host family events that need staff capable of engaging children in their efforts.

Where does what comes easily to you meet what the world needs? That could be your mission, should you choose to accept it.

~

Finding ways to integrate nature into our relational and erotic lives nurtures our awareness of the intimacy that extends beyond us and our lovers: the intimacy we share with our planet. It also helps us to refuel, to draw nourishment from that intimacy that replenishes our resources. And it reminds us to share our lives, and our aliveness, with the Earth. Thus, it supports not only our individual eroticism, but also our capacity to tend to that wider relationship, to tend our patch, to take action.

Some further ideas for including the natural world in your erotic explorations include the following:

- Breath and imagination exercises, like Sun Breathing, like the one described in the memory above, like reaching our roots down into the Earth to build our sexual energy
- Doing the Heart/Heart or Heart-Sex Breath Circuit with the Earth, or with a particular natural phenomenon such as a rock formation or a tree (check in first: Does it feel like you have consent from the entity in question?)
- Using natural ingredients in your play: Simulating the senses with objects from the natural world as we did in the Ecosensual Awakening; caressing

your beloveds with leaves, fallen feathers, catkins, petals; using bunches of stinging nettles or willow in your impact play

- Having sex in sunlight, in the rain, on the earth, against a tree, somewhere you can see the sky
- Bringing the natural world into the space where you usually have sex—rocks, flowers, fragrant greenery; bring the elements to your bedside table—vessels of water, of sand, of pebbles polished by the sea
- Dedicating the energy and pleasure from your lovemaking to the Earth; imagining it flowing into the ground below you from your hands, or your spine, or your feet

Heart/Heart Circuit Breathing with beings in the natural world

One of my favourite ways of basking in that planetary intimacy is the aforementioned ecowank. An ecowank is, quite simply, intentional self-pleasuring in nature, where the focus is the connection between you and the natural world.

Solo ecowanks can be combined beautifully with any of the breath, energy, and ecosensual stimulation ideas listed earlier. I like to make them into little rituals, and begin by setting an intention for what I wish to receive, and what I wish to give back. Sometimes, my focus will be on something I wish to call into my own life, but I'll offer the energy raised to the Earth at the end of my ritual; sometimes, my focus is on a gift I wish for the Earth, with a side helping of pleasure for me.

Group ecowanks benefit from a stated intention and an agreed structure as well. Decide why you are doing this; whether it will simply consist of whatever self-pleasuring means to each person, or whether you will also invite a particular breath or visualisation or activity; decide on practical considerations like location, length of time, and supplies; and establish any boundaries that need to be put in place to keep the group and the environment safe. All these things will help your wank run smoothly. That being said, ecowanks do not require a lot of detail to be powerful and pleasurable experiences. Their structure can be very simple, and yet there is extraordinary sweetness, sexiness, and a sense of community in every one.

And remember: if there's ever a time when taking time to receive, surrender, and simply be can lead to particularly beautiful experiences, it's at the end of an ecowank. Make sure you factor in time to lie back, look at the sky, and give thanks for your place on this Earth.

~

In this last chapter, I've invited you to expand your experience of intimacy to include the natural world around you. My wish for you is that you leave it having planted the seeds of a more conscious and more mutual relationship with our planet, and with the family of things without which we could not exist, or taste pleasure. Having dipped your toes into the possibility of intimacies with the manifest world, I invite you to take a further leap of faith, and journey with me now into intimacy with the unseen …

Chapter 10

Making Love with God

Dear reader, it's time. We're going there. Here comes the God bit. You don't have to read it of course, but I hope that you will. Because I am writing this—and in doing so realising a lifelong dream planted by my father when I was four or five years old—because of a relationship: a relationship I have been in since my early teens. That relationship has seen me tenderly through every tough time since then, as well as through processing the ones that came before; it has lifted me out of abuse, poverty, and pain; and it has carried me into some truly extraordinary, ecstatic, and life-expanding situations and experiences.

There are a number of moments I could trace it back to—several of them involving books, as it happens: paper portals of permission to love and be loved by the cosmos. I would love for this book to be such a portal. The moment that stands out to me when I look back now goes something like this:

Practical Magic: *It had been another rough day. My teenage years were not particularly kind, rich with xenophobic bullying and parenting that was based on the belief that what didn't kill me would make me stronger. Lying close to the ceiling in my bunkbed, I was crying and praying for change.*

In my mind's eye, my guardian angel appeared. He took me by the hand, and led me into a forest. It was a night-time landscape, but things twinkled in the trees, and there was a sense of anticipation in the air. He drew me into a clearing, and standing there were The Lord and Lady (forgive the gender-normativity of my thirteen-year-old pantheon—I was reading a lot of books on Wicca).

He was in the background, beautiful, broad and tall, the antlers on his head adding another couple of feet to his already substantial height. He was smiling, and warmth radiated from him like sunshine. She was in the foreground, little nut-brown hands outstretched to welcome me. Her fingers ended in neat, black claws that might have belonged to some small woodland creature, as might the eyes twinkling in her face. She took me into her arms and held me as I cried. I could not recall ever having felt so loved.

That experience of being held and loved so completely, so incomprehensibly, so unconditionally—that experience has inspired my work, my ministry, and my relating ever since. That experience is at the heart of what I am trying to facilitate for others in all that I do—and I want to emphasise that it is an experience, not a belief system. I'm not interested in the language or imagery you attach to that experience; I don't need you to see my stardusted Goddess, the Friend in all his antlered glory, or my wild or winged beloveds. I'm simply interested in creating spaces and sharing practices that might allow you to have that love experience. Perhaps it's an experience you've already gotten a taste of in some of the practices threaded through this book. The practices that follow are designed to facilitate it more specifically.

There are a lot of reasons that I cannot, will not, *shan't* separate out the god stuff from the rest of this work. The fact that, for me, sex has been a path to transcendence from my first kiss, and the fact that it is where so many of the practices mentioned in this book take me, are certainly high on that list. But the main reason I'm including this chapter is relationship. I know what it is to believe and to behave as though I'm in this on my own. I know how I feel, and I know how my life unfolds, when I get stuck in that place. And I know the transformation returning to relationship creates in me, and in my life. I know what it is to be trying to do it all by myself, and I know what it is to be working in partnership with something infinitely more than the self I am familiar with. The former option is exhausting, debilitating, stressful, and disconnecting—and I'm so thankful that I have an alternative in the latter.

That is what I'd like to offer you here. An alternative way to get out of bed in the morning.

∼

Before I move on then, let me say a little about my use of the G-word. I use this word primarily for two reasons. First, because it's a simple single syllable that is nonetheless imminently and eminently recognisable to the majority of people in our culture as a shorthand for divinity. Secondly, because I have a linguistic fetish: I like to take words that have been used to belittle, shame, and degrade us—especially in relation to our sexuality—and re-appropriate them for use in sexually empowering contexts.

It's not the language I use in relationship with my own sense of divinity. My primary deity can be traced back to those first experiences of unconditional of love, so I will tend to use terms of endearment like My Lady, mama, or Goddess. And it's not a language I require you to use in order to do this work. Any time I use the G-word, think of it as an open parenthesis into which you are welcome to insert your own descriptor for that experience of being loved.

Unconditional love

What follow are some of my favourite ways to access that experience.

⇒ PLAYTIME ⇐
Let Yourself Be Loved

Get comfortable.

Begin to take some full, deep, easeful breaths.

With each breath in, invite yourself into your present body, in this present moment.

With each breath out, let go of anything that is coming between you, your body, and this moment.

Breathe.

Notice what's up for you, what's worrying and scurrying its way around your mind.

Acknowledge it. Thank it for all its hard work. Then give it some breath, and feel it slowly soften, allowing you to sink deeper into your body with the breath.

Breathe.

Notice what you're feeling in this moment. Welcome it with kindness. Give it breath, and feel it soften, little by little, allowing you to follow your breath deeper into your body.

Breathe.

Notice what's happening in your body in this moment. Give your body a little more permission to be here, to be soft, to be supported.

Breathe.

Breath by breath, find your way to a still, quiet place within.

Breath by breath, settle into that still space, that inner temple.

Breath by breath, let the stillness of that place expand to fill your body, your senses, your experience.

Breathe.

Breathe.

Breathe.

Sit in this body, in this moment, in that still, quiet space within.

Whisper: Yes

And let God love you.

$\sim$

After a little practise, you may find that you can create a shorthand for this practice to reconnect you to that experience of being loved in your daily life. Taking a moment, a few deep breaths, and whispering "Yes" can take me there these days—even here, in the busy cafe in a coach station where I'm sitting after missing my coach, and writing this to you.

$\sim$

For those of you who are more visual, taking a journey like the one I took as a teenager all those years ago might be a more effective way to kindle connection with your own sense of divinity.

At the time, I was working fairly extensively with a visual representation of my inner landscape. This was an imaginary landscape where I would go in my mind's eye, which was populated by various guides and guardians, and aspects of myself. I would start on the same path, and invariably be led to where I needed to go.

Since then, I've also encountered the neo-shamanic map of other realms, which divides them into Middle World, Upper World, and Lower World. We visited the Lower World earlier to connect with an erotic ally, since this is the place associated with the Earth, the elements, and our more physical, carnal selves. The Middle World is akin to our own world. And the Upper World is the place we are likely to encounter deities, angels, and entities more connected with the spiritual aspect of ourselves and the cosmos.

So I'm going to give you two ways to do this, as I suspect each one will speak to and provide a more accessible route to different readers. And if you're getting impatient with all this breath and visualisation stuff, don't worry—we'll be doing this with pleasure in just a bit!

⇒ PLAYTIME ⇐
Meeting the Gods I—Into the Innerworld

Get comfortable somewhere you can be still for twenty to forty minutes without falling asleep if you close your eyes. Make sure you will be undisturbed. If you feel so drawn take a moment to create the space, and set your intention. The latter should be your own version of "I intend to meet an unconditionally loving deity/the god of my understanding." Allow yourself to relax into the space you're in, and, when you're ready, begin to take some full, conscious breaths.

Let go of your environment, and let your awareness follow the breath into the body. If you need to take a moment to breathe your way through any thoughts or feelings floating around on the surface, do so—until your awareness has settled into the warm, welcoming darkness of your body.

In that darkness, allow a door to take shape in front of you. Get curious, notice what its shape and colour, its texture and materials are. When you can see it fairly clearly, and you feel ready, open the door, and enter your inner landscape.

I don't know what you will find here. You might find yourself in a forest or a field, a street or a building, on top of a mountain, at the bottom of the ocean, or in an entirely fantastical new world. Step through the door, and get curious. Take the time to take in your surroundings. When you're ready, invite a guide to come and join you, and take you to meet the Divine being you've come here to meet. Your guide may take the form of a creature you're familiar with from our world, or a magical being from another. Greet it, have a conversation if you wish, and then allow it to lead you to meet the being you came here to meet.

The rest is up to you. Know that you are always in control, and can ask for things to be different, or stop your travels at any time. As much as possible, allow things to arise spontaneously, let yourself be surprised, and trust the process. When your encounter is complete, come back to the place you started from in your inner landscape, and thank your guide. Slowly, breathfully, with whatever small movements and stretches you need, find your way back into the space you're sitting in. Wriggle fingers and toes, feel the contact between you and the space, make sure you feel fully back in your body. Open your eyes last of all.

⇒ PLAYTIME ⇐
Meeting the Gods II—Into the Otherworld

As above, get comfortable somewhere you can be still for twenty to forty minutes without falling asleep if you close your eyes. Make sure you will be undisturbed. If you feel so drawn take a moment to create the space. Find a suitable drumming track to "ride" on your journey.

Choose a doorway, or something that could serve as a doorway, that you're familiar with from this world to be your portal into another. This could be a tree, a path or alleyway you've never taken but often wondered where it leads, a body of water, or a garden gate from your childhood. Make sure it's something you can visualise fairly clearly, that feels like it might have magical potential.

Set your intention—a single sentence along the lines of "I am journeying to meet the god of my understanding/a loving divinity."

Allow yourself to relax into the space you're in. Put on the drumming track you've chosen, and begin to take some full, conscious breaths. When you're feeling like you have managed to let go of your surroundings a little and follow your breath into your body, visualise your portal. Remind yourself of your intention. And then head on in.

You may feel like travelling downward as we did in the erotic ally exercise, or you may be guided to travel upward. Just see where you are drawn to go. You may find an ally appears to you early on, or you may decide you'd like to ask that one appear to guide you on your way—in which case, allow them to show you. Release your expectations, trust what arises, allow yourself to be surprised, and know that you are always in consent. If something doesn't feel right you can bring the encounter to a close.

When the experience feels complete, remember to come back the way you came in, thank your guide if one appeared, and exit through your portal. Take your time coming back into your body—take deeper breaths, feel your body move with the breath, wiggle your fingers and toes and stretch your limbs and spine, become aware of your contact with the space you're in. Only open your eyes when you feel like you're back where you started.

The subtle differences in the exercises above speak to some of the different ways we can think about divinity, ranging from beings from other worlds to aspects of our deep mind. Personally, I don't have any particular attachment to how you conceptualise any of the experiences you have as a result of the exercises above, or other experiences like them. What I'm interested in is whether those experiences give you access to a relationship that supports, inspires, and enriches you. I am inclined to answer questions such as "is it still god if I seem to access it through my imagination?" with other questions like "does it bring you a sense of peace, well-being, or, as Julia Cameron so eloquently puts it, Good Orderly Direction? [41] If yes, does it matter?"

As you may have noticed by now, I believe it's possible to find divinity in all manner of places, including ourselves, other people, and the natural world around us. My only caution to anyone who elects to look for the Divine solely in one of those places, perhaps solely in the one that feels most comfortable, would be to beware of not leaving any space for grace. I define grace as the love that finds me—not in those times and places where I am comfortable, where I feel aligned, where I am in flow, but in those moments when I'm at sea, when I am exhausted and stretched thin, when I feel broken or lesser or lost. And in my experience, grace enters in unexpected, unlooked for, unprecedented ways. So find god where you will—and also prepare for

41. Cameron, *The Artist's Way*, 3.

the extraordinary. Prepare for the Divine to be so much more wily and wonderful than you expected. Prepare for grace.

Transcendent pleasures

All right. You've been so terribly patient. So let's look at some of the ways we can encounter divinity through pleasure, and welcome the Divine into the erotic. Since most of us have forgotten that these things are so intimately interconnected, it can be helpful to set out with the explicit intention of bringing them together.

⇾PLAYTIME⇽
The Genital- and Gender-Free Orgasm

My gateway drug into all things sex magical has been the work of Barbara Carrellas, whom I have referred to a number of times throughout this book. It is from Barbara that I inherited my obsession with breath, and the breath practice at the core of her work is one she calls the Breath and Energy orgasm.[42] For me, and for countless other people, this practice has provided a direct experience of the correlation between the erotic and the transcendent. As an experience it can also be healing, cathartic, deeply emotional, or profoundly peaceful. As a practice, it can open doors to full body sensation and full being ecstasy.

It's also groovy because it requires no touch, no partner, no particular physical position or activity—it only requires the breath, and a willing imagination.

At its bare bones, the practice involves filling up the body with breath and energy, starting from the base, the perineum, or the root chakra, depending on what map you want to use, and moving up the body in stages. You can build energy using deep, full breaths (the Energising Breath is good for this one)—as well as the following:

• Sound, e.g., sighing, moaning
• Movement, e.g., rocking your pelvis, moving your hands up the body to guide the energy
• PC squeezes, which are squeezes of the pubococcygeus muscle: the muscle you might squeeze to stop the flow of urine, or contract during orgasm

---

42. Carrellas, *Urban Tantra*, 87.

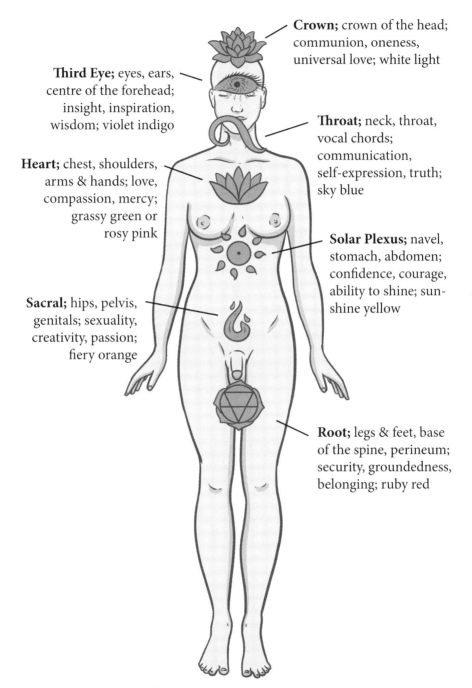

Crown; crown of the head; communion, oneness, universal love; white light

Third Eye; eyes, ears, centre of the forehead; insight, inspiration, wisdom; violet indigo

Throat; neck, throat, vocal chords; communication, self-expression, truth; sky blue

Heart; chest, shoulders, arms & hands; love, compassion, mercy; grassy green or rosy pink

Solar Plexus; navel, stomach, abdomen; confidence, courage, ability to shine; sunshine yellow

Sacral; hips, pelvis, genitals; sexuality, creativity, passion; fiery orange

Root; legs & feet, base of the spine, perineum; security, groundedness, belonging; ruby red

The body's energy centres

To do the practice, get comfortable, preferably lying down, with your feet flat on the floor and knees bent, so that you can move your pelvis as you breathe. Rhythmic music in the background can be useful. I like to imagine a root dropping down from the base of my spine into the centre of the Earth, like a tap root I can draw energy from. Once I've dropped my root down, I start by imagining deep red energy flowing up from the Earth and into the base of my spine, into my pelvis and hips. I use my breath and imagination to fill up that part of my body with red light, or heat, or pulsing—however visualising that energy works best. After a few minutes, when that part of my body feels full of energy, I'll imagine drawing orange energy up from that root into my genitals and belly, and so on, as per the illustration on the previous page.

If you let your breathing build, and pay attention to the energy flowing round your body, there may come a point where it feels like the energy is starting to flow upward of its own accord, rather than being something you need to do or push. You may notice your movements or sounds changing or accelerating as you move up the body. Let that happen, and feel free to build on it.

When you reach the crown, and once this too feels nice and energised, take thirty fuller, faster breaths—this is where that Breath of Fire comes in handy again. Then take three deep breaths. On the third deep breath, breathe in, and then hold the breath and clench all the muscles in your body (especially those around your genitals, your fists, and your face if you can). Wait for fifteen to thirty seconds, and then release the breath (this part of the practice is referred to by Barbara as the Clench and Hold, and is a potent magical alternative to orgasm).

Then comes the hard part: do nothing. Just breathe, notice the sensations in your body, and let yourself be.

You'll notice that this practice, with its energy raising, release, and surrender sections, lends itself very well to the sex magic model we've been looking at thus far.

As it's best approached with minimal expectations, an open mind, and a shit ton of curiosity (and breath!), I don't want to say too much more about what you might expect to experience as a result of giving this practice a go. But I do want to strongly encourage you to give it a go. And if, as I did initially, you don't find it really clicks when you try it alone, see if you can find a workshop to try it in. It's quite something experienced in a group setting! See the Resource section for links to workshops run by Barbara, and by me, that include this practice.

Messiness Alert!

Like other exercises that place a lot of breath and awareness in the body, the Genital- and Gender-Free Orgasm can bring us into contact with feelings or facets of ourselves we've been avoiding. When this happens, your only job is to keep breathing. If you need to, remember that energy is very flexible stuff; if a particular knot is too tight to undo in the moment, let the energy flow around it.

Sacred self-pleasure revisited

In the Making Love with Self section, we explored some of the ways in which we can bring our attention and our love back to our bodies, and touched on the possibility of also inviting the love of something greater to come in and hold us in our pleasure. I'm now going to offer some more explicit ways to invite the Divine into your masturbation adventures. It is my hope that you will discover that your pleasure is not just "allowed," it's not just "OK" in the eyes of that unconditionally loving presence—it's actively welcome, supported, and celebrated by the cosmos!

Leaning into Big Love

Before beginning to self-pleasure, take some time to breathe yourself into your body. Gradually follow the breath with your attention, through the layers of doubts and to-do lists in the mind, breathing yourself down into the heart. Initially just take some time to notice how your heart is feeling. Place a hand on the part of your body where you feel it to be, and get curious and compassionate with what's there. Whatever is there, offer it your breath, and make it welcome. When you feel more connected to your own heart, imagine that your heart is cradled in a much greater heart, like a leaf floating on an ocean of unconditional love. Let yourself lean back and float on that ocean. Say yes to that greater love that is available for you, and breathe it into your own heart. When you breathe out, let it flow round the rest of your body. If you find the prospect of letting yourself be loved a challenging one, this doesn't need to become another thing to "get right." Set yourself a smaller goal for now, and see if you can let that love just an inch or two under your skin, or just a little way into your heart. When you're feeling cradled, when you have taken in as much as you can of your own lovedness, begin to self-pleasure. Keep coming back to breathing in that greater love as you do so, noticing that it is available to you unconditionally, and allowing it to support you in building the pleasure and energy in your body with your breath. Let that take you where it will.

Receptive breath magic

Another way to include divine love in your self-pleasure practices is using the Heart/Sex Circuit Breath, very much as we did with the Sun Breathing. You can use this to simply receive love, energy, and support from the cosmos or your deities—or you can use it to welcome more of a particular quality, feeling, or experience into your body. For example, you might self-pleasure whilst breathing in through the sex, and welcoming divine love into your body, and breathing out through the heart and letting it spread through your system and back to your sex. Or, if you were working on cultivating a sense of your own right to pleasure, or inviting more joy into your life, or feeling more abundant, you could request that from that same universe/deity. Then, you could either breathe that in through your sex and out through your heart into your body, or in through your heart, and out through your sex into your life. Here, you are using your pleasure to open you up to the gifts life holds for you, and imagining how those might feel so that your system starts to adjust to them in this open and receptive state. This practice works well for creating shifts in yourself that take time, and integrating those changes in an enjoyable way.

Aspecting/visiting with your erotic ally

If big cosmic deities are not your thing, but when you embarked on any of the "journeying" adventures earlier in this section you did encounter an ally who feels like they are available to support you with your erotic explorations, try inviting them to join you in your self-pleasuring. You can do this either by inviting them into your body, or visiting them through an erotic journey or fantasy.

To do the former, before you begin, get comfortable, close your eyes, and breathe until you feel centred in the warm, welcoming darkness of your body. Then invite your ally to join you there, just as you did in the Erotic Shapeshifting exercise earlier. Take the time to let them take up space in you, to adapt to their shape and presence in your body. Then, see what pleasure you might enjoy together. When that feels complete, thank them, and take the time to release them from your body—perhaps by exhaling them into the Earth, and inhaling your own awareness back into your body.

You can also meet your ally in a fantasy world, or breathe your way back to that door to your inner landscape and meet them there. Find out what happens when you bring pleasure into your connection; see how your forms want to move together or co-create in your mind's eye; explore how this ally can inspire or support or contribute to your pleasure. Remember to take the time to give thanks, return to this reality, and get grounded when you're done.

Out into the cosmos

Practical Magic: *It's the final morning of our weekend away together in Fox Cottage. Sunbeams are wriggling in through the honeysuckle around the small window and caressing the bedsheets. I'm breathing them in, along with the sensations from your tongue running between my legs. I'm not sure how long we've been here for. We've entered some timeless place woven from sunlight and sensation, and I've already traversed a number of small crests of breath, energy, and emotion. When I finally climax, the sunbeams I've been breathing in seem to disperse through my body in waves of pleasure, and then melt outward through my skin, carrying my awareness with them. I travel into the walls of the cottage around us, so cool and thick. Then I'm the honeysuckle climbing the wall outside, basking in the heat. I float over the garden on the sunlight, feeling the startling green of the grass, the hum of the rose bushes, the warm presence of the neighbour's cat in his favourite spot in the flower bed. I feel for the kite that was circling above the garden the day before—I rather fancy flying with a kite—but it's not there ... so eventually I find my way back into the room, breathe myself back into my skin, and settle* *for gazing at you in wonder instead, as you describe how you felt my orgasm crashing through you like a wave…*

The previous exercises are primarily focused on inviting something in during pleasure experiences. However, practices like the Genital- and Gender-Free Orgasm have shown me that orgasm—and other peak erotic experiences—can be ejections of consciousness as well as injections of consciousness. This is to say that they don't just give us ways to be more in our bodies, and to commune with divinity therein; they also give us ways to fly. If we allow them to, if we open our lungs and our minds, they can take us deep into the Earth, into the bodies of our lovers, out into the stars, or into God/dess. I share the story above to give you a taste of what I'm talking about, as it can be hard to pin down the precise ingredients for journeys such as these. Again, breath, imagination, intention, and a willing companion—whether that's yourself or someone else—are likely to be your best allies on the journey. Or, in the words of Sir Terry Pratchett, "open your eyes, and then open your eyes again."[43] Open your eyes in pleasure—look within, and look without—and then look without from within, and see what the universe has been waiting to show you.

Greeting the gods together

All of the above can be adapted for two or more partners in pleasure. Here are some extra tips for finding transcendence in company:

Bring your respective pantheons, find a shared intention

When embarking on erotic journeys with transcendental intent together, it's worth finding a balance between welcoming each person's practices and beliefs, and agreeing on a shared intention for your adventures. Everyone involved will have something to contribute to the experience, and—if you're hoping to have a divine time—one way to achieve that is to let everyone involved invoke their own allies, deities, or at least the qualities they hope will be present (e.g., love, safety, bliss). At the same time, it's worth taking the time to agree on an intention for the experience that everyone can get behind. As we've discussed before, intentions have a life of their own, and can

---

43. Pratchett, *A Hat Full of Sky*, 57.

take us to unexpectedly and inexplicably magical places. The same is true of our unseen friends. Welcoming both into your love-making is an excellent way to create space for the sacred between you.

Come with an open heart, commit to the flow

It's hard to open to the unseen when we're being closed with the seen. By this I mean that shared transcendent experiences rely on those involved being open enough with one another to achieve three things: to clear anything from the space between them that needs to be said in order for them to make magic together; to get on the same page regarding the intention of the experience as above; and to feel the flow between them, and follow it into the magic.

Cultivating the openness, presence, and trust to be able to listen to what is unfolding in the space between you, instead of succumbing to the temptation to try and perform, is key to erotic transcendence. Committing to listening to, finding, and following that flow in each moment is what will take you into uncharted, and potentially ecstatic, territory. Staying open to communicating with each other about what you're feeling and where the flow is taking you is a vital part of getting to that territory together, co-creatively and consensually.

Create the container, leave space for the magic to happen

Another balance that needs to be struck when seeking those moments of erotic ecstasy in company is creating a container that's safe and sacred enough for everyone involved to open to the possibility of something magical taking place, whilst also leaving enough space for the magic to unfold. Revelation is synonymous with surprise for a reason: it is, by its very nature, unexpected. Which is why we need to learn to slow down, to breathe, to listen, to follow the flow—because if we fill every moment with passion and sensation, we leave no space for wonder.

∼

As I explained earlier in this chapter, one of my deepest wishes for this book is that it be a portal for you, a doorway into deeper intimacy—not just with yourself and other people, but with the world beyond and the spirit within.

I hope that you will be able to allow this work to surprise you, and that something from this chapter has surprised you with the experience of a new kind of relationship—a more present, constant intimacy that you can draw on to feel that you are loved, and to transform your life. And it is that life that we will be getting creative with next, as we look at how ritual practices and principles can be the tools from which we build a life we love to live.

Chapter 11

Making Love with Life

In this final section, we're going to look at how the principles of magic we've been exploring can transform our lives—not only through specific rituals, but day to day.

I use the phrase Making Love with God in my work not just to hint at the practices we explored in the previous section, but also because of the realisation that I needed to move away from reacting to life, and toward co-creating my life with God/dess. Thus, Making Love with God also speaks to striving to create—with love, kindness, and intention, and in collaboration with the world around me and the gods of my understanding.

One thing magic teaches us is that we're not in this alone. It can show us that we have greater agency, and therefore perhaps greater responsibility, than we know. But it also shows us that life is not "all on us." To live magically is to do what is ours to do in each moment, and to bring our intention, presence, and energy to it—knowing that there comes a point when it's not our job anymore. There comes a point when we must hand our efforts over to something else, and step back. When we must heed the mirror of the natural world, and take shelter, and rest, withdrawing into our fertile selves so that new seeds may be planted before we rush headlong into reaping again. And we must heed the call of our bodies—of our hearts and our spirits and our genitals—and indulge in the radical and consensual acts of pleasure, love, and creativity that make our lives worth living.

In short, magic teaches us about the bothness of things. It can show us how to hold the paradox that is living. It gives us a way to practice pouring our intention, presence, and energy into any given moment or activity—while also teaching us to let go, surrender, and trust that we are being carried toward our desire.

At a time when the world is veering toward polarisation, it's worth remembering how much of living and loving are made up of paradoxes such as these, and looking to the fundamentals of magic for ways to embrace paradox as the path.

Magical living

Creating Space

The first act of magic is to consciously and clearly delineate a piece of space and time, and to dedicate it to a purpose. In this simple act lies an invitation to choose, to take a stand on how we wish to spend our energy in a given moment, rather than being pulled hither and thither by to-do lists, obligations, or the allure of multitasking. Sometimes the things we value require us to get fully present with them to the exclusion of all else. This is particularly true of those things that our culture tends to devalue, but which happen to make life worth living—e.g., relating, parenting, creating, acts of pleasure and self-care.

If you're not in the habit of being choiceful with your time, find a way to practice. Pick a short daily practice, or a weekly date with yourself, and carve out time and space that is dedicated to your chosen activity and intention, and devoid of distraction.

You can also experiment with being more mindful with the things that matter to you. Whether this is stopping everything else for the ten minutes it takes your child, partner, or flat-mate to tell you about their day, or switching screens and comms off early for the evening to focus on reconnecting with yourself or your beloved—find out how it is to do only the thing that means the most to you in the moment. Experts in fields ranging from meditation to time-management all suggest that bringing all of yourself to one activity or experience at a time greatly enhances both pleasure and productivity. Explore how fully you can open yourself to that single experience, and gift it and you with your presence, attention, and love.

Invocation

The second act of magic is to ask for help. This is another invitation that runs counter to our current cultural habits in the West.

Capitalism defines success as private ownership. Thus it encourages us to go it alone, and relies on us conflating comfort, belonging, even love, with accrued stuff. Magic, on the other hand, suggests that anything important enough to do ritual for is going to be something we'll be needing assistance with—because "going it alone" is setting ourselves up to fail, and why would we do that with the things that matter?

Your life matters. Your dreams matter. Your pleasure matters. Your heart matters. Your labour matters. The changes you are longing to make matter. You matter. Don't try and hold all these precious and important things by yourself. Reach out.

For some of you, this may be as much an invitation to reach out to other people, to lean into your relationships or communities a little more, or to go in search of new collaborators in life, creativity, and pleasure, as it is an invitation to call upon the unseen. You know who you are. If you find it blisteringly diffi-cult to ask for help, or you can't imagine why you would need it, or you're just too busy giving it to others to get round to asking for some for you, then yes, by all means, invoke the internal, elemental, and divine support you need. But also, please know there are people out there who want to love you. Let them in.

For those of you who have spent a lifetime reaching for validation, affir-mation, and support from outside of yourself, reaching out in this instance may look more like reaching in. It might look like including your child self, or invoking your wise self, or inviting your empowered self to join you on your quests. It might mean building relationships with your natural environ-ment, with the Earth below and the sky above: relationships that remind you that you are welcome in this world. Or it might involve building relationships with an unseen support network of allies or ancestors, relationships that re-mind you that you are not alone, or relationships with deity(s) that remind you that you are loved.

Whatever it is for you, you do not have to go this alone. One of the loud-est and most repeated messages I receive when I make time to commune with my own guides is "we're here for you; call on us; ask us for help."

We're here for you. Call on us. Ask us for help.

Intention

Hopefully at this point on our journey together you've experienced how setting/stating an Intention can transform a conversation, a ritual, an erotic act. That same power can be applied to life.

Let me be clear here: intention is not expectation, nor is it entitlement. It's not the anticipation of things being just so, nor is it the assumption that they will be. Intention is the feeling we hope to have, the change that will have been made, the big picture, the prayer. To set an intention, and/or to live intentionally, is the very epitome of co-creation with the cosmos. By stating an intention, we express a threefold truth: that we plan to behave and take action in a manner that is aligned with this intention; that this intention is, or is aligned with, our desire; and that we are inviting the universe to line things up for us to make it so.

Expectation is a closed door. Intention leaves space for miracles.

Even if you're not up for making room for the miraculous, you can still lean into the power of intention. By setting intentions for your projects, your relationships, and/or your life, you give your conscious mind a compass toward which to orient itself when making decisions and taking action—while also planting a seed in your unconscious mind, which has a similar effect on those impulses and choices that you're less aware of. I particularly like to take advantage of the liminal spaces in the calendar for the setting of intentions. At the turning of the year, or key points on the wheel of the year—birthdays, anniversaries, solstices—I relish the invitation to pause, reflect, and chart a new course.

Being intentional is another way of inviting us into greater presence with life. With each intention we set, we become more focused, and also more engaged in our efforts on that intention's behalf. To be intentional is to be present, to be engaged, to get in the ring with life. It's also a powerful tool to wield in the face of the unknown. When starting out on new adventures, taking the road less travelled, squaring up to a challenge, or embarking on a path where we can only see one or two steps ahead, setting an intention can point us to both a guiding light and our holy grail.

No matter where you find yourself in life, no matter where you live in relation to the intersections of power and oppression, you can still set an intention for something new. And I promise you, intentions are magical things.

Raising Energy

The practice of raising energy offers two core teachings for living.

First, it shows us how to be present with the things that matter, by giving us a chance to practice and experience throwing all the energy and attention we have available in the moment into a single thing. This is not a way many of us are encouraged to live. We're encouraged to be cool, collected, reserved. We're encouraged to be flawless, poreless, perfectly made up, perfectly masked. We're encouraged to perform—whether it's strength or sexiness, power or purity.

Instead, magic invites us to be present, and gives us permission to be alive.

Second, by becoming better versed in energy we become better versed in ourselves. We're able to connect with our feelings, find our flow, and feel into where to go next. We can sense whether a potential choice or activity will be an energy gain, or an energy drain,[44] by imagining it, and noticing whether doing so makes us feel energised or weary/wary. We can become better versed in our own energy levels, and make choices that nurture and sustain them. We can feel into our belly to find out what truly fires us up, and take that into account when making the decisions that shape our lives. As well as practising aliveness, when we work with energy, we're also practising the discernment that will guide us toward a life well-lived.

Release

Pleasure is a radical act.

And so is pain.

Insofar as we are willing to feel each of them with our whole selves.

I wrote in the Letting Go chapter about Grief the Friend. Here is what grief the friend has taught me: contrary to what we are taught about grief and joy—that they are a binary, that they are opposites, that to feel one is to fail, and to feel the other is to succeed—I have found them to be comrades in arms. The

---

44. Carrellas, *Ecstasy is Necessary*, 100.

more I embrace the one, the more vulnerable I am to the other. And the more I let the other crack me open, the more deeply I can feel the one. If I can keep breathing when they visit, separately or together; if I can lean my body, my attention, my whole self into them; if I can open wide, and make them welcome; then both of them can be an ecstatic experience. And this applies to any other epic symphonies of emotion, sensation, or revelation that come my way. It also applies to the little notes that symphonies are built from.

To find ecstasy in living this life, this one right here—that is a truly radical act.

Surrender

Magic, sex, and nature all remind us that we're not just here for the doing. We are cyclical beings, round and curvy and wavy and seasonal. Contrary to the constant growth model currently dragging us all out of bed and into an unsustainable future in the West, when we look into the eyes of nature, dive into the depths of sex, or get our magician on and make ritual, we discover that without the peaks, the pauses, the profound stillness, the doing is meaningless.

The Surrender component of magic invites us to do what is ours to do—and then hand it over. It assures us we are not alone, and tomorrow is not our job today. It is an invitation into detached creativity: do what you can, let it go, allow space for the unseen to play its part.

Handing it over can be an exhale, or clocking off, or a leaning back. My favourite rituals of handing over also include: Breathing that which I wish to include God/dess in, seek her help with, or hand over to her entirely, into my hands, and then placing my hands on my altar, and handing it over; breathing each individual concern into a small candle, setting the candle alight, and letting it burn down and release itself into the loving hands of the cosmos; and standing in the shower, letting the water pool in my cupped hands, imagining my fears and doubts collecting there, and then releasing them down the plug hole, and letting the flow wash me clean.

To Surrender is also to let in. After we've handed over, we can receive. It's the reminder to lean back, and breathe in the view; to stop chasing the climax, and instead receive the sensation; to pause in the rush of things and notice your own aliveness; to try "good enough," "I don't know," and "fuck it" on for size; to curl up, cuddle, snuggle, snooze, sleep.

It's the invitation, having planted the seed, to walk away, and let it be. Let it go, honey. You did the best you could. Let yourself be.

Giving Thanks

Giving Thanks is not just the conclusion of ritual, it's also its summation. Giving Thanks brings us present, and is all an intentional act. It's both a doing, and a receiving. When we give thanks we take positive, choiceful action—and we also open to the mystery.

More than this, by practising gratitude, we practise relationship. We acknowledge that we are connected with the world around us, that we are interdependent, that we need others. From gratitude stems humility, recognition, appreciation, and compassion. Gratitude, in short, opens us up, and invites us to be kind. Whether we are opening to other people, and allowing ourselves to be moved by them; or opening up to the natural world, and realising our interconnectedness with and responsibility to all things; or opening up to the Divine—whatever that means to us—and being inspired to share the blessings we have; or opening up to ourselves, realising at last that we are lovable and loved, and treating ourselves accordingly. By being grateful for what we receive, we let ourselves be opened by it. We discover more space in us for receiving, and have more to give in our turn.

Finally, gratitude is self-perpetuating. Plant the seed of thanks, and watch kindness bloom in its wake.

Magic for life

Having explored how the fundamentals of magic can be applied to transform the way we live, I want to acknowledge that of course there will be times when you are doing sex magic for the purpose of changing your life, rather than for your love life.

The sex magic structures we explored in both the Making Love with Self and Making Love with Each Other chapter can both be adapted for such a purpose, and I've touched explicitly on that with each of them. However, I wanted to pull together the threads we've covered in previous sections, to look specifically at how you might craft a ritual focused on the change you want to see in the world—whether that's the microcosm of your own world, or the macrocosm of the world we share.

So, one more time, with feeling, and an extra dash of creativity and permission to play…

Creating Space

By now, you're well-versed in the importance of creating space that is separate, sacred, and safe(r). You can go simple, or you can get creative. If all you feel available and/or drawn to offer this piece of magic is an hour or two of your time, you can pack all the punch you need into that time. You could also:

- Give your ritual a more extended stretch of time, letting your preparations, your dreaming and visioning of your intention, and/or your energy raising spread luxuriously over the course of a day or a weekend.
- Gift yourself and your intention with a series of rituals. You could stretch those rituals over a day or two, or place them at regular intervals.
- You can create an altar for your intention, a shrine to your desires, and feed it at regular intervals. You can feed it with ritual, with breath, with offerings, and/or with orgasms—fuelling your vision over an extended period of time.
- You can create a miniature ritual that is portable and repeatable. A ritual that can be done in the five minutes before you go out the door, or every time you go for a walk, or before you do something that scares you, or each time you cum. Little rituals like these utilise the power of repetition to plant the seeds of change in our psychosomatic selves.

Invocation

Hopefully you have a clearer sense now of who or what you're willing to call on for support in your rituals, and of how to call them in. Invocation possibilities include the following:

- A quality—e.g., Universal Love
- An energy or element—e.g., Fire, or the Fires of Transformation
- A part of yourself—e.g., your Wise Self or creative power
- A guide—e.g., an angel, an animal guide, the spirit of a fictional character
- An ancestor—e.g., someone from your bloodline, or an ancestor you feel a connection or lineage with

- A deity—e.g., the god of your understanding, or a deity from a particular tradition
- That which unites us all—e.g., Spirit, The Universe

Sometimes, when you're making magic for something that feels very new, or in a new way, or embarking on a new path, you may wish to journey to meet a new ally to support you with that new change, or send a prayer out to the Cosmos for the perfect divine co-conspirator to make themselves known to you.

Setting Intention

What will your intention be, and how will you speak it to your deep mind and/or to the gods of your understanding?

Your intention can relate to your internal or external worlds, or to the world at large. It can be for a change in feeling, circumstances, resources, relationships. However, in magic, as in sex, consent is nonnegotiable. You cannot do magic that either wills someone else to feel or behave in a way they don't want to, or that wills something for them that they do not want. You can create ritual that supports change within you, or invites the world lovingly to change; you can do ritual for someone else if they wish it, and you can certainly do it in support of your relationships with others. But don't go trying to bend someone's will with magic. Karma is a bitch, and with the infinite possibilities magic makes available to us, there is always a better solution to be imagined than the one that goes against someone else's consent.

Ways to encapsulate your intention that we have looked at include the following:

- A word or sentence
- An imagined image or physical object
- A feeling. When working with feeling, the trick is to use your imagination to conjure that feeling as clearly as you can during your ritual. Feelings pack an energetic punch, so the more you can really "feel" the outcome you're working for, the better.
- A sigil
- An altar or shrine

Remember clarity, strength of desire, and feeling: these are your friends when it comes to Setting Intention. Begin your ritual by planting the seed of your intention in yourself, the space, and anyone sharing it with you. State it clearly, and set it in your mind's eye, on your or someone else's body, or in plain sight.

Raising Energy

How will you spark, fuel, and build energy to feed or fire up your intention? What's going to make you sweat, get you wet, help you fly? Whether it's building a rhythm with breath or body or impact play, or building sensation with pleasure or pain. Whether it's solo or together, or some or all of the above, make sure you pick something you love. Something you can commit to; something you can get lost in; something you'll enjoy so much that— when the end of the ritual comes around—you can release your intention with love, because you're too busy revelling in inhabiting your own skin to need to cling to anything in that moment. Build it, build it, build it. Get high. Exhaust yourself. Let it go.

Release

Let it go. How you do this is up to you. How you crest the wave, open to the Universe, hit that wall of exhaustion. It could be the last in a series of intense sensations, or an orgasm. If in doubt, I like to call on the last section of the Genital- and Gender-Free Orgasm: first deep breath, second deep breath, breathe in and hold the third deep breath. Count to fifteen or so. Clench everything. Let it go.

Let it go. You can breathe your intention out into the stars, or place your hands on the ground to plant it in the Earth. You can see it floating away from you, or feel it explode from your body. You can set it on fire—in your mind's eye, or, if you're using a sentence or image that's written on paper, or a nontoxic flammable object, literally set it on fire. Or float it away on water— again, imaginatively, or literally. Whatever it takes to hand it over. Surrender. Your work here is done.

Surrender

Your work here is done. Neither dwell on it, nor rush to be up and on with your day. Instead, wait a while. Listen to your body. Let yourself be, and let yourself be here, and let yourself be loved. Let it in. You've done enough. You are enough. Let it in.

Giving Thanks

Finally, give thanks.

Thank any unseen collaborators you called in.

Thank your stardusted co-conspirators in pleasure and ecstasy.

Thank the Earth who held you with such constancy and unconditionality.

And thank yourself. You brave and extraordinary creature.

You made it. Through that ritual, and through this book, with me. Thank you.

Thank you for your time, your trust, and your willingness to give it a try. I do so ardently hope you have found something herein to arouse, empower, and inspire you. You've been such wonderful company. Until we meet again...

The circle is open, but never broken. We are the people, we are the power. Merry meet, merry part, and merry meet again.

The Infinite Possibilities of Sex Magic

Afterword—A Permission Slip

By the power invested in me by the God/dess, the Earth, and my genitals, I hereby grant you permission to play with the Divine.

I invite you to take the god of your understanding by the hand, and embark on a co-created lifelong playdate in search of your empowered, erotic, and ecstatic self, in the knowledge that:

You are loved.

You are loved not in spite of, but because of.

Not because you are tolerated, but because you are celebrated.

You are celebrated in all that you are.

In all of your beauty, in all of your mess, in all the ways you seek out—and also in all the ways you turn away from—the pleasure that is your birthright.

You are celebrated and you are welcome on this Earth. You are wanted, here, by this Earth that made you.

By the Earth and the trees and the stars and the seas you are wanted,

And you are blessed.

Blessed are your desires, and your capacity to fulfil them.

Blessed is your creativity, and your capacity to flow.

Blessed is your body, and your capacity to listen to yourself.

Blessed is your heart, and your capacity to share its treasures with us all.

You are love.

You are loved.

You are loved right now.

The Friend awaits you.

Go play.

Resources

Sex Magic Events

Koinonia (UK)

Elemental Ritual Pleasure Spaces welcoming participants of all genders, orientations, bodies, and backgrounds.

Find out more at makinglovewithgod.co.uk.

Sacred Kink Immersion & Queer Sacred Kink Immersion (US)

Events weaving together Tantra and kink in a safe, structured environment, which begin as a guided experiential workshop, and transition into a facilitated play party. All genders, orientations, bodies, and races welcome, with the Queer edition dedicated to LGBTQI+ individuals and our partners.

Find out more at AlexSMorgan.com/events.

Quintasensual (UK)

The queer spirituality, sexuality, and Tantra festival.

Find out more at quintasensual.org.

Camp Crucible (US)

Nine days and eight nights of hedonism, kink, and camping! Play. Relax. Explore. Enjoy.

Find out more at campcrucible.com.

Sex Magic Trainings

Making Love with God—The Art of Sex Magic (UK)

Making Love with God is a body of work that unites the spiritual with the sensual, supporting personal and collective transformation through pleasure. Offerings include sex magic intensives for building radical relationships with yourself, your beloveds, the Earth, and divinity.

Find out more at makinglovewithgod.co.uk.

The Urban Tantra® Experience and the Urban Tantra® Professional Training Program (US, Europe, Australia)

Workshops for spiritual seekers and erotic explorers who know that there is "something more" to sex and spirit—and an international training program that is also a community, a philosophy, and an inclusive sacred sexuality practice supporting both personal and professional goals.

Find out more at barbaracarrellas.com—where you can also find a guided meditation of the Genital- and Gender-Free Orgasm!

Sex Therapists

Cyndi Darnell (New York, US)

Online and face-to-face sex and relationship counselling and coaching for individuals, couples, and pods. Also online sex education and personal/relationship development courses.

Find out more at www.cyndidarnell.com.

The London Gender, Sexual & Relationship Diversity Practice (London, UK)

A London-based practice of counsellors, psychotherapists, psychologists, coaches, mentors, and trainers who offer sex and relationship support across gender, sexual, and relationship diversity in person and online.

Find out more at www.londonsexrelationshiptherapy.com.

Somatic Sex Educators and Sexological Bodyworkers

Meredith Reynolds (London, UK)

Meredith's particular areas of teaching interest include: use of breath and mindfulness to be here "in the now"; use of breath and touch variation to learn to prolong pleasure states; expressing boundaries; learning to notice, honour, and ask for what you want; exploration of parts of the body that hold both pleasure and shame; supporting people with trans and altered bodies to integrate changes.

Find out more at www.meredith-reynolds.com.

Kim Loliya (London, UK)

Kim Loliya is a sex educator, body-based coach, and consultant specialising in women's sexuality and empowerment, supporting clients with trauma, pelvic pain, scar tissue, relationship difficulties, and much more. Using simple and practical tools, Kim creates a gentle healing space for women and couples that offers new avenues for intimacy, joy, and healing.

Find out more at www.pleasureinstitute.org.

Beck Thom (Midlands, UK)

Beck offers Sex Coaching, Somatic Sex Education, and Sexological Bodywork (including integrated ScarWork) to "anybody with a body"—in particular LGBT, queer, and trans folk—in the Midlands, UK.

Find out more at www.body-curious-sexcoach.co.uk.

Caffyn Jesse (Salt Spring Island, Canada)

Leading teacher of somatic sex education, trauma-informed practice, and dimensions of intimacy. Author of books and video trainings on somatic sex education.

Find out more at www.erospirit.ca.

Ecosexuals

Elise Bish

Elise is a sex educator, family constellations facilitator, and desire catalyst offering conscious sexuality education grounded and resourced by the Earth.

She runs ecosexual retreats and workshops across the United States, and offers private coaching for those seeking to cultivate a sacred connection to their desire and the natural world.

Find out more at elisebish.com.

Annie Sprinkle and Elizabeth Stephens

Writing, education, art, and activism about ecosexuality—changing the metaphor from Earth as Mother to Earth as Lover, and making environmentalism sexier and more diverse.

Find out more at sexecology.org.

Consent Pioneers

Betty Martin (US)

Betty offers training and support to other practitioners through the School of Consent, which also offers information and workshops for individuals and couples.

Find our more at schoolofconsent.org.

Meg-John Barker (UK)

Meg-John offers writings on consent and mentorship and supervision of practitioners working and writing in related areas.

Find out more at rewriting-the-rules.com/conflict-break-up/consensual-relationships-revisited.

Good Introductory Books

Conscious Relating/Sacred Sexuality

Barker, M-J. (2018). *Rewriting the Rules: An Anti-Self-Help Guide to Love, Sex and Relationships.* London: Routledge.

Carrellas, B. (2012). *Ecstasy Is Necessary.* New York, NY: Hay House Inc.

Carrellas, B. (2017). *Urban Tantra: Sacred Sex for the Twenty-First Century.* Berkeley, CA: Ten Speed Press.

Geraghty, A. (2003). *How Loving Relationships Work: Understanding Love's Living* Force. London: Vega Books.

Michaels, M. A. & Johnson, P. (2014). *Partners in Passion: A Guide to Great Sex, Emotional Intimacy, and Long-Term Love.* Jersey City, NJ: Cleis Press.

BDSM and Conscious Kink

Easton, D. & Hardy, J. W. (2011). *Radical Ecstasy.* Emeryville, CA: Greenery Press.

Harrington, L. & Williams, M. (2013). *Playing Well with Others: Your Field Guide to Discovering, Navigating and Exploring the Kink, Leather and BDSM Communities.* Emeryville, CA: Greenery Press.

Kaldera, R. (2015). *Sacred Power, Holy Surrender: Living a Spiritual Power Dynamic.* Morrisville, NC: Lulu.com.

Taormino, T. (2012). *The Ultimate Guide to Kink: BDSM, Role Play and the Erotic Edge.* Jersey City, NJ: Cleis Press.

Gender

Bornstein, K. (2016). *Gender Outlaw: On Men, Women, and the Rest of Us.* New York: Vintage.

Bornstein, K. & Bergman, S. B. (2016). *Gender Outlaws: The Next Generation.* Boston: Seal Press.

Iantaffi, A. & Barker, M-J. (2017). *How to Understand Your Gender: A Practical Guide for Exploring Who You Are.* London: Jessica Kingsley.

Magic

Fries, J. (2007). *Visual Magick: A Manual of Freestyle Shamanism.* Oxford: Mandrake.

Harrington, L. & Kulystin, T. F. (Eds.) (2018). *Queer Magic: Power Beyond Binaries.* Anchorage, AK: taikulystin.com

Creativity

Cameron, J. (2012). *The Artist's Way: A Spiritual Path to Higher Creativity.* London: Souvenir Press.

Gilbert, E. (2015). *Big Magic: Creative Living Beyond Fear.* London: Bloomsbury.

Radical Self-Love

brown, a. m. (2019). *Pleasure Activism: The Politics of Feeling Good*. Chico, CA: AK Press.

Brown, B. (2013). *Daring Greatly: How the Courage to Be Vulnerable Transforms the Way We Live, Love, Parent, and Lead*. London: Penguin.

Lorde, A. (2012). *Sister Outsider: Essays and Speeches*. Canada: Crossing Press.

Taylor, S. R. (2018). *The Body Is Not an Apology: The Power of Radical Self-Love*. Oakland, CA: Berrett-Koehler Publishers.

Welwood, J. (2007). *Perfect Love, Imperfect Relationships: Healing the Wound of the Heart*. Boulder, CO: Shambhala Publications Inc.

All of the Above

Brezsny, R. (2009). *Pronoia Is the Antidote for Paranoia, Revised and Expanded: How the Whole World Is Conspiring to Shower You with Blessings*. Berkeley, CA: North Atlantic Books.

Online Resources

Queer Body Love talks

How do we love ourselves, our bodies, and each other in the face of oppression? Video interviews with queer & trans leaders exploring this essential question.

Find out more at thequeerbodyloveseries.com.

Sex+

A team of sex enthusiasts from various countries and walks of life have taken their thoughts, explorations, and conversations and poured them into this intersectional, sex positive, inclusive, honest zine.

Find out more at sexpluszine.com.

Appendix—
Sample Erotic Checklist

Create your own checklist or use the one below, with columns like Yes, No, Maybe, Solo, Together, If... and Notes next to it. Complete it for yourself, or share the exercise with a partner, as a first step toward new erotic adventures.

Anal penetration
Biting
Blindfolds
Bondage (cuffs/tape)
Bondage (rope)
Breathing together
Breath play
Butt plugs/anal beads
Caning
Caressing
Clitoral stimulation
Clothes-pegs
Cock and ball play/torture
Cock rings
Costumes
Cross-dressing
Cuddling

Dildos

Domination

Double-penetration

Dry-humping

Ejaculating on partner

Electrical play

Energy play

Erotic dancing

Exhibitionism

Eye-contact

Face slapping

Fantasising

Female ejaculation

Fingering (vagina/anus)

Fisting (vaginal/anal)

Flogging

Following orders

Food play

Foot worship

Furry play

Gags

Group sex

G-spot stimulation/play

Hair pulling

Hand jobs

Ice cubes

Kissing

Leather clothing

Lingerie (wearing)

Marking/bruising

Massage

Multiple orgasms

Mutual masturbation

Needles/piercing

Nipple stimulation/play

Torture
Oral sex
Outdoor sex
Pain play
Penis stimulation/strokes
Phone sex
Pinching
Porn (making)
Porn (watching)
Prostate stimulation/play
Public displays of affection
Public sex
Punching
Punishment play
Reading erotica
Rimming
Role play
Rubber/latex clothing
Scratching
Sensory deprivation
Serving/being served
Sex parties
Sex workshops
Sharing fantasies
Spanking (hands/paddles/crops)
Strap-on play
Squeezing/kneading
Submission
Swallowing semen
Swinging
Talking dirty
Testes stimulation
Threesome
Tickling
Tribadism/scissoring

Triple penetration

Vaginal penetration

Vibrators

Voyeurism

Wax play

Whips

Wrestling

Bibliography

Brown, Brené. *Daring Greatly*. New York: Portfolio Penguin, 2012.

———. *Rising Strong*. London: Vermillion, 2015.

———. *The Gifts of Imperfection*. Center City, MN: Hazelden, 2010.

Cameron, Julia. *The Artist's Way*. New York: Jeremy P. Tarcher/Putnam, 2002.

Carrellas, Barbara. *Ecstasy Is Necessary*. New York: Hay House, 2012.

———. *Urban Tantra*. Berkeley, CA: Ten Speed Press, 2017.

Chapman, Gary. *The Five Love Languages*. Chicago: Northfield Publishing, 1992.

Crowe, Cameron, dir. *We Bought a Zoo*. 2011; Los Angeles: 20th Century Fox, 2011. DVD.

Cunsolo, Ashlee & Neville R. Ellis. "Ecological grief as a mental health response to climate change-related loss," nature.com, https://www.nature .com/articles/s41558-018-0092-2. Accessed August 21, 2018.

Darnell, Cindy. "The Atlas of Erotic Anatomy and Arousal," cyndidarnell .com, https://cyndidarnell.com/atlas-of-erotic-anatomy-arousal/. Accessed August 21, 2018.

David, Susan. "The Gift and Power of Emotional Courage," susandavid.com, http://www.susandavid.com/the-talks. Accessed August 21, 2018.

Easton, Dossie and Janet Hardy. *Radical Ecstasy*. Oakland, CA: Greenery Press, 2004.

Estés, Clarissa Pinkola. *Women Who Run with the Wolves: Myths and Stories of the Wild Woman Archetype*. London: Rider, 1993.

Fries, Jan. *Visual Magic*. Oxford: Mandrake, 1992.

Geraghty, Anne. *How Loving Relationships Work*. London: Vega, 2003.

Howitt, Hollie, "Genitals Do Not Equal Gender," hhowitt.com, http://hhowitt.com/2016/11/genitals-do-not-equal-gender-a-talk-by-hollie-howitt-escape-the-binary/. Accessed August 21, 2018.

Kirkpatrick, Bill. *The Creativity of Listening*. London: Darton, Longman, and Todd Ltd, 2005.

Knight, Sarah. "The Magic of Not Giving a F***," nofucksgivenguides.com, http://nofucksgivenguides.com/audio-video/. Accessed August 21, 2018.

Lockhart, E. *We Were Liars*. London: Hot Key Books, 2014.

Lorde, Audre. *A Burst of Light: Essays*. Ithaca, NY: Firebrand Books, 1988.

———. *Sister Outsider: Essays and Speeches*. Trumansburg, NY: Crossing Press, 1984.

Macy, Joanna. *Coming Back to Life*. Gabriola Island, BC: New Society Publishers, 2014.

Martin, Betty. "The Pleasure in Your Hands," bettymartin.org, https://bettymartin.org/videos/#4. Accessed August 21, 2018.

Michaels, Mark and Patricia Johnson. *Partners in Passion*. Berkeley, CA: Cleis Press, 2014.

Oliver, Mary. *Dream Work*. New York: The Atlantic Monthly Press, 1986.

Pratchett, Terry. *A Hat Full of Sky*. London: Doubleday, 2004.

Rao, Srikumar. "Plug into Your Hard-Wired Happiness," TED.com, https://www.ted.com/talks/srikumar_rao_plug_into_your_hard_wired_happiness/transcript?language=en. Accessed August 21, 2018.

Schleifer, Hedy. "The Power of Connection," hedyyumi.com, https://www.hedyyumi.com/about-us/ted-talk/. Accessed August 21, 2018.

Smith, DeAnne. "DeAnne Smith Melbourne International Comedy Festival Gala 2017," deannesmith.com, http://www.deannesmith.com/videos/. Accessed August 21, 2018.

Sonnenburg, Justin and Erica Sonnenburg. *Gut Reactions*. London: Transworld Publishers, 2017.

Stephens, Beth and Annie Sprinkle, dir. *Goodbye Gauley Mountain*. 2014; Fecund Arts, 2014. DVD.

Taymor, Julie, dir. *Frida*. 2002; Los Angeles: Miramax Films, 2002. DVD.

To Write to the Author

If you wish to contact the author or would like more information about this book, please write to the author in care of Llewellyn Worldwide Ltd. and we will forward your request. Both the author and the publisher appreciate hearing from you and learning of your enjoyment of this book and how it has helped you. Llewellyn Worldwide Ltd. cannot guarantee that every letter written to the author can be answered, but all will be forwarded. Please write to:

Rev. Rowan Bombadil
℅ Llewellyn Worldwide
2143 Wooddale Drive
Woodbury, MN 55125-2989

Please enclose a self-addressed stamped envelope for reply,
or $1.00 to cover costs. If outside the U.S.A., enclose
an international postal reply coupon.

Many of Llewellyn's authors have websites with additional
information and resources. For more information,
please visit our website at http://www.llewellyn.com

GET MORE AT LLEWELLYN.COM

Visit us online to browse hundreds of our books and decks, plus sign up to receive our e-newsletters and exclusive online offers.

- Free tarot readings • Spell-a-Day • Moon phases
- Recipes, spells, and tips • Blogs • Encyclopedia
- Author interviews, articles, and upcoming events

GET SOCIAL WITH LLEWELLYN

Find us on     @LlewellynBooks

www.Facebook.com/LlewellynBooks

GET BOOKS AT LLEWELLYN

LLEWELLYN ORDERING INFORMATION

 Order online: Visit our website at www.llewellyn.com to select your books and place an order on our secure server.

 Order by phone:
- Call toll free within the US at 1-877-NEW-WRLD (1-877-639-9753)
- We accept VISA, MasterCard, American Express, and Discover.

 Order by mail:
Send the full price of your order (MN residents add 6.875% sales tax) in US funds plus postage and handling to: Llewellyn Worldwide, 2143 Wooddale Drive, Woodbury, MN 55125-2989

POSTAGE AND HANDLING

STANDARD (US):(Please allow 12 business days)
$30.00 and under, add $6.00.
$30.01 and over, FREE SHIPPING.

CANADA:
We cannot ship to Canada. Please shop your local bookstore or Amazon Canada.

INTERNATIONAL:
Customers pay the actual shipping cost to the final destination, which includes tracking information.

Visit us online for more shipping options. Prices subject to change.

FREE CATALOG!

To order, call
1-877-
NEW-WRLD
ext. 8236
or visit our
website